Oxford Young Reader's Spelling Dictionary

Robert Allen

OXFORD
UNIVERSITY PRESS

OXFORD
UNIVERSITY PRESS

Great Clarendon Street, Oxford OX2 6DP

Oxford University Press is a department of the University of Oxford. It furthers the University's objective of excellence in research, scholarship, and education by publishing worldwide in

Oxford New York
Auckland Cape Town Dar es Salaam Hong Kong Karachi
Kuala Lumpur Madrid Melbourne Mexico City Nairobi New Delhi
Shanghai Taipei Toronto

with offices in

Argentina Austria Brazil Chile Czech Republic France Greece
Guatemala Hungary Italy Japan South Korea Poland Portugal
Switzerland Thailand Turkey Ukraine Vietnam

Oxford Young Reader's Spelling Dictionary is an enlarged edition of the *Oxford Pocket Spelling Dictionary* 2004 edition

Database right Oxford University Press (maker)

British Library cataloguing in Publication Data

Data available

ISBN 13: 978-0-19-911327-9

ISBN 10: 0-19-911327-0

10 9 8 7 6 5 4 3 2 1

Typeset in Arial

Printed in India

Introduction

The *Oxford Young Reader's Spelling Dictionary* is a special dictionary designed to help students with their spelling. Generally speaking there are three main areas of spelling difficulty for users of English whatever their age.

- Some words are difficult because they have unusual or unpredictable features. **Eighth**, **guard**, and **niece** are often spelt wrongly because they have awkward letter sequences. **Disappear** and **embarrass** are confusing because some letters are doubled while others are not. Words such as **desperate** and **separate** seeminconsistent because one has an **e** in the middle where the other has an **a** for no apparent reason.
- Then there are words that are easily confused. **Vain**, **vein**, and **vane** sound the same but have very different meanings. Some words change their spelling according to how they are used. For example, **dependant** as a *noun* is spelt with an **a**, but as an *adjective*, it is spelt with an **e**.
- The third type of difficulty arises when suffixes and endings are added to words. It is not easy to remember to keep an **e** in **changeable**, to replace **y** with **i** in **happily**, and not to double the **p** in **galloping**.

With increased interest in spelling, reading, and writing in schools today we hope that the *Oxford Young Reader's Spelling Dictionary* will provide a valuable tool offering useful strategies for dealing with spelling difficulties. We also hope that it will support teachers and parents whose task is to enable young writers to become confident, accurate spellers and to express themselves with a voice of their own.

How to use this book

Entries

Words are listed alphabetically in **bold** and the part of speech or word class (e.g. *noun*, *verb*, *adjective*) follows in italic. If the word has endings (called inflections), these are also listed in black below the headword.

Decide on the first sound of the word you are looking for. Some first sounds can be confusing. If you cannot find the word you are looking for, use the **Try also** tips which will guide you to other possible spellings.

Footnotes

Some words have footnotes attached to them. These identify words that you need to check that you have the right meaning. For example, at **bite** you will find a footnote to tell you that there is another word that sounds like it but is spelt a different way, **!byte**. Words that sound the same but are spelt differently are called homophones. Some footnotes also give extra information on usage and grammar.

Panels

There are about 250 panels which highlight particular problems. For example, you may want to know which words are spelt **-able** like **bendable**, and which ones are spelt **-ible** like **accessible**. Or you may want to know how you form plurals of nouns ending in **-f** such as **calf** or **roof**. Use these information panels to build your knowledge of spelling rules and practices.

It may be useful to keep a spelling jotter for new words. When using a new word, say it aloud several times before you write it down. When you go on to use it in your writing, try not to copy it but to write the word from memory.

Thumb index

Try also

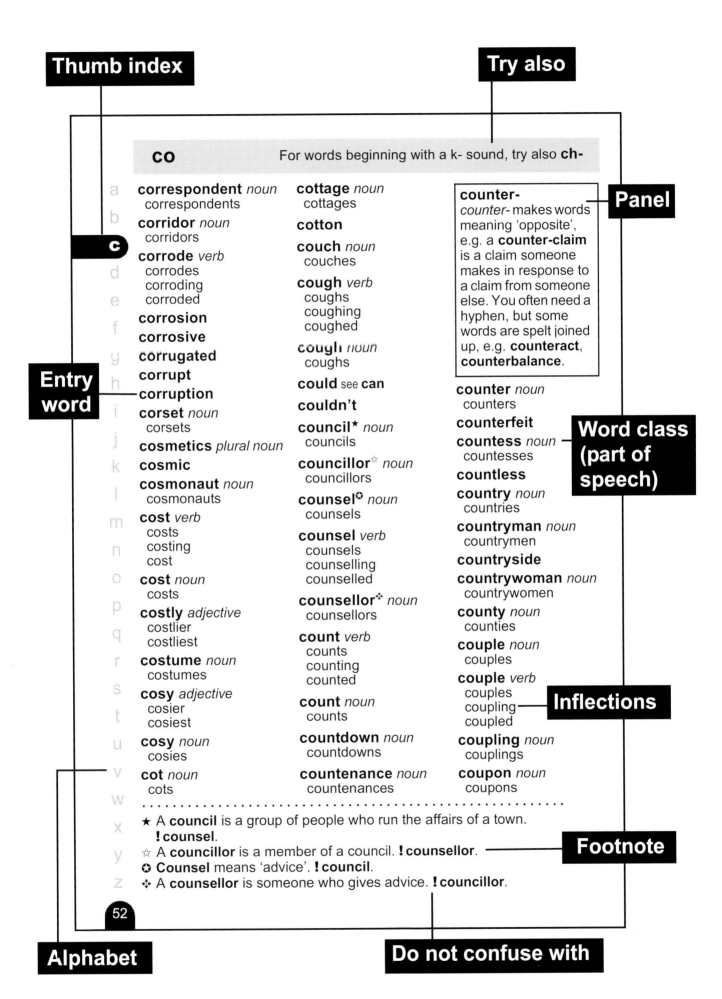

a b **c** d e f g h i j k l m n o p q r s t u v w x y z

correspondent *noun*
correspondents

corridor *noun*
corridors

corrode *verb*
corrodes
corroding
corroded

corrosion

corrosive

corrugated

corrupt

corruption

corset *noun*
corsets

cosmetics *plural noun*

cosmic

cosmonaut *noun*
cosmonauts

cost *verb*
costs
costing
cost

cost *noun*
costs

costly *adjective*
costlier
costliest

costume *noun*
costumes

cosy *adjective*
cosier
cosiest

cosy *noun*
cosies

cot *noun*
cots

cottage *noun*
cottages

cotton

couch *noun*
couches

cough *verb*
coughs
coughing
coughed

cough *noun*
coughs

could see **can**

couldn't

council★ *noun*
councils

councillor☆ *noun*
councillors

counsel✪ *noun*
counsels

counsel *verb*
counsels
counselling
counselled

counsellor✣ *noun*
counsellors

count *verb*
counts
counting
counted

count *noun*
counts

countdown *noun*
countdowns

countenance *noun*
countenances

> **counter-**
> *counter-* makes words meaning 'opposite', e.g. a **counter-claim** is a claim someone makes in response to a claim from someone else. You often need a hyphen, but some words are spelt joined up, e.g. **counteract**, **counterbalance**.

counter *noun*
counters

counterfeit

countess *noun*
countesses

countless

country *noun*
countries

countryman *noun*
countrymen

countryside

countrywoman *noun*
countrywomen

county *noun*
counties

couple *noun*
couples

couple *verb*
couples
coupling
coupled

coupling *noun*
couplings

coupon *noun*
coupons

★ A **council** is a group of people who run the affairs of a town. **! counsel**.
☆ A **councillor** is a member of a council. **! counsellor**.
✪ **Counsel** means 'advice'. **! council**.
✣ A **counsellor** is someone who gives advice. **! councillor**.

Panel

Entry word

Word class (part of speech)

Inflections

Footnote

Alphabet

Do not confuse with

Aa

-a
Most nouns ending in *-a*, e.g. **amoeba**, **gala**, have plurals ending in *-as*, e.g. **amoebas**, **galas**. A few technical words have plurals ending in *-ae*, e.g. **antennae**.

aback

abacus *noun*
abacuses

abandon *verb*
abandons
abandoning
abandoned

abbey *noun*
abbeys

abbot *noun*
abbots

abbreviate *verb*
abbreviates
abbreviating
abbreviated

abbreviation *noun*
abbreviations

abdomen *noun*
abdomens

abdominal

abduct *verb*
abducts
abducting
abducted

abide *verb*
abides
abiding
abided

ability *noun*
abilities

ablaze

able *adjective*
abler
ablest

-able and **-ible**
You add *-able* to a verb to make an adjective that means 'able to be done', e.g. **bendable** means 'able to be bent'. Some adjectives that have this meaning end in *-ible*, e.g. **accessible**, **convertible**, and **incredible**. You cannot use *-ible* to make new words as you can with *-able*.

ably

abnormal
abnormally

abnormality *noun*
abnormalities

aboard

abode *noun*
abodes

abolish *verb*
abolishes
abolishing
abolished

abolition

abominable

aboriginal

Aborigines

abort *verb*
aborts
aborting
aborted

abortion *noun*
abortions

abound *verb*
abounds
abounding
abounded

about

above

abrasive

abreast

abroad

abrupt

abscess *noun*
abscesses

abseil *verb*
abseils
abseiling
abseiled

absence *noun*
absences

absent

absentee *noun*
absentees

absent-minded
absent-mindedly

absolute
absolutely

absorb *verb*
absorbs
absorbing
absorbed

absorbent

absorption

abstract *adjective* and *noun*
abstracts

abstract *verb*
abstracts
abstracting
abstracted

absurd
absurdly

absurdity *noun*
absurdities

abundance

abundant

abuse *verb*
abuses
abusing
abused

abuse *noun*
abuses

abusive
abusively

abysmal

abyss *noun*
abysses

academic

academy *noun*
academies

accelerate *verb*
accelerates
accelerating
accelerated

acceleration

accelerator *noun*
accelerators

accent *noun*
accents

accent *verb*
accents
accenting
accented

accept★ *verb*
accepts
accepting
accepted

acceptable

acceptance

access *noun*
accesses

access *verb*
accesses
accessing
accessed

accessibility

accessible

accession *noun*
accessions

accessory *noun*
accessories

accident *noun*
accidents

accidental
accidentally

acclaim *verb*
acclaims
acclaiming
acclaimed

accommodate *verb*
accommodates
accommodating
accommodated

accommodation

accompaniment
noun
accompaniments

accompanist *noun*
accompanists

accompany *verb*
accompanies
accompanying
accompanied

accomplish *verb*
accomplishes
accomplishing
accomplished

accomplished

accomplishment
noun
accomplishments

accord *noun*
accords

according
accordingly

accordion *noun*
accordions

account *noun*
accounts

account *verb*
accounts
accounting
accounted

accountancy

accountant *noun*
accountants

accumulate *verb*
accumulates
accumulating
accumulated

accumulation

accuracy

accurate
accurately

accusation *noun*
accusations

accuse *verb*
accuses
accusing
accused

accustomed

ace *noun*
aces

ache *noun*
aches

ache *verb*
aches
aching
ached

achieve *verb*
achieves
achieving
achieved

achievement
achievements

acid *noun*
acids

acidic

acidity *noun*

★ To **accept** something is to take it. **! except**.

acknowledge *verb*
acknowledges
acknowledging
acknowledged

acknowledgement *noun*
acknowledgements

acne

acorn *noun*
acorns

acoustic

acoustics

acquaint *verb*
acquaints
acquainting
acquainted

acquaintance *noun*
acquaintances

acquire *verb*
acquires
acquiring
acquired

acquisition *noun*
acquisitions

acquit *verb*
acquits
acquitting
acquitted

acquittal *noun*
acquittals

acre *noun*
acres

acrobat *noun*
acrobats

acrobatic *adjective*
acrobatically

acrobatics

acronym *noun*
acronyms

across *adverb* and *preposition*

act *noun*
acts

act *verb*
acts
acting
acted

action *noun*
actions

activate *verb*
activates
activating
activated

active

activity *noun*
activities

actor *noun*
actors

actress *noun*
actresses

actual
actually

acupuncture

acute

Adam's apple *noun*
Adam's apples

adapt *verb*
adapts
adapting
adapted

adaptable

adaptation

adaptor *noun*
adaptors

add *verb*
adds
adding
added

adder *noun*
adders

addict *noun*
addicts

addicted

addiction *noun*
addictions

addictive

addition *noun*
additions

additional

additive *noun*
additives

address *noun*
addresses

address *verb*
addresses
addressing
addressed

adenoids

adequate

adhere *verb*
adheres
adhering
adhered

adhesive *noun*
adhesives

adhesion

adhesive

Adi Granth

adjacent

adjective *noun*
adjectives

adjourn *verb*
adjourns
adjourning
adjourned

adjournment

adjudicate *verb*
adjudicates
adjudicating
adjudicated

adjudication

adjudicator

adjust *verb*
adjusts
adjusting
adjusted

adjustment *noun*
adjustments

administer *verb*
administers
administering
administered

administration *noun*
administrations

administrative

administrator

admirable
admirably

admiral *noun*
admirals

admiration

admire *verb*
admires
admiring
admired

admirer *noun*
admirers

admission *noun*
admissions

admit *verb*
admits
admitting
admitted

admittance

admittedly

ado

adolescence

adolescent *noun*
adolescents

adopt *verb*
adopts
adopting
adopted

adoption

adoptive

adorable
adorably

adoration

adore *verb*
adores
adoring
adored

adorn *verb*
adorns
adorning
adorned

adornment

adrenalin

adrift

adult *noun*
adults

adulterer

adultery

advance *noun*
advances

advance *verb*
advances
advancing
advanced

advanced

advantage *noun*
advantages

advantageous

Advent★

adventure *noun*
adventures

adventurous *adjective*
adventurously

adverb *noun*
adverbs

adversary *noun*
adversaries

adverse

adversity *noun*
adversities

advertise *verb*
advertises
advertising
advertised

advertisement *noun*
advertisements

advice

advisable

advise *verb*
advises
advising
advised

adviser *noun*
advisers

advisory

advocate *noun*
advocates

advocate *verb*
advocates
advocating
advocated

aerial *adjective* and *noun*
aerials

> **aero-**
> You use *aero-* to make words to do with the air or aircraft, e.g. **aerobatics**.
> If the word is a long one you spell it with a hyphen, e.g. **aero-engineering**.

aerobatic

aerobatics

aerobics

aeronautical

aeronautics

aeroplane *noun*
aeroplanes

aerosol *noun*
aerosols

aesthetic
aesthetically

★ Use a capital A when you mean the period before Christmas.

affair *noun*
affairs

affect★ *verb*
affects
affecting
affected

affection *noun*
affections

affectionate
affectionately

afflict *verb*
afflicts
afflicting
afflicted

affliction
afflictions

affluence

affluent

afford *verb*
affords
affording
afforded

afforestation

afloat *adjective* and *adverb*

afraid

afresh

African *adjective* and *noun*
Africans

aft

after

afternoon *noun*
afternoons

afterwards

again

against

age *noun*
ages

age *verb*
ages
ageing
aged

aged

agency *noun*
agencies

agenda *noun*
agendas

agent *noun*
agents

aggravate *verb*
aggravates
aggravating
aggravated

aggravation

aggression

aggressive
aggressively

aggressor
aggressors

agile

agility

agitate *verb*
agitates
agitating
agitated

agitation

agitator *noun*
agitators

agnostic *noun*
agnostics

ago

agonizing

agony *noun*
agonies

agree *verb*
agrees
agreeing
agreed

agreeable

agreement *noun*
agreements

agriculture

agricultural

aground

ahead

ahoy

aid *noun*
aids

aid *verb*
aids
aiding
aided

Aids☆

ailing

ailment *noun*
ailments

aim *verb*
aims
aiming
aimed

aim *noun*
aims

aimless
aimlessly

air✪ *noun*
airs

air *verb*
airs
airing
aired

airborne

air-conditioned

air-conditioning

aircraft *noun*
aircraft

Airedale *noun*
Airedales

★ **Affect** means 'to make something change'. **! effect**.
☆ Use a capital A when you mean the disease.
✪ You can use a plural in the phrase *to put on airs*.

a b c d e f g h i j k l m n o p q r s t u v w x y z

airfield *noun*
airfields
air force *noun*
air forces
airgun *noun*
airguns
airline *noun*
airlines
airlock *noun*
airlocks
airmail
airman *noun*
airmen
airport *noun*
airports
airship *noun*
airships
airstream *noun*
airstreams
airtight
airy *adjective*
airier
airiest
airily
aisle★ *noun*
aisles
ajar
akela☆ *noun*
akelas
alarm *verb*
alarms
alarming
alarmed
alarm *noun*
alarms
alas
albatross *noun*
albatrosses
album *noun*
albums

alcohol
alcoholic *adjective* and *noun*
alcoholics
alcoholism
alcove *noun*
alcoves
ale✪ *noun*
ales
alert *verb*
alerts
alerting
alerted
alert *adjective* and *noun*
alerts
algebra
algebraic
alias *noun*
aliases
alibi *noun*
alibis
alien *adjective* and *noun*
aliens
alienate *verb*
alienates
alienating
alienated
alienation
alight
alike
alive
alkali *noun*
alkalis
alkaline
alkalinity
Allah
allegation *noun*
allegations

allege *verb*
alleges
alleging
alleged
allegedly
allegiance *noun*
allegiances
allegorical
allegory *noun*
allegories
allergic
allergy *noun*
allergies
alley *noun*
alleys
alliance *noun*
alliances
allied
alligator *noun*
alligators
allot *verb*
allots
allotting
allotted
allotment *noun*
allotments
allow *verb*
allows
allowing
allowed
allowance *noun*
allowances
alloy *noun*
alloys
all right
all-round
all-rounder
ally *noun*
allies

★ An **aisle** is a passage in a church or cinema. **! isle**.
☆ **Akela** is a Scout leader.
✪ You can use a plural when you mean 'different types of ale'.

ally *verb*
allies
allying
allied
almighty
almond *noun*
almonds
almost
aloft
alone
along
alongside
aloud★
alphabet *noun*
alphabets
alphabetical
alphabetically
alpine
already
Alsatian *noun*
Alsatians
also
altar☆ *noun*
altars
alter✪ *verb*
alters
altering
altered
alteration
alternate
alternate *verb*
alternates
alternating
alternated
alternately
alternation
alternating current
alternative *noun*
alternatives
alternative
alternator *noun*
alternators
although *conjunction*
altitude *noun*
altitudes
altogether
aluminium
always
amalgamate *verb*
amalgamates
amalgamating
amalgamated
amalgamation
amateur *adjective* and *noun*
amateurs
amateurish
amaze *verb*
amazes
amazing
amazed
amazement
ambassador *noun*
ambassadors
amber
ambiguity
ambiguities
ambiguous
ambiguously
ambition *noun*
ambitions
ambitious
ambitiously
amble *verb*
ambles
ambling
ambled
ambulance *noun*
ambulances
ambush *noun*
ambushes
ambush *verb*
ambushes
ambushing
ambushed
amen
amend *verb*
amends
amending
amended
amendment
amenity *noun*
amenities
American *adjective* and *noun*
Americans
amiable
amiably
amicable
amicably
amid✣
amidships
ammonia
ammunition
amnesty *noun*
amnesties
amoeba *noun*
amoebas
among✺
amount *noun*
amounts

★ **Aloud** means 'in a voice that can be heard'. **! allowed**.
☆ An **altar** is a raised surface in religious ceremonies. **! alter**.
✪ **Alter** means to change something. **! altar**.
✣ You can also spell this word *amidst*.
✺ You can also spell this word *amongst*.

a b c d e f g h i j k l m n o p q r s t u v w x y z

amount *verb*
amounts
amounting
amounted

amphibian *adjective* and *noun*
amphibians

amphibious

ample *adjective*
ampler
amplest
amply

amplification

amplfiier *noun*
amplifiers

amplify *verb*
amplifies
amplifying
amplified

amputate *verb*
amputates
amputating
amputated

amputation

amuse *verb*
amuses
amusing
amused

amusement *noun*
amusements

amusing

an★

anaemia

anaemic

anaesthetic *noun*
anaesthetics

anaesthetist

anaesthetize *verb*
anaesthetizes
anaesthetizing
anaesthetized

anagram *noun*
anagrams

analogous

analogue☆

analogy *noun*
analogies

analyse *verb*
analyses
analysing
analysed

analysis *noun*
analyses

analytical

anarchism

anarchist *noun*
anarchists

anarchy

anatomical

anatomy

> **-ance** and **-ence**
> Most nouns ending in *-ance* come from verbs, e.g. **disturbance**, **endurance**. Some nouns end in *-ence*, e.g. **dependence**, **obedience**, and you need to be careful not to misspell these.

ancestor *noun*
ancestors

ancestral

ancestry *noun*
ancestries

anchor *noun*
anchors

anchorage *noun*
anchorages

ancient

anemone *noun*
anemones

angel *noun*
angels

angelic

anger

angle *noun*
angles

angle *verb*
angles
angling
angled

angler *noun*
anglers

Anglican *adjective* and *noun*
Anglicans

Anglo-Saxon *adjective* and *noun*
Anglo-Saxons

angry *adjective*
angrier
angriest
angrily

anguish

angular

animal *noun*
animals

animated

animation

★ You use **an** instead of *a* before a word beginning with a vowel, e.g. *an apple*, or before an abbreviation that sounds as though it begins with a vowel, e.g. *an MP*.

☆ You will sometimes see the spelling *analog*, especially when it is about computers.

animosity *noun*
animosities

aniseed

ankle *noun*
ankles

annex *verb*
annexes
annexing
annexed

annexation

annexe *noun*
annexes

annihilate *verb*
annihilates
annihilating
annihilated

annihilation

anniversary *noun*
anniversaries

announce *verb*
announces
announcing
announced

announcer

announcement *noun*
announcements

annoy *verb*
annoys
annoying
annoyed

annoyance *noun*
annoyances

annual *adjective*
annually

annual *noun*
annuals

anonymity★

anonymous
anonymously

anorak *noun*
anoraks

anorexia

anorexic

another

answer *noun*
answers

answer *verb*
answers
answering
answered

> **-ant** and **-ent**
> Many adjectives end in *-ant*, e.g. **abundant**, **important**. Some adjectives end in *-ent*, e.g. **dependent** (**dependant** is a noun), **permanent**, and you need to be careful not to misspell these.

antagonism

antagonistic

antagonize *verb*
antagonizes
antagonizing
antagonized

Antarctic *adjective* and *noun*

anteater *noun*
anteaters

antelope☆ *noun*
antelope *or* antelopes

antenna *noun*
antennae *or* antennas

anthem *noun*
anthems

anthill *noun*
anthills

anthology *noun*
anthologies

anthracite

anthropologist

anthropology

> **anti-**
> *anti-* at the beginning of a word makes a word meaning 'against something' or 'stopping something', e.g. **antifreeze** means 'a liquid that stops water from freezing'. If the word you are adding *anti-* to begins with a vowel, you use a hyphen, e.g. **anti-aircraft**.

antibiotic *noun*
antibiotics

anticipate *verb*
anticipates
anticipating
anticipated

anticipation

anticlimax *noun*
anticlimaxes

anticlockwise *adverb* and *adjective*

anticyclone *noun*
anticyclones

antidote *noun*
antidotes

antifreeze

★ The noun from **anonymous**.
☆ You use **antelope** when you mean a lot of animals and **antelopes** when you mean several you are thinking about separately.

antipodes★
antiquated
antique *adjective* and *noun*
antiques
antiseptic *noun*
antiseptics
antler *noun*
antlers
anus *noun*
anuses
anvil *noun*
anvils
anxiety *noun*
anxieties
anxious
anxiously
anybody
anyhow
anyone
anything
anyway
anywhere
apart
apartment *noun*
apartments
apathetic
apathy
ape *noun*
apes
aphid *noun*
aphids
apiece
apologetic
apologetically
apologize *verb*
apologizes
apologizing
apologized

apology *noun*
apologies
apostle *noun*
apostles
apostrophe *noun*
apostrophes
appal *verb*
appals
appalling
appalled
appalling
apparatus *noun*
apparatuses
apparent
apparently
appeal *verb*
appeals
appealing
appealed
appeal *noun*
appeals
appear *verb*
appears
appearing
appeared
appearance *noun*
appearances
appease *verb*
appeases
appeasing
appeased
appeasement
appendicitis
appendix☆
appendixes *or* appendices
appetite *noun*
appetites
appetizing

applaud *verb*
applauds
applauding
applauded
applause
apple *noun*
apples
appliance *noun*
appliances
applicable
applicant *noun*
applicants
application *noun*
applications
applied
apply *verb*
applies
applying
applied
appoint *verb*
appoints
appointing
appointed
appointment *noun*
appointments
appraisal
appraisals
appraise *verb*
appraises
appraising
appraised
appreciate *verb*
appreciates
appreciating
appreciated
appreciation
appreciative
apprehension *noun*
apprehensive

★ A word Europeans use for Australia and New Zealand.
☆ You use **appendixes** when you mean organs of the body and **appendices** when you mean parts of a book.

apprentice *noun*
apprentices
apprenticeship
approach *verb*
approaches
approaching
approached
approach *noun*
approaches
approachable
appropriate
approval
approve *verb*
approves
approving
approved
approximate
approximately
apricot *noun*
apricots
April
apron *noun*
aprons
aptitude *noun*
aptitudes
aquarium *noun*
aquariums
aquatic
aqueduct *noun*
aqueducts
Arab★ *noun*
Arabs
Arabian★ *adjective*
Arabic☆
arabic☆
arable
arbitrary

arbitrate *verb*
arbitrates
arbitrating
arbitrated
arbitration
arbitrator
arc✪ *noun*
arcs
arcade *noun*
arcades
arch *noun*
arches
arch *verb*
arches
arching
arched
archaeology
archaeological
archaeologist
archbishop *noun*
archbishops
archer *noun*
archers
archery
architect *noun*
architects
architecture

-archy
-archy at the end of a word means 'rule or government', e.g. **anarchy** (= a lack of rule) and **monarchy** (= rule by a king or queen). The plural form is *-archies*, e.g. **monarchies**.

Arctic
are
area *noun*
areas
arena *noun*
arenas
aren't *abbreviation*
argue *verb*
argues
arguing
argued
argument *noun*
arguments
arid
aridity
arise *verb*
arises
arising
arose
arisen
aristocracy *noun*
aristocracies
aristocrat *noun*
aristocrats
aristocratic
arithmetic
arithmetical
ark✣ *noun*
arks
arm *noun*
arms
arm *verb*
arms
arming
armed
armada *noun*
armadas

★ You use **Arab** when you mean a person or the people, and **Arabian** when you mean the place, e.g. *the Arabian desert*.
☆ You use **Arabic** when you mean the language, and **arabic** when you mean numbers, e.g. *arabic numerals*.
✪ **Arc** means a curve. **! ark**.
✣ **Ark** means a boat. **! arc**.

a b c d e f g h i j k l m n o p q r s t u v w x y z

armadillo *noun*
armadillos

armaments

armchair *noun*
armchairs

armful *noun*
armfuls

armistice *noun*
armistices

armour

armoured

armpit *noun*
armpits

army *noun*
armies

aroma *noun*
aromas

aromatic

arose see **arise**

around

arouse *verb*
arouses
arousing
aroused

arrange *verb*
arranges
arranging
arranged

arrangement

array *noun*
arrays

arrears

arrest *verb*
arrests
arresting
arrested

arrest *noun*
arrests

arrival

arrive *verb*
arrives
arriving
arrived

arrogance

arrogant

arrow *noun*
arrows

arsenal *noun*
arsenals

arsenic

arson

artefact *noun*
artefacts

artery *noun*
arteries

artful
artfully

arthritic

arthritis

article *noun*
articles

articulate *adjective*

articulate *verb*
articulates
articulating
articulated

artificial
artificially

artillery *noun*
artilleries

artist *noun*
artists

artiste *noun*
artistes

artistic

artistry

asbestos

ascend *verb*
ascends
ascending
ascended

ascent *noun*
ascents

ash★ *noun*
ashes

ashamed

ashen

ashore

ashtray *noun*
ashtrays

Asian *adjective* and *noun*
Asians

aside

ask *verb*
asks
asking
asked

asleep

aspect *noun*
aspects

asphalt☆

aspirin *noun*
aspirins

ass *noun*
asses

assassin *noun*
assassins

assassinate *verb*
assassinates
assassinating
assassinated

assassination *noun*
assassinations

assault *verb*
assaults
assaulting
assaulted

★ The tree and the burnt powder.
☆ Note that this word is not spelt *ash-*.

assault *noun*
assaults
assemble *verb*
assembles
assembling
assembled
assembly *noun*
assemblies
assent
assert *verb*
asserts
asserting
asserted
assertion
assertive
assess *verb*
assesses
assessing
assessed
assessment
assessor
asset *noun*
assets
assign *verb*
assigns
assigning
assigned
assignment *noun*
assignments
assist *verb*
assists
assisting
assisted
assistance
assistant *noun*
assistants
associate *verb*
associates
associating
associated
associate *noun*
associates

association *noun*
associations
assorted
assortment
assume *verb*
assumes
assuming
assumed
assumption *noun*
assumptions
assurance *noun*
assurances
assure *verb*
assures
assuring
assured
asterisk *noun*
asterisks
asteroid *noun*
asteroids
asthma
asthmatic *adjective*
and *noun*
asthmatics
astonish *verb*
astonishes
astonishing
astonished
astonishment
astound *verb*
astounds
astounding
astounded
astride
astrologer
astrological
astrology
astronaut *noun*
astronauts
astronomer
astronomical
astronomy

-asy
Not many words end in *-asy*. The most important are **ecstasy**, **fantasy**, **idiosyncrasy**. There are a lot of words ending in *-acy*, however, e.g. **accuracy**.

ate★ see **eat**
atheist *noun*
atheists
atheism
athlete *noun*
athletes
athletic
athletics
atlas *noun*
atlases
atmosphere *noun*
atmospheres
atmospheric
atoll *noun*
atolls
atom *noun*
atoms
atomic
atrocious
atrociously
atrocity *noun*
atrocities
attach *verb*
attaches
attaching
attached
attached
attachment *noun*
attachments

★ **Ate** is the past tense of eat e.g. *I ate an apple*. **! eight**.

a b c d e f g h i j k l m n o p q r s t u v w x y z

attack *verb*
attacks
attacking
attacked

attack *noun*
attacks

attain *verb*
attains
attaining
attained

attainment

attempt *verb*
attempts
attempting
attempted

attempt *noun*
attempts

attend *verb*
attends
attending
attended

attendance *noun*
attendances

attendant *noun*
attendants

attention

attentive

attic *noun*
attics

attitude *noun*
attitudes

attract *verb*
attracts
attracting
attracted

attraction *noun*
attractions

attractive

auburn

auction *noun*
auctions

auctioneer

audibility

audible

audience *noun*
audiences

> **audio-**
> *audio-* makes words with 'sound' or 'hearing' in their meaning. Some of them have hyphens, e.g. **audio-visual** (= to do with hearing and seeing).

audio-visual

audition *noun*
auditions

auditorium *noun*
auditoriums

August

aunt *noun*
aunts

auntie★ *noun*
aunties

au pair☆ *noun*
au pairs

aural✪

austere

austerity

Australian *adjective* and *noun*
Australians

authentic
authentically

authenticity

author *noun*
authors

authority *noun*
authorities

authorize *verb*
authorizes
authorizing
authorized

autistic

> **auto-**
> *auto-* at the beginning of a word means 'self', e.g. **autobiography** (= a biography of yourself), **automatic** (= done by itself). But some words beginning with *auto-* are to do with cars, e.g. **autocross** (= car racing across country).

autobiography *noun*
autobiographies

autograph *noun*
autographs

automate *verb*
automates
automating
automated

automatic
automatically

automation

automobile *noun*
automobiles

autumn *noun*
autumns

autumnal

auxiliary *adjective* and *noun*
auxiliaries

★ You can also spell this word *aunty*.

☆ **Au pair** means a young person from another country who works in your house.

✪ **Aural** means 'to do with hearing'. **! oral**.

availability
available
avalanche *noun*
avalanches
avenue *noun*
avenues
average *adjective* and *noun*
averages
average *verb*
averages
averaging
averaged
avert *verb*
averts
averting
averted
aviary *noun*
aviaries
aviation
avid
avoid *verb*
avoids
avoiding
avoided
avoidance
await *verb*
awaits
awaiting
awaited
awake *adjective*
awake *verb*
awakes
awaking
awoke
awoken
awaken *verb*
awakens
awakening
awakened
award *noun*
awards
award *verb*
awards
awarding
awarded
aware
awareness
awash
away
awe
awed
awful
awfully
awhile★
awkward
awoke see **awake**
awoken see **awake**
axe *noun*
axes
axe *verb*
axes
axing
axed
axis *noun*
axes
axle *noun*
axles
Aztec *noun*
Aztecs
azure *adjective*

Bb

babble *verb*
babbles
babbling
babbled
baboon *noun*
baboons
baby *noun*
babies
babyish
babysit *verb*
babysits
babysitting
babysat
babysitter *noun*
babysitters
bachelor *noun*
bachelors
back *noun*
backs
back *verb*
backs
backing
backed
backache *noun*
backaches
backbone *noun*
backbones
background *noun*
backgrounds
backing
backlash *noun*
backlashes
backlog *noun*
backlogs
backside *noun*
backsides
backstroke
backward *adjective* and *adverb*
backwards *adverb*
backwater *noun*
backwaters
backyard *noun*
backyards
bacon
bacteria
bacterial

★ **Awhile** means 'for a short time', e.g. *Wait here awhile*. You spell it as two words in e.g. *a short while*.

a b c d e f g h i j k l m n o p q r s t u v w x y z

bad *adjective*
worse
worst
badly

baddy *noun*
baddies

badge *noun*
badges

badger *noun*
badgers

badger *verb*
badgers
badgering
badgered

badminton

baffle *verb*
baffles
baffling
baffled

bag *noun*
bags

bag *verb*
bags
bagging
bagged

bagel *noun*
bagels

baggage

baggy *adjective*
baggier
baggiest

bagpipes

bail★ *noun*
bails

bail☆ *verb*
bails
bailing
bailed

Bairam *noun*
Bairams

Baisakhi

bait *noun*

bait *verb*
baits
baiting
baited

bake *verb*
bakes
baking
baked

baker *noun*
bakers

bakery *noun*
bakeries

baking powder

balance *noun*
balances

balance *verb*
balances
balancing
balanced

balcony *noun*
balconies

bald *adjective*
balder
baldest

bale✪ *noun*
bales

bale✣ *verb*
bales
baling
baled

ballad *noun*
ballads

ballerina *noun*
ballerinas

ballet *noun*
ballets

ballistic *adjective*

balloon *noun*
balloons

ballot *noun*
ballots

ballpoint *noun*
ballpoints

ballroom *noun*
ballrooms

balsa

bamboo *noun*
bamboos

ban *verb*
bans
banning
banned

banana *noun*
bananas

band *noun*
bands

band *verb*
bands
banding
banded

bandage *noun*
bandages

bandit *noun*
bandits

bandstand *noun*
bandstands

bandwagon *noun*
bandwagons

bandy *adjective*
bandier
bandiest

★ **Bail** means 'money paid to let a prisoner out of prison' and 'a piece of wood put on the stumps in cricket'. **! bale**.

☆ **Bail** means 'to pay money to let a prisoner out of prison' and 'to scoop water out of a boat'. **! bale**.

✪ **Bale** means 'a large bundle'. **! bail**.

✣ **Bale** means 'to jump out of an aircraft'. **! bail**.

bang *noun*
bangs

bang *verb*
bangs
banging
banged

banger *noun*
bangers

banish *verb*
banishes
banishing
banished

banishment

banisters

banjo *noun*
banjos

bank *noun*
banks

bank *verb*
banks
banking
banked

banknote *noun*
banknotes

bankrupt

bankruptcy

banner *noun*
banners

banquet *noun*
banquets

baptism *noun*
baptisms

Baptist★ *noun*
Baptists

baptize *verb*
baptizes
baptizing
baptized

bar *noun*
bars

bar *verb*
bars
barring
barred

barb *noun*
barbs

barbarian *noun*
barbarians

barbaric

barbarism

barbarity *noun*
barbarities

barbarous *adjective*

barbecue *noun*
barbecues

barber *noun*
barbers

bar code *noun*
bar codes

bard *noun*
bards

bare☆ *adjective*
barer
barest

bareback

barely

bargain *noun*
bargains

bargain *verb*
bargains
bargaining
bargained

barge *noun*
barges

barge *verb*
barges
barging
barged

baritone *noun*
baritones

bark *noun*
barks

bark *verb*
barks
barking
barked

barley

barman *noun*
barmen

bar mitzvah *noun*
bar mitzvahs

barnacle *noun*
barnacles

barnyard *noun*
barnyards

barometer *noun*
barometers

barometric

baron *noun*
barons

baroness *noun*
baronesses

baronial

barrack *verb*
barracks
barracking
barracked

barracks✪ *plural noun*

barrage *noun*
barrages

barrel *noun*
barrels

★ You use a capital B when you mean a member of the Christian Church.

☆ **Bare** means 'naked' or 'not covered'. **! bear**.

✪ **Barracks** is plural but sometimes has a singular verb, e.g. *The barracks is over there.*

a **b** c d e f g h i j k l m n o p q r s t u v w x y z

barren

barricade *noun*
barricades

barricade *verb*
barricades
barricading
barricaded

barrier *noun*
barriers

barrister *noun*
barristers

barrow *noun*
barrows

barter *verb*
barters
bartering
bartered

base★ *noun*
bases

base *verb*
bases
basing
based

baseball *noun*
baseballs

basement *noun*
basements

bash *verb*
bashes
bashing
bashed

bash *noun*
bashes

bashful
bashfully

basic
basically

basin *noun*
basins

basis *noun*
bases

bask *verb*
basks
basking
basked

basket *noun*
baskets

basketball *noun*
basketballs

basketful *noun*
basketfuls

bass☆ *noun*
basses

bassoon *noun*
bassoons

bastard *noun*
bastards

bat *noun*
bats

bat *verb*
bats
batting
batted

batch *noun*
batches

bath *noun*
baths

bath *verb*
baths
bathing
bathed

bathe *verb*
bathes
bathing
bathed

bathroom *noun*
bathrooms

baton✪ *noun*
batons

batsman *noun*
batsmen

battalion *noun*
battalions

batten✣ *noun*
battens

batter *verb*
batters
battering
battered

batter *noun*

battery *noun*
batteries

battle *noun*
battles

battlefield *noun*
battlefields

battlements

battleship *noun*
battleships

bawl *verb*
bawls
bawling
bawled

bay *noun*
bays

bayonet *noun*
bayonets

bazaar *noun*
bazaars

beach✺ *noun*
beaches

beacon *noun*
beacons

bead *noun*
beads

★ **Base** means 'a place where things are controlled'. **! bass**.
☆ **Bass** means 'a singer with a low voice'. **! base**.
✪ A **baton** is a stick used by a conductor in an orchestra. **! batten**.
✣ A **batten** is a flat strip of wood. **! baton**.
✺ **Beach** means 'sandy part of the seashore'. **! beech**.

beady *adjective*
beadier
beadiest
beagle *noun*
beagles
beak *noun*
beaks
beaker *noun*
beakers
beam *noun*
beams
beam *verb*
beams
beaming
beamed
bean★ *noun*
beans
bear☆ *verb*
bears
bearing
bore
borne
bear☆ *noun*
bears
bearable
beard *noun*
beards
bearded
bearing *noun*
bearings
beast *noun*
beasts
beastly
beat *verb*
beats
beating
beat
beaten
beat *noun*
beats

beautiful
beautifully
beautify *verb*
beautifies
beautifying
beautified
beauty *noun*
beauties
beaver *noun*
beavers
becalmed
became see **become**
because
beckon *verb*
beckons
beckoning
beckoned
become *verb*
becomes
becoming
became
become
bedclothes
bedding
bedlam
bedraggled
bedridden
bedroom *noun*
bedrooms
bedside
bedspread *noun*
bedspreads
bedstead *noun*
bedsteads
bedtime
bee *noun*
bees
beech✪ *noun*
beeches

beef
beefburger *noun*
beefburgers
beefeater *noun*
beefeaters
beefy *adjective*
beefier
beefiest
beehive *noun*
beehives
beeline
been✣ see **be**
beer *noun*
beers
beet *noun*
beet *or* beets
beetle *noun*
beetles
beetroot *noun*
beetroot
before
beforehand
beg *verb*
begs
begging
begged
began see **begin**
beggar *noun*
beggars
begin *verb*
begins
beginning
began
begun
beginner *noun*
beginners
beginning *noun*
beginnings

★ A **bean** is a vegetable. **! been**.
☆ To **bear** something is to carry it and a **bear** is an animal. **! bare**.
✪ **Beech** means 'a tree'. **! beach**.
✣ You use **been** in e.g. *I've been to the zoo.* **! bean**.

a
b
c
d
e
f
g
h
i
j
k
l
m
n
o
p
q
r
s
t
u
v
w
x
y
z

begrudge *verb*
begrudges
begrudging
begrudged

begun see **begin**

behalf

behave *verb*
behaves
behaving
behaved

behaviour

behead *verb*
beheads
beheading
beheaded

behind *adverb* and *preposition*

behind *noun*
behinds

beige *noun*

being *noun*
beings

belch *verb*
belches
belching
belched

belch *noun*
belches

belfry *noun*
belfries

belief *noun*
beliefs

believe *verb*
believes
believing
believed

believable

believer

bellow *verb*
bellows
bellowing
bellowed

bellows

belly *noun*
bellies

belong *verb*
belongs
belonging
belonged

belongings

beloved

below

belt *noun*
belts

belt *verb*
belts
belting
belted

bench *noun*
benches

bend *verb*
bends
bending
bent

bend *noun*
bends

beneath

benefaction

benefactor *noun*
benefactors

benefit *noun*
benefits

beneficial
beneficially

benevolence

benevolent

bent see **bend**

bequeath *verb*
bequeaths
bequeathing
bequeathed

bequest

bereaved★

bereavement

bereft☆

beret *noun*
berets

berry *noun*
berries

berserk

berth *noun*
berths

beside

besides

besiege *verb*
besieges
besieging
besieged

bestseller *noun*
bestsellers

bet *noun*
bets

bet *verb*
bets
betting
bet
betted

betray *verb*
betrays
betraying
betrayed

betrayal

better *adjective* and *adverb*

★ You use **bereaved** when you mean a person with a close relative who has died. **! bereft**.

☆ You use **bereft** when you mean 'deprived of something', e.g. *bereft of hope*. **! bereaved**.

better *verb*
betters
bettering
bettered

between

beware★ *verb*

bewilder *verb*
bewilders
bewildering
bewildered

bewilderment

bewitch *verb*
bewitches
bewitching
bewitched

beyond

bi-
bi- at the beginning of a word means 'two', e.g. **bicycle** (= a machine with two wheels), **bilateral** (= having two sides).

bias *noun*
biases

biased

bib *noun*
bibs

Bible *noun*
Bibles

biblical

bicycle *noun*
bicycles

bid *noun*
bids

bid *verb*
bids
bidding
bid

bide *verb*
bides
biding
bided

big *adjective*
bigger
biggest

bigamist

bigamous

bigamy

bike *noun*
bikes

bikini *noun*
bikinis

bile

bilge *noun*
bilges

bilingual

billiards

billion *noun*
billions

billionth

billow *noun*
billows

billow *verb*
billows
billowing
billowed

billy goat *noun*
billy goats

binary

bind *verb*
binds
binding
bound

bingo

binoculars

bio-
bio- at the beginning of a word means 'life', e.g. **biography** (= a story of a person's life), **biology** (= the study of living things).

biodegradable
biographer
biographical
biography *noun*
biographies
biological
biologist
biology
bionic
biosphere
birch *noun*
birches
bird *noun*
birds
birdseed
Biro *noun*
Biros
birth *noun*
births
birth control
birthday *noun*
birthdays
birthmark *noun*
birthmarks
birthplace *noun*
birthplaces
biscuit *noun*
biscuits
bisect *verb*
bisects
bisecting
bisected
bishop *noun*
bishops

★ **Beware** has no other forms.

a b c d e f g h i j k l m n o p q r s t u v w x y z

bison *noun*
bison

bit *noun*
bits

bit see **bite**

bitch *noun*
bitches

bitchy *adjective*
bitchier
bitchiest

bite *verb*
bites
biting
bit
bitten

bite★ *noun*
bites

bitter

black *adjective*
blacker
blackest

black *noun*
blacks

blackberry *noun*
blackberries

blackbird *noun*
blackbirds

blackboard *noun*
blackboards

blacken *verb*
blackens
blackening
blackened

blackmail *verb*
blackmails
blackmailing
blackmailed

blackout *noun*
blackouts

blacksmith *noun*
blacksmiths

bladder *noun*
bladders

blade *noun*
blades

blame *verb*
blames
blaming
blamed

blame *noun*

blancmange *noun*
blancmanges

blank *adjective* and *noun*
blanks

blanket *noun*
blankets

blare *verb*
blares
blaring
blared

blaspheme *verb*
blasphemes
blaspheming
blasphemed

blasphemous

blasphemy

blast *noun*
blasts

blast *verb*
blasts
blasting
blasted

blast-off

blaze *noun*
blazes

blaze *verb*
blazes
blazing
blazed

blazer *noun*
blazers

bleach *noun*
bleaches

bleach *verb*
bleaches
bleaching
bleached

bleak *adjective*
bleaker
bleakest

bleary *adjective*
blearier
bleariest
blearily

bleat *noun*
bleats

bleat *verb*
bleats
bleating
bleated

bleed *verb*
bleeds
bleeding
bled

bleep *noun*
bleeps

blemish *noun*
blemishes

blend *verb*
blends
blending
blended

blend *noun*
blends

bless *verb*
blesses
blessing
blessed

blessing *noun*
blessings

blew☆ see **blow**

blight *noun*
blights

★ A **bite** is an act of biting. **! byte**.

☆ You use **blew** in e.g. *the wind blew hard*. **! blue**.

blind *adjective*
blinder
blindest

blind *verb*
blinds
blinding
blinded

blind *noun*
blinds

blindfold *noun*
blindfolds

blindfold *verb*
blindfolds
blindfolding
blindfolded

blink *verb*
blinks
blinking
blinked

bliss

blissful
blissfully

blister *noun*
blisters

blitz *noun*
blitzes

blizzard *noun*
blizzards

bloated

block *noun*
blocks

block *verb*
blocks
blocking
blocked

blockade *noun*
blockades

blockage *noun*
blockages

blond *adjective*
blonder
blondest

blonde★ *noun*
blondes

blood

bloodhound *noun*
bloodhounds

bloodshed

bloodshot

bloodstream

bloodthirsty *adjective*
bloodthirstier
bloodthirstiest

bloody *adjective*
bloodier
bloodiest

bloom *verb*
blooms
blooming
bloomed

bloom *noun*
blooms

blossom *noun*
blossoms

blossom *verb*
blossoms
blossoming
blossomed

blot *noun*
blots

blot *verb*
blots
blotting
blotted

blotch *noun*
blotches

blotchy *adjective*
blotchier
blotchiest

blouse *noun*
blouses

blow *noun*
blows

blow *verb*
blows
blowing
blew
blown

blowlamp *noun*
blowlamps

blowtorch *noun*
blowtorches

blue *adjective*
bluer
bluest

blue☆ *noun*
blues

bluebell *noun*
bluebells

bluebottle *noun*
bluebottles

blueprint *noun*
blueprints

bluff *verb*
bluffs
bluffing
bluffed

bluff *noun*
bluffs

blunder *verb*
blunders
blundering
blundered

blunder *noun*
blunders

blunt *adjective*
blunter
bluntest

blur *verb*
blurs
blurring
blurred

★ You use **blonde** when you are talking about a girl or woman.
☆ **Blue** is the colour. **! blew**.

a b c d e f g h i j k l m n o p q r s t u v w x y z

blur *noun*
blurs
blush *verb*
blushes
blushing
blushed
bluster *verb*
blusters
blustering
blustered
blustery
boa constrictor *noun*
boa constrictors
boar★ *noun*
boars
board☆ *noun*
boards
board *verb*
boards
boarding
boarded
boarder *noun*
boarders
board game *noun*
board games
boast *verb*
boasts
boasting
boasted
boastful
boastfully
boat *noun*
boats
boating
bob *verb*
bobs
bobbing
bobbed
bobble *noun*
bobbles
bobsled *noun*
bobsleds
bobsleigh *noun*
bobsleighs
bodice *noun*
bodices
bodily
body *noun*
bodies
bodyguard *noun*
bodyguards
boggy *adjective*
boggier
boggiest
bogus
boil *verb*
boils
boiling
boiled
boil *noun*
boils
boiler *noun*
boilers
boisterous
boisterously
bold *adjective*
bolder
boldest
bollard *noun*
bollards
bolster *verb*
bolsters
bolstering
bolstered
bolster *noun*
bolsters
bolt *noun*
bolts
bolt *verb*
bolts
bolting
bolted
bomb *noun*
bombs
bomb *verb*
bombs
bombing
bombed
bombard *verb*
bombards
bombarding
bombarded
bombardment
bomber *noun*
bombers
bond *noun*
bonds
bondage
bone *noun*
bones
bonfire *noun*
bonfires
bonnet *noun*
bonnets
bonus *noun*
bonuses
bony *adjective*
bonier
boniest
boo *verb*
boos
booing
booed
booby *noun*
boobies
book *noun*
books
book *verb*
books
booking
booked
bookcase *noun*
bookcases
booklet *noun*
booklets

★ A **boar** is a wild pig. **! bore**.
☆ A **board** is a piece of wood. **! bored**.

bookmaker *noun*
bookmakers

bookmark *noun*
bookmarks

boom *noun*
booms

boom *verb*
booms
booming
boomed

boomerang *noun*
boomerangs

boost *verb*
boosts
boosting
boosted

booster *noun*
boosters

boot *noun*
boots

boot *verb*
boots
booting
booted

booth *noun*
booths

border *noun*
borders

borderline

bore *verb*
bores
boring
bored

bore★ *noun*
bores

boredom

boring

born☆

borne✪ see **bear**

borough *noun*
boroughs

borrow *verb*
borrows
borrowing
borrowed

bosom *noun*
bosoms

boss *noun*
bosses

boss *verb*
bosses
bossing
bossed

bossy *adjective*
bossier
bossiest

botanical

botanist

botany

both

bother *verb*
bothers
bothering
bothered

bother *noun*

bottle *noun*
bottles

bottle *verb*
bottles
bottling
bottled

bottleneck *noun*
bottlenecks

bottom *noun*
bottoms

bottomless

bough✣ *noun*
boughs

bought

boulder *noun*
boulders

bounce *verb*
bounces
bouncing
bounced

bounce *noun*
bounces

bouncing

bouncy *adjective*
bouncier
bounciest

bound *verb*
bounds
bounding
bounded

bound *adjective* and *noun*
bounds

bound see **bind**

boundary *noun*
boundaries

bounds

bouquet *noun*
bouquets

bout *noun*
bouts

boutique *noun*
boutiques

bow✹ *noun*
bows

★ **Bore** means 'something boring'. **! boar**.

☆ You use **born** in e.g. *He was born in June*. **! borne**.

✪ You use **borne** in e.g. *She has borne three children* and *The cost is borne by the government*. **! born**.

✣ A **bough** is a part of a tree. **! bow**.

✹ A **bow** is a knot with loops and rhymes with 'go'. A **bow** is also the front of a ship or a bending of the body and rhymes with 'cow'.

a b c d e f g h i j k l m n o p q r s t u v w x y z

bow★ *verb*
bows
bowing
bowed

bowels

bowl *noun*
bowls

bowl *verb*
bowls
bowling
bowled

bow-legged

bowler *noun*
bowlers

bowling

bowls

bow tie *noun*
bow ties

box *noun*
boxes

box *verb*
boxes
boxing
boxed

boxer *noun*
boxers

Boxing Day *noun*

boy *noun*
boys

boycott *verb*
boycotts
boycotting
boycotted

boyfriend *noun*
boyfriends

boyhood

boyish

bra *noun*
bras

brace *noun*
braces

bracelet *noun*
bracelets

braces

bracken

bracket *noun*
brackets

bracket *verb*
brackets
bracketing
bracketed

brag *verb*
brags
bragging
bragged

braid *noun*
braids

braille

brain *noun*
brains

brainy *adjective*
brainier
brainiest

brake☆ *noun*
brakes

bramble *noun*
brambles

branch *noun*
branches

branch *verb*
branches
branching
branched

brand *noun*
brands

brand *verb*
brands
branding
branded

brandish *verb*
brandishes
brandishing
brandished

brand new

brandy *noun*
brandies

brass

brassière *noun*
brassières

brassy *adjective*
brassier
brassiest

brave *adjective*
braver
bravest

brave *noun*
braves

bravery

brawl *noun*
brawls

brawn

brawny *adjective*
brawnier
brawniest

bray *verb*
brays
braying
brayed

brazen

brazier *noun*
braziers

breach✪ *noun*
breaches

bread

breadth *noun*
breadths

breadwinner *noun*
breadwinners

★ To **bow** is to bend the body and rhymes with 'cow'.
☆ A **brake** is what makes a car stop. **! break**.
✪ A **breach** is a gap or a breaking of a rule. **! breech**.

break★ *verb*
breaks
breaking
broke
broken
break *noun*
breaks
breakable
breakage *noun*
breakages
breakdown *noun*
breakdowns
breaker *noun*
breakers
breakfast *noun*
breakfasts
breakneck
breakthrough *noun*
breakthroughs
breakwater *noun*
breakwaters
breast *noun*
breasts
breaststroke
breath *noun*
breaths
breathalyse
breathalyses
breathalysing
breathalysed
breathalyser *noun*
breathalysers
breathe *verb*
breathes
breathing
breathed
breather *noun*
breathers
breathless
breathtaking
bred see **breed**
breech☆ *noun*
breeches
breeches *plural noun*
breed *verb*
breeds
breeding
bred
breed *noun*
breeds
breeder *noun*
breeders
breeze *noun*
breezes
breezy *adjective*
breezier
breeziest
brethren
brevity
brew *verb*
brews
brewing
brewed
brewer *noun*
brewers
brewery *noun*
breweries
briar✪ *noun*
briars
bribe *noun*
bribes
bribe *verb*
bribes
bribing
bribed
bribery
brick *noun*
bricks
bricklayer *noun*
bricklayers
bride *noun*
brides
bridal✣
bridegroom *noun*
bridegrooms
bridesmaid *noun*
bridesmaids
bridge *noun*
bridges
bridle✹ *noun*
bridles
brief *adjective*
briefer
briefest
brief *noun*
briefs
brief *verb*
briefs
briefing
briefed
briefcase *noun*
briefcases
brigade *noun*
brigades
brigadier *noun*
brigadiers
brigand *noun*
brigands
bright *adjective*
brighter
brightest

★ To **break** something is to make it go into pieces. **! brake**.
☆ A **breech** is a part of a gun. **! breach**.
✪ **Briar** means 'a prickly bush' and 'a pipe'. You will sometimes see it spelt *brier*.
✣ **Bridal** means 'to do with a bride'. **! bridle**.
✹ A **bridle** is part of a horse's harness. **! bridal**.

a b c d e f g h i j k l m n o p q r s t u v w x y z

brighten *verb*
brightens
brightening
brightened

brilliance

brilliant

brim *noun*
brims

brimming

brine

bring *verb*
brings
bringing
brought

brink

brisk *adjective*
brisker
briskest

bristle *noun*
bristles

bristly
bristlier
bristliest

British

Briton *noun*
Britons

brittle *adjective*
brittler
brittlest

broach★ *verb*
broaches
broaching
broached

broad *adjective*
broader
broadest
broadly

broadcast *noun*
broadcasts

broadcast *verb*
broadcasts
broadcasting
broadcast

broadcaster

broaden *verb*
broadens
broadening
broadened

broad-minded

broadside *noun*
broadsides

brochure *noun*
brochures

brogue *noun*
brogues

broke see **break**

broken see **break**

bronchitis

bronze

brooch☆ *noun*
brooches

brood *noun*
broods

brood *verb*
broods
brooding
brooded

broody *adjective*
broodier
broodiest

brook *noun*
brooks

broom *noun*
brooms

broomstick *noun*
broomsticks

broth *noun*
broths

brother *noun*
brothers

brotherly

brother-in-law *noun*
brothers-in-law

brought see **bring**

brow *noun*
brows

brown *adjective*
browner
brownest

brownie✪ *noun*
brownies

Brownie✢ *noun*
Brownies

browse *verb*
browses
browsing
browsed

bruise *noun*
bruises

bruise *verb*
bruises
bruising
bruised

brunette *noun*
brunettes

brush *noun*
brushes

brush *verb*
brushes
brushing
brushed

Brussels sprout *noun*
Brussels sprouts

brutal
brutally

brutality
brutalities

★ **Broach** means 'to mention something'. **! brooch**.
☆ A **brooch** is an ornament you wear. **! broach**.
✪ A **brownie** is a chocolate cake.
✢ A **Brownie** is a junior Guide.

brute *noun*
brutes
bubble *noun*
bubbles
bubble *verb*
bubbles
bubbling
bubbled
bubble gum
bubbly *adjective*
bubblier
bubbliest
buccaneer *noun*
buccaneers
buck *noun*
bucks
buck *verb*
bucks
bucking
bucked
bucket *noun*
buckets
bucketful *noun*
bucketfuls
buckle *noun*
buckles
buckle *verb*
buckles
buckling
buckled
bud *noun*
buds
Buddhism
Buddhist
budding
budge *verb*
budges
budging
budged
budgerigar *noun*
budgerigars
budget *noun*
budgets
budget *verb*
budgets
budgeting
budgeted
budgie *noun*
budgies
buff
buffalo *noun*
buffalo *or* buffaloes
buffer *noun*
buffers
buffet *noun*
buffets
bug *noun*
bugs
bug *verb*
bugs
bugging
bugged
bugle *noun*
bugles
bugler *noun*
buglers
build *verb*
builds
building
built
builder *noun*
builders
building *noun*
buildings
built-in
built-up
bulb *noun*
bulbs
bulge *noun*
bulges
bulge *verb*
bulges
bulging
bulged
bulk
bulky *adjective*
bulkier
bulkiest
bull *noun*
bulls
bulldog *noun*
bulldogs
bulldoze *verb*
bulldozes
bulldozing
bulldozed
bulldozer *noun*
bulldozers
bullet *noun*
bullets
bulletin *noun*
bulletins
bulletproof
bullfight *noun*
bullfights
bullfighter
bullion
bullock *noun*
bullocks
bull's-eye *noun*
bull´s-eyes
bully *verb*
bullies
bullying
bullied
bully *noun*
bullies
bulrush *noun*
bulrushes
bulwark★ *noun*
bulwarks
bulwarks☆ *plural noun*
bum *noun*
bums

★ A **bulwark** is a strong wall.
☆ **Bulwarks** are the sides of a ship.

a b c d e f g h i j k l m n o p q r s t u v w x y z

bumblebee *noun*
bumblebees
bump *verb*
bumps
bumping
bumped
bump *noun*
bumps
bumper *adjective* and *noun*
bumpers
bumpy *adjective*
bumpier
bumpiest
bunch *noun*
bunches
bundle *noun*
bundles
bundle *verb*
bundles
bundling
bundled
bung *verb*
bungs
bunging
bunged
bung *noun*
bungs
bungalow *noun*
bungalows
bungle *verb*
bungles
bungling
bungled
bungler *noun*
bunglers
bunk *noun*
bunks
bunk bed *noun*
bunk beds
bunker *noun*
bunkers
bunny *noun*
bunnies
bunsen burner *noun*
bunsen burners
buoy *noun*
buoys
buoyancy
buoyant
burden *noun*
burdens
burdensome
bureau★ *noun*
bureaux
burglar *noun*
burglars
burglary *noun*
burglaries
burgle *verb*
burgles
burgling
burgled
burial *noun*
burials
burly *adjective*
burlier
burliest
burn☆ *verb*
burns
burning
burnt *or* burned
burn *noun*
burns
burner *noun*
burners
burning
burp *noun*
burps
burp *verb*
burps
burping
burped
burr *noun*
burrs
burrow *noun*
burrows
burrow *verb*
burrows
burrowing
burrowed
burst *verb*
bursts
bursting
burst
burst *noun*
bursts
bury *verb*
buries
burying
buried
bus *noun*
buses
bus stop *noun*
bus stops
bush *noun*
bushes
bushy *adjective*
bushier
bushiest
busily
business *noun*
businesses
businesslike
busker *noun*
buskers

★ **Bureau** is a French word used in English. It means 'a writing desk' or 'an office'.

☆ You use **burned** in e.g. *I burned the cakes*. You use **burnt** in e.g. *I can smell burnt cakes*. You use **burned** or **burnt** in e.g. *I have burned/burnt the cakes*.

bust *verb*
busts
busting
bust
bust *noun*
busts
bust *adjective*
bustle *verb*
bustles
bustling
bustled
busy *adjective*
busier
busiest
busybody *noun*
busybodies
but★
butcher *noun*
butchers
butchery
butler *noun*
butlers
butt☆ *noun*
butts
butt✪ *verb*
butts
butting
butted
butter
buttercup *noun*
buttercups
butterfingers *noun*
butterfingers
butterfly *noun*
butterflies
butterscotch *noun*
butterscotches

buttocks
button *noun*
buttons
button *verb*
buttons
buttoning
buttoned
buttonhole *noun*
buttonholes
buttress *noun*
buttresses
buy *verb*
buys
buying
bought
buy *noun*
buys
buyer *noun*
buyers
buzz *noun*
buzzes
buzz *verb*
buzzes
buzzing
buzzed
buzzard *noun*
buzzards
buzzer *noun*
buzzers
by✣ *preposition*
bye✹ *noun*
byes
bye-bye
by-election *noun*
by-elections
by-law *noun*
by-laws

bypass *noun*
bypasses
by-product *noun*
by-products
bystander *noun*
bystanders
byte❈ *noun*

Cc

CAB *abbreviation*
cab *noun*
cabs
cabaret *noun*
cabarets
cabbage *noun*
cabbages
cabin *noun*
cabins
cabinet *noun*
cabinets
cable *noun*
cables
cackle *verb*
cackles
cackling
cackled
cackle *noun*
cackles
cactus *noun*
cacti
caddie⊙ *noun*
caddies

★ You use **but** in e.g. *I like fish but I´m not hungry.* **! butt**.
☆ A **butt** is a barrel or part of a gun. **! but**.
✪ **Butt** means 'to hit with your head' **! but**.
✣ You use **by** in e.g. *a book by J. K. Rowling*. **! bye**.
✹ You use **bye** in e.g *bye for now*. **! by**.
❈ A **byte** is a unit in computing. **! bite**.
⊙ A **caddie** is a person who helps a golfer. **! caddy**..

a b c d e f g h i j k l m n o p q r s t u v w x y z

a b **c** d e f g h i j k l m n o p q r s t u v w x y z

caddy★ *noun*
caddies

cadet *noun*
cadets

cadge *verb*
cadges
cadging
cadged

cafe *noun*
cafes

cafeteria *noun*
cafeterias

caffeine

caftan *noun*
caftans use **kaftan**

cage *noun*
cages

cagey *adjective*
cagier
cagiest

cagoule *noun*
cagoules

cake *noun*
cakes

caked

calamine

calamitous

calamity *noun*
calamities

calcium

calculate *verb*
calculates
calculating
calculated

calculation *noun*
calculations

calculator *noun*
calculators

calendar *noun*
calendars

calf☆ *noun*
calves

calico

call *noun*
calls

call *verb*
calls
calling
called

calling *noun*
callings

callipers *plural noun*

callous

calm *adjective*
calmer
calmest
calmly

calmness

calorie *noun*
calories

calves✪ see **calf**

calypso *noun*
calypsos

camcorder *noun*
camcorders

came see **come**

camel *noun*
camels

camera *noun*
cameras

cameraman *noun*
cameramen

camouflage

camp *noun*
camps

camp *verb*
camps
camping
camped

campaign *noun*
campaigns

campaign *verb*
campaigns
campaigning
campaigned

camper *noun*
campers

campsite *noun*
campsites

campus *noun*
campuses

can *verb*
could

can✣ *verb*
cans
canning
canned

can *noun*
cans

canal *noun*
canals

canary *noun*
canaries

cancel *verb*
cancels
cancelling
cancelled

cancellation *noun*
cancellations

cancer *noun*
cancers

candidate *noun*
candidates

★ A **caddy** is a container for tea. **! caddie**.
☆ **Calf** means 'a young cow' and 'a part of your leg'.
✪ **Calves** is the plural of calf. **! carves**.
✣ This verb **can** means 'to put food in a can', and it has normal forms.

candle *noun*
candles
candlelight
candlestick *noun*
candlesticks
candy *noun*
candies
candyfloss
cane *noun*
canes
cane *verb*
canes
caning
caned
canine
cannabis
canned music
cannibal *noun*
cannibals
cannibalism
cannon★ *noun*
cannon *or* cannons
cannonball *noun*
cannonballs
cannot
canoe *noun*
canoes
canoe *verb*
canoes
canoeing
canoed
canoeist
canon☆ *noun*
canons
canopy *noun*
canopies
can't *verb*

canteen *noun*
canteens
canter *verb*
canters
cantering
cantered
canton *noun*
cantons
canvas✪ *noun*
canvases
canvass✣ *verb*
canvasses
canvassing
canvassed
canyon *noun*
canyons
cap *verb*
caps
capping
capped
cap *noun*
caps
capable
capably
capability
capacity *noun*
capacities
cape *noun*
capes
caper *verb*
capers
capering
capered
caper *noun*
capers
capital *noun*
capitals
capitalism

capitalist
capsize *verb*
capsizes
capsizing
capsized
capsule *noun*
capsules
captain *noun*
captains
caption *noun*
captions
captivating
captive *adjective* and *noun*
captives
captivity
captor *noun*
captors
capture *verb*
captures
capturing
captured
capture *noun*
car *noun*
cars
caramel *noun*
caramels
carat *noun*
carats
caravan *noun*
caravans
carbohydrate *noun*
carbohydrates
carbon
car boot sale *noun*
car boot sales

★ A **cannon** is a gun. **! canon**. You use **cannons** in e.g. *There are ten cannons on the walls* and **cannon** in e.g. *They use all their cannon*.
☆ A **canon** is a member of the clergy. **! cannon**.
✪ **Canvas** means ‘a strong cloth’. **! canvass**.
✣ **Canvass** means ‘to ask people for their support’. **! canvas**.

a b c d e f g h i j k l m n o p q r s t u v w x y z

carburettor *noun*
carburettors

carcass *noun*
carcasses

card *noun*
cards

cardboard

cardigan *noun*
cardigans

cardinal *noun*
cardinals

cardphone *noun*
cardphones

care *noun*
cares

care *verb*
cares
caring
cared

career *noun*
careers

career *verb*
careers
careering
careered

carefree

careful *adjective*
carefully

careless *adjective*
carelessly
carelessness

caress *verb*
caresses
caressing
caressed

caress *noun*
caresses

caretaker *noun*
caretakers

cargo *noun*
cargoes

Caribbean

caricature *noun*
caricatures

carnation *noun*
carnations

carnival *noun*
carnivals

carnivore *noun*
carnivores

carnivorous

carol *noun*
carols

caroller *noun*
carollers

carolling

carp *noun*
carp

carpenter *noun*
carpenters

carpentry

carpet *noun*
carpets

carriage *noun*
carriages

carriageway *noun*
carriageways

carrier *noun*
carriers

carrot *noun*
carrots

carry *verb*
carries
carrying
carried

cart *noun*
carts

cart *verb*
carts
carting
carted

carthorse *noun*
carthorses

cartilage

carton *noun*
cartons

cartoon *noun*
cartoons

cartoonist *noun*
cartoonists

cartridge *noun*
cartridges

cartwheel *noun*
cartwheels

carve★ *verb*
carves
carving
carved

cascade *noun*
cascades

case *noun*
cases

cash *verb*
cashes
cashing
cashed

cash *noun*

cashier *noun*
cashiers

cash register *noun*
cash registers

cask *noun*
casks

casket *noun*
caskets

casserole *noun*
casseroles

cassette *noun*
cassettes

cast *verb*
casts
casting
cast

cast *noun*
casts

castanets *plural noun*

★ You use **carves** in e.g. *He carves the meat with a knife.* **! calves**.

castaway *noun*
castaways
castle *noun*
castles
castor *noun*
castors
castor sugar
casual *adjective*
casually
casualty *noun*
casualties
cat *noun*
cats
catalogue *noun*
catalogues
catalyst *noun*
catalysts
catamaran *noun*
catamarans
catapult *noun*
catapults
catastrophe *noun*
catastrophes
catastrophic
catch *verb*
catches
catching
caught
catch *noun*
catches
catching
catchphrase *noun*
catchphrases
catchy *adjective*
catchier
catchiest
category *noun*
categories
cater *verb*
caters
catering
catered
caterer *noun*
caterers
caterpillar *noun*
caterpillars
cathedral *noun*
cathedrals
Catherine wheel *noun*
Catherine wheels
cathode *noun*
cathodes
Catholic *adjective* and *noun*
Catholics
catkin *noun*
catkins
Cat's-eye *noun*
Cat´s-eyes
cattle
caught see **catch**
cauldron *noun*
cauldrons
cauliflower *noun*
cauliflowers
cause *verb*
causes
causing
caused
cause *noun*
causes
caution *noun*
cautions
cautious *adjective*
cautiously
cavalier *noun*
cavaliers
cavalry *noun*
cavalries
cave *noun*
caves
cave *verb*
caves
caving
caved
caveman *noun*
cavemen
cavern *noun*
caverns
cavity *noun*
cavities
CD
CD-ROM *noun*
CD-ROMs
cease *verb*
ceases
ceasing
ceased
ceasefire *noun*
ceasefires
ceaseless *adjective*
ceaselessly
cedar *noun*
cedars
ceiling *noun*
ceilings
celebrate *verb*
celebrates
celebrating
celebrated
celebration *noun*
celebrations
celebrity *noun*
celebrities
celery
cell★ *noun*
cells
cellar *noun*
cellars
cello *noun*
cellos
cellular
celluloid
cellulose

★ A **cell** is a small room or a part of an organism. **! sell**.

a b c d e f g h i j k l m n o p q r s t u v w x y z

Celsius
Celt *noun*
Celts
Celtic
cement
cemetery *noun*
cemeteries
censor *verb*
censors
censoring
censored
censor★ *noun*
censors
censorship
censure *verb*
censures
censured
censuring
censure☆ *noun*
census *noun*
censuses
cent✪ *noun*
cents
centenary *noun*
centenaries
centigrade
centimetre *noun*
centimetres
centipede *noun*
centipedes
central *adjective*
centrally
centre *noun*
centres
centrifugal force
centurion *noun*
centurions
century *noun*
centuries
ceramic *adjective*
ceramics *plural noun*
cereal✣ *noun*
cereals
ceremony *noun*
ceremonies
ceremonial *adjective*
ceremonially
certain
certainly
certainty *noun*
certainties
certificate *noun*
certificates
certify *verb*
certifies
certifying
certified
chaffinch *noun*
chaffinches
chain *noun*
chains
chair *noun*
chairs
chairlift *noun*
chairlifts
chairman *noun*
chairmen
chairperson *noun*
chairpersons
chalet *noun*
chalets
chalk *noun*
chalks
chalky *adjective*
chalkier
chalkiest
challenge *verb*
challenges
challenging
challenged
challenge *noun*
challenges
challenger *noun*
challengers
chamber *noun*
chambers
champagne
champion *noun*
champions
championship *noun*
championships
chance *noun*
chances
chancel *noun*
chancels
chancellor *noun*
chancellors
Chancellor of the Exchequer
chandelier *noun*
chandeliers
change *verb*
changes
changing
changed
change *noun*
changes
changeable
channel *noun*
channels
chant *noun*
chants

★ A **censor** is someone who makes sure books and films are suitable for people to see. **! censure**.
☆ **Censure** means 'harsh criticism'. **! censor**.
✪ A **cent** is a coin used in America. **! scent**, **sent**.
✣ A **cereal** is something you eat. **! serial**.

chant *verb*
chants
chanting
chanted
chaos
chaotic *adjective*
chaotically
chap *noun*
chaps
chapatti *noun*
chapattis
chapel *noun*
chapels
chapped
chapter *noun*
chapters
char *verb*
chars
charring
charred
character *noun*
characters
characteristic *adjective*
characteristically
characteristic *noun*
characteristics
characterize *verb*
characterizes
characterizing
characterized
charades *plural noun*
charcoal
charge *verb*
charges
charging
charged
charge *noun*
charges
chariot *noun*
chariots

charioteer *noun*
charioteers
charitable *adjective*
charitably
charity *noun*
charities
charm *verb*
charms
charming
charmed
charm *noun*
charms
charming
chart *noun*
charts
charter *noun*
charters
charter *verb*
charters
chartering
chartered
charwoman *noun*
charwomen
chase *verb*
chases
chasing
chased
chase *noun*
chases
chasm *noun*
chasms
chassis *noun*
chassis
chat *verb*
chats
chatting
chatted
chat *noun*
chats

chatty *adjective*
chattier
chattiest
chateau★ *noun*
chateaux
chatter *verb*
chatters
chattering
chattered
chauffeur *noun*
chauffeurs
chauvinism
chauvinist
cheap☆ *adjective*
cheaper
cheapest
cheat *verb*
cheats
cheating
cheated
cheat *noun*
cheats
check *verb*
checks
checking
checked
check *noun*
checks
checkmate *noun*
checkmates
checkout *noun*
checkouts
check-up *noun*
check-ups
cheek *noun*
cheeks
cheek *verb*
cheeks
cheeking
cheeked

★ **Chateau** is a French word used in English. It means 'a castle or large house'.
☆ **Cheap** means 'not costing much'. **! cheep**.

a b c d e f g h i j k l m n o p q r s t u v w x y z

cheeky *adjective*
cheekier
cheekiest
cheekily

cheep★ *verb*
cheeps
cheeping
cheeped

cheer *verb*
cheers
cheering
cheered

cheer *noun*
cheers

cheerful *adjective*
cheerfully

cheerio

cheese *noun*
cheeses

cheesy *adjective*
cheesier
cheesiest

cheetah *noun*
cheetahs

chef *noun*
chefs

chemical *adjective*
chemically

chemical *noun*
chemicals

chemist *noun*
chemists

chemistry

cheque *noun*
cheques

chequebook *noun*
chequebooks

chequered

cherish *verb*
cherishes
cherishing
cherished

cherry *noun*
cherries

chess

chest *noun*
chests

chestnut *noun*
chestnuts

chest of drawers *noun*
chests of drawers

chew *verb*
chews
chewing
chewed

chewy *adjective*
chewier
chewiest

chic☆

chick *noun*
chicks

chicken *noun*
chickens

chicken *verb*
chickens
chickening
chickened

chickenpox

chief *adjective*
chiefly

chief *noun*
chiefs

chieftain *noun*
chieftains

chilblain *noun*
chilblains

child *noun*
children

childhood *noun*
childhoods

childish

childminder *noun*
childminders

childproof

chill *noun*
chills

chill *verb*
chills
chilling
chilled

chilli✪ *noun*
chillies

chilly✣ *adjective*
chillier
chilliest

chime *noun*
chimes

chime *verb*
chimes
chiming
chimed

chimney *noun*
chimneys

chimpanzee *noun*
chimpanzees

chin *noun*
chins

china

★ **Cheep** is the noise a bird makes. **! cheap**.

☆ Chic is a French word and means 'smart or elegant'. There is no word *chicly*.

✪ A **chilli** is a type of hot pepper, added to meat or vegetable dishes. **! chilly**.

✣ You use **chilly** to describe cold, bleak weather or atmosphere. **! chilli**.

chink *noun*
chinks

chip *noun*
chips

chip *verb*
chips
chipping
chipped

chirp *verb*
chirps
chirping
chirped

chirpy *adjective*
chirpier
chirpiest

chisel *noun*
chisels

chisel *verb*
chisels
chiselling
chiselled

chivalrous *adjective*
chivalrously

chivalry

chlorine

chlorophyll

choc ice *noun*
choc ices

chock-a-block

chock-full

chocolate *noun*
chocolates

choice *noun*
choices

choir *noun*
choirs

choirboy *noun*
choirboys

choirgirl *noun*
choirgirls

choke *verb*
chokes
choking
choked

choke *noun*
chokes

cholera

cholesterol

choose *verb*
chooses
choosing
chose
chosen

choosy *adjective*
choosier
choosiest

chop *verb*
chops
chopping
chopped

chop *noun*
chops

chopper *noun*
choppers

choppy *adjective*
choppier
choppiest

chopsticks

choral

chord★ *noun*
chords

chore *noun*
chores

chorister *noun*
choristers

chorus *noun*
choruses

chose see **choose**

chosen see **choose**

christen *verb*
christens
christening
christened

christening

Christian *adjective* and *noun*
Christians

Christianity

Christmas *noun*
Christmases

chrome

chromium

chromosome *noun*
chromosomes

chronic *adjective*
chronically

chronicle *noun*
chronicles

chronological *adjective*
chronologically

chronology

chrysalis *noun*
chrysalises

chrysanthemum *noun*
chrysanthemums

chubby *adjective*
chubbier
chubbiest

chuck *verb*
chucks
chucking
chucked

chuckle *verb*
chuckles
chuckling
chuckled

chuckle *noun*
chuckles

chug *verb*
chugs
chugging
chugged

chum *noun*
chums

★ A **chord** is a number of musical notes played together. **! cord**.

chummy *adjective*
chummier
chummiest

chunk *noun*
chunks

chunky *adjective*
chunkier
chunkiest

church *noun*
churches

churchyard *noun*
churchyards

churn *noun*
churns

churn *verb*
churns
churning
churned

chute★ *noun*
chutes

chutney *noun*
chutneys

cider *noun*
ciders

cigar *noun*
cigars

cigarette *noun*
cigarettes

cinder *noun*
cinders

cine camera *noun*
cine cameras

cinema *noun*
cinemas

cinnamon

circle *noun*
circles

circle *verb*
circles
circling
circled

circuit *noun*
circuits

circular *adjective* and *noun*
circulars

circulate *verb*
circulates
circulating
circulated

circulation *noun*
circulations

circumference *noun*
circumferences

circumstance *noun*
circumstances

circus *noun*
circuses

cistern *noun*
cisterns

citizen *noun*
citizens

citizenship

citric acid

citrus

city *noun*
cities

civic

civil

civilian *noun*
civilians

civilization *noun*
civilizations

civilize *verb*
civilizes
civilizing
civilized

clad

claim *verb*
claims
claiming
claimed

claim *noun*
claims

claimant *noun*
claimants

clam *noun*
clams

clamber *verb*
clambers
clambering
clambered

clammy *adjective*
clammier
clammiest

clamp *noun*
clamps

clamp *verb*
clamps
clamping
clamped

clan *noun*
clans

clang *verb*
clangs
clanging
clanged

clanger *noun*
clangers

clank *verb*
clanks
clanking
clanked

clap *verb*
claps
clapping
clapped

clap *noun*
claps

clapper *noun*
clappers

clarification

clarify *verb*
clarifies
clarifying
clarified

★ A **chute** is a funnel for sending things down. **! shoot**.

clarinet *noun*
clarinets
clarinettist
clarity
clash *verb*
clashes
clashing
clashed
clash *noun*
clashes
clasp *verb*
clasps
clasping
clasped
clasp *noun*
clasps
class *noun*
classes
class *verb*
classes
classing
classed
classic *noun*
classics
classic
classical *adjective*
classically
classification
classified
classify *verb*
classifies
classifying
classified
classmate *noun*
classmates
classroom *noun*
classrooms
clatter *noun*
clatter *verb*
clatters
clattering
clattered
clause★ *noun*
clauses
claw☆ *noun*
claws
claw✪ *verb*
claws
clawing
clawed
clay
clayey
clean *adjective*
cleaner
cleanest
cleanly
clean *verb*
cleans
cleaning
cleaned
cleaner *noun*
cleaners
cleanliness
cleanse *verb*
cleanses
cleansing
cleansed
cleanser
clear *adjective*
clearer
clearest
clearly
clear *verb*
clears
clearing
cleared
clearance *noun*
clearances
clearing *noun*
clearings
clef *noun*
clefs
clench *verb*
clenches
clenching
clenched
clergy
clergyman *noun*
clergymen
clergywoman *noun*
clergywomen
clerical
clerk *noun*
clerks
clever *adjective*
cleverer
cleverest
cliché *noun*
clichés
click *noun*
clicks
client *noun*
clients
cliff *noun*
cliffs
cliffhanger *noun*
cliffhangers
climate *noun*
climates
climatic
climax *noun*
climaxes
climb *verb*
climbs
climbing
climbed

★ A **clause** is a part of a sentence or contract. **! claws**.
☆ **Claws** are the hard sharp nails that some animals have on their feet. **! clause**.
✪ To **claw** is to scratch, maul, or pull a person or thing.

a b **c** d e f g h i j k l m n o p q r s t u v w x y z

climb *noun*
climbs
climber *noun*
climbers
cling *verb*
clings
clinging
clung
clingfilm
clinic *noun*
clinics
clink *verb*
clinks
clinking
clinked
clip *verb*
clips
clipping
clipped
clip *noun*
clips
clipboard *noun*
clipboards
clipper *noun*
clippers
clippers *plural noun*
clipping *noun*
clippings
cloak *noun*
cloaks
cloakroom *noun*
cloakrooms
clobber *verb*
clobbers
clobbering
clobbered
clock *noun*
clocks
clockwise
clockwork
clog *verb*
clogs
clogging
clogged
clog *noun*
clogs
cloister *noun*
cloisters
clone *noun*
clones
clone *verb*
clones
cloning
cloned
close *verb*
closes
closing
closed
close *adjective* and *noun*
closer
closest
closely
close *noun*
closes
close-up *noun*
close-ups
closure *noun*
closures
clot *noun*
clots
clot *verb*
clots
clotting
clotted
cloth *noun*
cloths
clothe *verb*
clothes
clothing
clothed
clothes
clothing
cloud *noun*
clouds
cloud *verb*
clouds
clouding
clouded
cloudless
cloudy *adjective*
cloudier
cloudiest
clout *verb*
clouts
clouting
clouted
clove *noun*
cloves
clover
clown *noun*
clowns
clown *verb*
clowns
clowning
clowned
club *noun*
clubs
club *verb*
clubs
clubbing
clubbed
cluck *verb*
clucks
clucking
clucked
clue *noun*
clues
clueless
clump *noun*
clumps
clumsiness
clumsy *adjective*
clumsier
clumsiest
clumsily
clung see **cling**
cluster *noun*
clusters
clutch *verb*
clutches
clutching
clutched

clutch *noun*
clutches
clutter *verb*
clutters
cluttering
cluttered
clutter *noun*

co-
co- makes words meaning 'together', e.g. a **co-pilot** is another pilot who sits together with the chief pilot. You often need a hyphen, e.g. **co-author**, **co-driver**, but some words are spelt joined up, e.g. **cooperate**, **coordinate**.

coach *verb*
coaches
coaching
coached
coach *noun*
coaches
coal
coarse★ *adjective*
coarser
coarsest
coarsely
coast *noun*
coasts
coast *verb*
coasts
coasting
coasted
coastal
coastguard *noun*
coastguards
coastline
coat *noun*
coats
coat *verb*
coats
coating
coated
coating *noun*
coatings
coax *verb*
coaxes
coaxing
coaxed
cobalt
cobbled
cobbler *noun*
cobblers
cobbles *plural noun*
cobblestone *noun*
cobblestones
cobra *noun*
cobras
cobweb *noun*
cobwebs
cock *noun*
cocks
cock *verb*
cocks
cocking
cocked
cockerel *noun*
cockerels
cocker spaniel *noun*
cocker spaniels
cockle *noun*
cockles
cockney *noun*
cockneys
cockpit *noun*
cockpits
cockroach *noun*
cockroaches
cocky *adjective*
cockier
cockiest
cocoa *noun*
cocoas
coconut *noun*
coconuts
cocoon *noun*
cocoons
cod☆ *noun*
cod
code *noun*
codes
code *verb*
codes
coding
coded
coeducation
coeducational
coffee *noun*
coffees
coffin *noun*
coffins
cog *noun*
cogs
cohort *noun*
cohorts
coil *verb*
coils
coiling
coiled
coil *noun*
coils
coin *noun*
coins
coin *verb*
coins
coining
coined
coinage *noun*
coinages

★ **Coarse** means 'rough' or 'crude'. **! course**.
☆ You use **cod** for the plural: *The sea is full of cod.*

a b c d e f g h i j k l m n o p q r s t u v w x y z

coincide *verb*
coincides
coinciding
coincided

coincidence *noun*
coincidences

coincidentally

coke

cola *noun*
colas

colander *noun*
colanders

cold *adjective*
colder
coldest
coldly

cold *noun*
colds

cold-blooded

coldness

coleslaw

collaborate *verb*
collaborates
collaborating
collaborated

collaboration

collaborator

collage *noun*
collages

collapse *verb*
collapses
collapsing
collapsed

collapse *noun*
collapses

collapsible

collar *noun*
collars

collate *verb*
collates
collating
collated

colleague *noun*
colleagues

collect *verb*
collects
collecting
collected

collection *noun*
collections

collective

collector

college *noun*
colleges

collide *verb*
collides
colliding
collided

collie *noun*
collies

collision *noun*
collisions

colloquial *adjective*
colloquially

colon *noun*
colons

colonel★ *noun*
colonels

colonial

colonist *noun*
colonists

colony *noun*
colonies

colossal *adjective*
colossally

colour *noun*
colours

colour *verb*
colours
colouring
coloured

colour-blind

coloured

colourful *adjective*
colourfully

colouring

colourless

colt *noun*
colts

column *noun*
columns

coma *noun*
comas

comb *noun*
combs

comb *verb*
combs
combing
combed

combat *noun*
combats

combat *verb*
combats
combating
combated

combatant *noun*
combatants

combination *noun*
combinations

combine *verb*
combines
combining
combined

combine *noun*
combines

combustion

come *verb*
comes
coming
came

comeback *noun*
comebacks

comedian *noun*
comedians

comedy *noun*
comedies

★ A **colonel** is an army officer. **! kernel**.

comet *noun*
comets
comfort *verb*
comforts
comforting
comforted
comfort *noun*
comforts
comfortable *adjective*
comfortably
comic *adjective* and *noun*
comics
comical *adjective*
comically
comma *noun*
commas
command *verb*
commands
commanding
commanded
command *noun*
commands
commander *noun*
commanders
commandment *noun*
commandments
commando *noun*
commandos
commemorate *verb*
commemorates
commemorating
commemorated
commemoration
commence *verb*
commences
commencing
commenced
commencement
commend *verb*
commends
commending
commended
commendable
commendation

comment *verb*
comments
commenting
commented
comment *noun*
comments
commentary *noun*
commentaries
commentate
commentator *noun*
commentators
commerce
commercial *adjective*
commercially
commercial *noun*
commercials
commercialized
commit *verb*
commits
committing
committed
commitment *noun*
commitments
committee *noun*
committees
commodity *noun*
commodities
common *adjective*
commoner
commonest
common *noun*
commons
commonplace
commonwealth *noun*
commonwealths
commotion *noun*
commotions
communal *adjective*
communally
commune *noun*
communes
communicate *verb*
communicates
communicating
communicated

communication *noun*
communications
communicative
communion *noun*
communions
communism
communist *noun*
communists
community *noun*
communities
commute
commuter *noun*
commuters
compact *adjective*
compactly
compact *noun*
compacts
compact disc *noun*
compact discs
companion *noun*
companions
companionship
company *noun*
companies
comparable *adjective*
comparably
comparative *adjective*
comparatively
comparative *noun*
comparatives
compare *verb*
compares
comparing
compared
comparison *noun*
comparisons
compartment *noun*
compartments
compass *noun*
compasses
compassion

compassionate *adjective*
compassionately

compatible *adjective*
compatibly

compel *verb*
compels
compelling
compelled

compensate *verb*
compensates
compensating
compensated

compensation *noun*
compensations

compère *noun*
compères

compete *verb*
competes
competing
competed

competence

competent *adjective*
competently

competition *noun*
competitions

competitive *adjective*
competitively

competitor *noun*
competitors

compilation *noun*
compilations

compile *verb*
compiles
compiling
compiled

compiler *noun*
compilers

complacent *adjective*
complacently

complain *verb*
complains
complaining
complained

complaint *noun*
complaints

complement★ *noun*
complements

complementary☆

complete *adjective*
completely

complete *verb*
completes
completing
completed

completion

complex *adjective* and *noun*
complexes

complexion *noun*
complexions

complexity *noun*
complexities

complicated

complication *noun*
complications

compliment✪ *noun*
compliments

complimentary✣

component *noun*
components

compose *verb*
composes
composing
composed

composer *noun*
composers

composition *noun*
compositions

compost

compound *noun*
compounds

comprehend *verb*
comprehends
comprehending
comprehended

comprehension *noun*
comprehensions

comprehensive *adjective*
comprehensively

comprehensive *noun*
comprehensives

compress *verb*
compresses
compressing
compressed

compression

comprise *verb*
comprises
comprising
comprised

compromise *noun*
compromises

★ A **complement** is a thing that completes something. **! compliment**.
☆ Something **complementary** completes something. **! complimentary**.
✪ A **compliment** is something good you say about someone. **! complement**.
✣ Something **complimentary** praises someone. **! complementary**.

compromise *verb*
compromises
compromising
compromised
compulsory
computation
compute *verb*
computes
computing
computed
computer *noun*
computers
comrade *noun*
comrades
comradeship
con *verb*
cons
conning
conned
concave
conceal *verb*
conceals
concealing
concealed
concealment
conceit
conceited
conceive *verb*
conceives
conceiving
conceived
concentrate *verb*
concentrates
concentrating
concentrated
concentrated
concentration *noun*
concentrations
concentric
concept *noun*
concepts
conception *noun*
conceptions
concern *verb*
concerns
concerning
concerned
concern *noun*
concerns
concerning
concert *noun*
concerts
concertina *noun*
concertinas
concerto *noun*
concertos
concession *noun*
concessions
concise *adjective*
concisely
conclude *verb*
concludes
concluding
concluded
conclusion *noun*
conclusions
concrete *adjective* and *noun*
concussion
condemn *verb*
condemns
condemning
condemned
condemnation
condensation
condense *verb*
condenses
condensing
condensed
condition *noun*
conditions
condom *noun*
condoms
conduct *verb*
conducts
conducting
conducted
conduct *noun*
conduction
conductor *noun*
conductors
cone *noun*
cones
confectioner *noun*
confectioners
confectionery
confer *verb*
confers
conferring
conferred
conference *noun*
conferences
confess *verb*
confesses
confessing
confessed
confession *noun*
confessions
confetti
confide *verb*
confides
confiding
confided
confidence *noun*
confidences
confident *adjective*
confidently
confidential *adjective*
confidentially
confine *verb*
confines
confining
confined
confinement
confirm *verb*
confirms
confirming
confirmed
confirmation
confiscate *verb*
confiscates
confiscating
confiscated

confiscation *noun*
confiscations
conflict *verb*
conflicts
conflicting
conflicted
conflict *noun*
conflicts
conform *verb*
conforms
conforming
conformed
conformity
confront *verb*
confronts
confronting
confronted
confrontation *noun*
confrontations
confuse *verb*
confuses
confusing
confused
confusion *noun*
confusions
congested
congestion
congratulate *verb*
congratulates
congratulating
congratulated
congratulations *plural noun*
congregation *noun*
congregations
congress *noun*
congresses
congruence
congruent
conical
conifer *noun*
conifers
coniferous
conjunction *noun*
conjunctions
conjure *verb*
conjures
conjuring
conjured
conjuror *noun*
conjurors
conker★ *noun*
conkers
connect *verb*
connects
connecting
connected
connection *noun*
connections
conning tower *noun*
conning towers
conquer☆ *verb*
conquers
conquering
conquered
conqueror *noun*
conquerors
conquest *noun*
conquests
conscience
conscientious *adjective*
conscientiously
conscious *adjective*
consciously
consciousness
conscription
consecutive *adjective*
consecutively
consensus
consent *verb*
consents
consenting
consented
consent *noun*
consequence *noun*
consequences
consequently
conservation
conservationist
conservative
Conservative✪ *noun*
Conservatives
conservatory *noun*
conservatories
conserve *verb*
conserves
conserving
conserved
consider *verb*
considers
considering
considered
considerable *adjective*
considerably
considerate *adjective*
considerately
consideration *noun*
considerations
consist *verb*
consists
consisting
consisted
consistency *noun*
consistencies
consistent *adjective*
consistently
consolation *noun*
consolations

★ A **conker** is the fruit of a horse chestnut tree. **! conquer**.
☆ To **conquer** means ‘to invade or take over’. **! conker**.
✪ Use a capital C when you mean a member of the political party.

console *verb*
consoles
consoling
consoled
consonant *noun*
consonants
conspicuous *adjective*
conspicuously
conspiracy *noun*
conspiracies
conspirator
conspire *verb*
conspires
conspiring
conspired
constable *noun*
constables
constancy
constant *adjective*
constantly
constant *noun*
constants
constellation *noun*
constellations
constipated
constipation
constituency *noun*
constituencies
constituent *noun*
constituents
constitute *verb*
constitutes
constituting
constituted
constitution *noun*
constitutions
constitutional
construct *verb*
constructs
constructing
constructed
construction *noun*
constructions
constructive

consul *noun*
consuls
consult *verb*
consults
consulting
consulted
consultant *noun*
consultants
consultation *noun*
consultations
consume *verb*
consumes
consuming
consumed
consumer *noun*
consumers
consumption
contact *noun*
contacts
contact *verb*
contacts
contacting
contacted
contagious
contain *verb*
contains
containing
contained
container *noun*
containers
contaminate *verb*
contaminates
contaminating
contaminated
contamination
contemplate *verb*
contemplates
contemplating
contemplated
contemplation
contemporary *adjective* and *noun*
contemporaries
contempt

contemptible *adjective*
contemptibly
contemptuous *adjective*
contemptuously
contend *verb*
contends
contending
contended
contender *noun*
contenders
content *adjective* and *noun*
contented *adjective*
contentedly
contentment
contents *plural noun*
contest *verb*
contests
contesting
contested
contest *noun*
contests
contestant *noun*
contestants
context *noun*
contexts
continent *noun*
continents
continental
continual *adjective*
continually
continuation
continue *verb*
continues
continuing
continued
continuous *adjective*
continuously
continuity
contour *noun*
contours
contraception

contraceptive *noun*
contraceptives

contract *verb*
contracts
contracting
contracted

contract *noun*
contracts

contraction *noun*
contractions

contractor *noun*
contractors

contradict *verb*
contradicts
contradicting
contradicted

contradiction *noun*
contradictions

contradictory

contraflow *noun*
contraflows

contraption *noun*
contraptions

contrary *adjective* and *noun*

contrast *verb*
contrasts
contrasting
contrasted

contrast *noun*
contrasts

contribute *verb*
contributes
contributing
contributed

contribution *noun*
contributions

contributor *noun*
contributors

contrivance *noun*
contrivances

contrive *verb*
contrives
contriving
contrived

control *verb*
controls
controlling
controlled

control *noun*
controls

controller *noun*
controllers

controversial *adjective*
controversially

controversy *noun*
controversies

conundrum *noun*
conundrums

convalescence

convalescent

convection

convector *noun*
convectors

convenience *noun*
conveniences

convenient *adjective*
conveniently

convent *noun*
convents

convention *noun*
conventions

conventional *adjective*
conventionally

converge *verb*
converges
converging
converged

conversation *noun*
conversations

conversational *adjective*
conversationally

converse *verb*
converses
conversing
conversed

converse *noun*

conversion *noun*
conversions

convert *verb*
converts
converting
converted

convert *noun*
converts

convertible

convex

convey *verb*
conveys
conveying
conveyed

conveyor belt *noun*
conveyor belts

convict *verb*
convicts
convicting
convicted

convict *noun*
convicts

conviction *noun*
convictions

convince *verb*
convinces
convincing
convinced

convoy *noun*
convoys

cook *verb*
cooks
cooking
cooked

cook *noun*
cooks

cooker *noun*
cookers

cookery

cool *adjective*
cooler
coolest
coolly

cool *verb*
cools
cooling
cooled
cooler
coolness
coop *noun*
coops
cooperate *verb*
cooperates
cooperating
cooperated
cooperation
cooperative
coordinate *verb*
coordinates
coordinating
coordinated
coordinate *noun*
coordinates
coordination
coordinator *noun*
coordinators
coot *noun*
coots
cop *verb*
cops
copping
copped
cop *noun*
cops
cope *verb*
copes
coping
coped
copier *noun*
copiers
copper *noun*
coppers
copper sulphate

copy *verb*
copies
copying
copied
copy *noun*
copies
coral
cord★ *noun*
cords
cordial *adjective*
cordially
cordial *noun*
cordials
cordiality
corduroy
core *noun*
cores
corgi *noun*
corgis
cork *noun*
corks
corkscrew *noun*
corkscrews
cormorant *noun*
cormorants
corn *noun*
corns
corned beef
corner *noun*
corners
corner *verb*
corners
cornering
cornered
cornet *noun*
cornets
cornfield *noun*
cornfields
cornflakes
cornflour

cornflower *noun*
cornflowers
Cornish
Cornish pasty *noun*
Cornish pasties
corny *adjective*
cornier
corniest
coronation *noun*
coronations
coroner *noun*
coroners
corporal *noun*
corporals
corporal *adjective*
corporation *noun*
corporations
corps☆ *noun*
corps
corpse✪ *noun*
corpses
corpuscle *noun*
corpuscles
corral *noun*
corrals
correct *adjective*
correctly
correct *verb*
corrects
correcting
corrected
correction *noun*
corrections
correctness
correspond *verb*
corresponds
corresponding
corresponded
correspondence

★ A **cord** is a piece of thin rope. **! chord**.
☆ A **corps** is a unit of soldiers. **! corpse**.
✪ A **corpse** is a dead body. **! corps**.

a b **c** d e f g h i j k l m n o p q r s t u v w x y z

a b c d e f g h i j k l m n o p q r s t u v w x y z

correspondent *noun*
correspondents

corridor *noun*
corridors

corrode *verb*
corrodes
corroding
corroded

corrosion

corrosive

corrugated

corrupt

corruption

corset *noun*
corsets

cosmetics *plural noun*

cosmic

cosmonaut *noun*
cosmonauts

cost *verb*
costs
costing
cost

cost *noun*
costs

costly *adjective*
costlier
costliest

costume *noun*
costumes

cosy *adjective*
cosier
cosiest

cosy *noun*
cosies

cot *noun*
cots

cottage *noun*
cottages

cotton

couch *noun*
couches

cough *verb*
coughs
coughing
coughed

cough *noun*
coughs

could see **can**

couldn't

council★ *noun*
councils

councillor☆ *noun*
councillors

counsel✪ *noun*
counsels

counsel *verb*
counsels
counselling
counselled

counsellor✣ *noun*
counsellors

count *verb*
counts
counting
counted

count *noun*
counts

countdown *noun*
countdowns

countenance *noun*
countenances

counter-
counter- makes words meaning 'opposite', e.g. a **counter-claim** is a claim someone makes in response to a claim from someone else. You often need a hyphen, but some words are spelt joined up, e.g. **counteract**, **counterbalance**.

counter *noun*
counters

counterfeit

countess *noun*
countesses

countless

country *noun*
countries

countryman *noun*
countrymen

countryside

countrywoman *noun*
countrywomen

county *noun*
counties

couple *noun*
couples

couple *verb*
couples
coupling
coupled

coupling *noun*
couplings

coupon *noun*
coupons

★ A **council** is a group of people who run the affairs of a town. **! counsel**.

☆ A **councillor** is a member of a council. **! counsellor**.

✪ **Counsel** means 'advice'. **! council**.

✣ A **counsellor** is someone who gives advice. **! councillor**.

courage
courageous *adjective*
courageously
courgette *noun*
courgettes
courier *noun*
couriers
course★ *noun*
courses
court *noun*
courts
court *verb*
courts
courting
courted
courteous *adjective*
courteously
courtesy *noun*
courtesies
court martial *noun*
courts martial
courtship
courtyard *noun*
courtyards
cousin *noun*
cousins
cove *noun*
coves
cover *verb*
covers
covering
covered
cover *noun*
covers
coverage
cover-up *noun*
cover-ups
cow *noun*
cows
coward *noun*
cowards
cowardice
cowardly
cowboy *noun*
cowboys
cowslip *noun*
cowslips
cox *noun*
coxes
coxswain *noun*
coxswains
coy *adjective*
coyly
coyness
crab *noun*
crabs
crack *verb*
cracks
cracking
cracked
crack *noun*
cracks
cracker *noun*
crackers
crackle *verb*
crackles
crackling
crackled
crackling
cradle *noun*
cradles
craft *noun*
crafts
craftsman *noun*
craftsmen
craftsmanship
crafty *adjective*
craftier
craftiest
craftily
craftiness
crag *noun*
crags
craggy *adjective*
craggier
craggiest
cram *verb*
crams
cramming
crammed
cramp *verb*
cramps
cramping
cramped
cramp *noun*
cramps
crane *noun*
cranes
crane *verb*
cranes
craning
craned
crane fly *noun*
crane flies
crank *verb*
cranks
cranking
cranked
crank *noun*
cranks
cranky *adjective*
crankier
crankiest
cranny *noun*
crannies
crash *verb*
crashes
crashing
crashed
crash *noun*
crashes
crate *noun*
crates
crater *noun*
craters

★ You use **course** in e.g. *a French course.* **! coarse**.

a b c d e f g h i j k l m n o p q r s t u v w x y z

crave *verb*
craves
craving
craved

crawl *verb*
crawls
crawling
crawled

crawl *noun*
crawls

crayon *noun*
crayons

craze *noun*
crazes

craziness

crazy *adjective*
crazier
craziest
crazily

creak *verb*
creaks
creaking
creaked

creak *noun*
creaks

creaky *adjective*
creakier
creakiest

cream *noun*
creams

creamy *adjective*
creamier
creamiest

crease *verb*
creases
creasing
creased

crease *noun*
creases

create *verb*
creates
creating
created

creation *noun*
creations

creative *adjective*
creatively

creativity

creator *noun*
creators

creature *noun*
creatures

crèche *noun*
crèches

credibility

credible *adjective*
credibly

credit *verb*
credits
crediting
credited

credit *noun*

creditable *adjective*
creditably

creditor *noun*
creditors

creed *noun*
creeds

creek *noun*
creeks

creep *verb*
creeps
creeping
crept

creep *noun*
creeps

creeper *noun*
creepers

creepy *adjective*
creepier
creepiest

cremate *verb*
cremates
cremating
cremated

cremation *noun*
cremations

crematorium *noun*
crematoria

creosote

crêpe *noun*
crêpes

crept see **creep**

crescendo *noun*
crescendos

crescent *noun*
crescents

cress

crest *noun*
crests

crevice *noun*
crevices

crew *noun*
crews

crib *verb*
cribs
cribbing
cribbed

crib *noun*
cribs

cricket★ *noun*
crickets

cricketer *noun*
cricketers

cried see **cry**

crime *noun*
crimes

criminal *adjective* and *noun*
criminals

crimson

crinkle *verb*
crinkles
crinkling
crinkled

★ **Cricket** means 'a game' and 'an insect like a grasshopper'.

crinkly *adjective*
crinklier
crinkliest

cripple *verb*
cripples
crippling
crippled

cripple *noun*
cripples

crisis *noun*
crises

crisp *adjective*
crisper
crispest

crisp *noun*
crisps

criss-cross *adjective*

critic *noun*
critics

critical *adjective*
critically

criticism *noun*
criticisms

criticize *verb*
criticizes
criticizing
criticized

croak *verb*
croaks
croaking
croaked

croak *noun*
croaks

crochet★ *noun*

crock *noun*
crocks

crockery

crocodile *noun*
crocodiles

crocus *noun*
crocuses

croft *noun*
crofts

crofter

croissant *noun*
croissants

crook *noun*
crooks

crook *verb*
crooks
crooking
crooked

crooked

croon *verb*
croons
crooning
crooned

crop *noun*
crops

crop *verb*
crops
cropping
cropped

cross-
cross- makes words meaning 'across', e.g. a *cross-channel ferry* is one that goes across the English Channel. You usually need a hyphen, but some words are spelt joined up, e.g. **crossroads** and **crosswind**.

cross *adjective*
crossly

cross *verb*
crosses
crossing
crossed

cross *noun*
crosses

crossbar *noun*
crossbars

crossbow *noun*
crossbows

cross-country

cross-examine *verb*
cross-examines
cross-examining
cross-examined

cross-examination *noun*
cross-examinations

cross-eyed

crossing *noun*
crossings

cross-legged

crossness

crossroads *noun*
crossroads

cross-section *noun*
cross-sections

crosswise

crossword *noun*
crosswords

crotchet☆ *noun*
crotchets

crouch *verb*
crouches
crouching
crouched

crow *noun*
crows

crow *verb*
crows
crowing
crowed

crowbar *noun*
crowbars

crowd *noun*
crowds

★ **Crochet** is a kind of needlework. **! crotchet**.
☆ A **crotchet** is a note in music. **! crochet**.

a b **c** d e f g h i j k l m n o p q r s t u v w x y z

crowd *verb*
crowds
crowding
crowded

crown *noun*
crowns

crown *verb*
crowns
crowning
crowned

crow's-nest *noun*
crow´s-nests

crucial *adjective*
crucially

crucifix *noun*
crucifixes

crucifixion★ *noun*
crucifixions

crucify *verb*
crucifies
crucifying
crucified

crude *adjective*
cruder
crudest

cruel *adjective*
crueller
cruellest
cruelly

cruelty *noun*
cruelties

cruise *verb*
cruises
cruising
cruised

cruise *noun*
cruises

cruiser *noun*
cruisers

crumb *noun*
crumbs

crumble *verb*
crumbles
crumbling
crumbled

crumbly *adjective*
crumblier
crumbliest

crumpet *noun*
crumpets

crumple *verb*
crumples
crumpling
crumpled

crunch *noun*
crunches

crunch *verb*
crunches
crunching
crunched

crunchy *adjective*
crunchier
crunchiest

crusade *noun*
crusades

crusader *noun*
crusaders

crush *verb*
crushes
crushing
crushed

crush *noun*
crushes

crust *noun*
crusts

crustacean *noun*
crustaceans

crutch *noun*
crutches

cry *verb*
cries
crying
cried

cry *noun*
cries

crypt *noun*
crypts

crystal *noun*
crystals

crystalline

crystallize *verb*
crystallizes
crystallizing
crystallized

cub *noun*
cubs

cubbyhole *noun*
cubbyholes

cube *noun*
cubes

cube *verb*
cubes
cubing
cubed

cubic

cubicle *noun*
cubicles

cuboid *noun*
cuboids

cuckoo *noun*
cuckoos

cucumber *noun*
cucumbers

cud

cuddle *verb*
cuddles
cuddling
cuddled

cuddly

cue☆ *noun*
cues

cuff *verb*
cuffs
cuffing
cuffed

★ Use a capital C when you are talking about Christ.
☆ A **cue** is a signal for action or a stick used in snooker. **! queue**.

cuff *noun*
cuffs
cul-de-sac *noun*
cul-de-sacs *or*
culs-de-sac
culminate *verb*
culminates
culminating
culminated
culmination
culprit *noun*
culprits
cult *noun*
cults
cultivate *verb*
cultivates
cultivating
cultivated
cultivation
cultivated
culture *noun*
cultures
cultural *adjective*
culturally
cultured
cunning
cup *noun*
cups
cup *verb*
cups
cupping
cupped
cupboard *noun*
cupboards
cupful *noun*
cupfuls
curate *noun*
curates
curator *noun*
curators
curb★ *verb*
curbs
curbing
curbed
curd *noun*
curds
curdle *verb*
curdles
curdling
curdled
cure *verb*
cures
curing
cured
cure *noun*
cures
curfew *noun*
curfews
curiosity *noun*
curiosities
curious *adjective*
curiously
curl *verb*
curls
curling
curled
curl *noun*
curls
curly *adjective*
curlier
curliest
currant☆ *noun*
currants
currency *noun*
currencies
current✪ *noun*
currents
current *adjective*
currently
curriculum *noun*
curriculums *or*
curricula
curry *verb*
curries
currying
curried
curry *noun*
curries
curse *verb*
curses
cursing
cursed
curse *noun*
curses
cursor *noun*
cursors
curtain *noun*
curtains
curtsy *verb*
curtsies
curtsying
curtsied
curtsy *noun*
curtsies
curvature *noun*
curvatures
curve *verb*
curves
curving
curved
curve *noun*
curves
cushion *noun*
cushions
cushion *verb*
cushions
cushioning
cushioned
custard

★ To **curb** a feeling is to restrain it. **! kerb**.
☆ A **currant** is a small dried grape. **! current**.
✪ A **current** is a flow of water, air, or electricity. **! currant**.

custom *noun*
customs

customary *adjective*
customarily

customer *noun*
customers

customize *noun*
customizes
customizing
customized

cut *verb*
cuts
cutting
cut

cut *noun*
cuts

cute *adjective*
cuter
cutest

cutlass *noun*
cutlasses

cutlery

cutlet *noun*
cutlets

cut-out *noun*
cut-outs

cut-price

cutter *noun*
cutters

cutting *noun*
cuttings

cycle *noun*
cycles

cycle *verb*
cycles
cycling
cycled

cyclist *noun*
cyclists

cyclone *noun*
cyclones

cyclonic

cygnet★ *noun*
cygnets

cylinder *noun*
cylinders

cylindrical

cymbal *noun*
cymbals

cynic *noun*
cynics

cynical *adjective*
cynically

cynicism

cypress *noun*
cypresses

Dd

dab *verb*
dabs
dabbing
dabbed

dab *noun*
dabs

dabble *verb*
dabbles
dabbling
dabbled

dachshund *noun*
dachshunds

dad *noun*
dads

daddy *noun*
daddies

daddy-long-legs *noun*
daddy-long-legs

daffodil *noun*
daffodils

daft *adjective*
dafter
daftest

dagger *noun*
daggers

dahlia *noun*
dahlias

daily *adjective* and *adverb*

daintiness

dainty *adjective*
daintier
daintiest
daintily

dairy *noun*
dairies

daisy *noun*
daisies

dale *noun*
dales

Dalmatian *noun*
Dalmatians

dam *noun*
dams

dam☆ *verb*
dams
damming
dammed

damage *verb*
damages
damaging
damaged

damage *noun*

damages *plural noun*

Dame✪ *noun*
Dames

★ A **cygnet** is a young swan. **! signet**.
☆ **Dam** means 'to build a dam across water'. **! damn**.
✪ Use a capital D when it is a title, e.g. *Dame Jane Smith*.

dame★ *noun*
dames

damn☆ *verb*
damns
damning
damned

damned

damp *adjective* and *noun*
damper
dampest

dampen *verb*
dampens
dampening
dampened

damson *noun*
damsons

dance *verb*
dances
dancing
danced

dance *noun*
dances

dancer *noun*
dancers

dandelion *noun*
dandelions

dandruff

danger *noun*
dangers

dangerous *adjective*
dangerously

dangle *verb*
dangles
dangling
dangled

dappled

dare *verb*
dares
daring
dared

dare *noun*
dares

daredevil *noun*
daredevils

daring

dark *adjective* and *noun*
darker
darkest

darken *verb*
darkens
darkening
darkened

darkness

darkroom *noun*
darkrooms

darling *noun*
darlings

darn *verb*
darns
darning
darned

dart *noun*
darts

dartboard *noun*
dartboards

dash *verb*
dashes
dashing
dashed

dash *noun*
dashes

dashboard *noun*
dashboards

data✪ *plural noun*

database *noun*
databases

date *noun*
dates

date *verb*
dates
dating
dated

daughter *noun*
daughters

dawdle *verb*
dawdles
dawdling
dawdled

dawn *noun*
dawns

dawn *verb*
dawns
dawning
dawned

day *noun*
days

daybreak

daydream *verb*
daydreams
daydreaming
daydreamed

daylight

day-to-day

daze *verb*
dazes
dazing
dazed

daze *noun*

dazzle *verb*
dazzles
dazzling
dazzled

★ Use a small d when you mean a pantomime woman played by a man.

☆ **Damn** means 'to say that something is very bad'. **! dam**.

✪ **Data** is strictly a plural noun, but is often used as a singular noun: *Here is the data.*

de-
de- makes verbs with an opposite meaning, e.g. **deactivate** means 'to stop something working'. You need a hyphen when the word begins with an *e* or *i*, e.g. **de-escalate**, **de-ice**.

dead

deaden *verb*
deadens
deadening
deadened

dead end *noun*
dead ends

deadline *noun*
deadlines

deadlock

deadly *adjective*
deadlier
deadliest

deaf *adjective*
deafer
deafest

deafness

deafen *verb*
deafens
deafening
deafened

deal *verb*
deals
dealing
dealt

deal *noun*
deals

dealer *noun*
dealers

dean *noun*
deans

dear★ *adjective*
dearer
dearest

death *noun*
deaths

deathly

debatable

debate *noun*
debates

debate *verb*
debates
debating
debated

debris

debt *noun*
debts

debtor *noun*
debtors

debug *verb*
debugs
debugging
debugged

début *noun*
débuts

decade *noun*
decades

decay *verb*
decays
decaying
decayed

decay *noun*

deceased

deceit

deceitful *adjective*
deceitfully

deceive *verb*
deceives
deceiving
deceived

December

decency

decent *adjective*
decently

deception *noun*
deceptions

deceptive

decibel *noun*
decibels

decide *verb*
decides
deciding
decided

deciduous

decimal *noun*
decimals

decimalization

decimalize *verb*
decimalizes
decimalizing
decimalized

decipher *verb*
deciphers
deciphering
deciphered

decision *noun*
decisions

decisive *adjective*
decisively

deck *noun*
decks

deckchair *noun*
deckchairs

declaration *noun*
declarations

declare *verb*
declares
declaring
declared

decline *verb*
declines
declining
declined

★ **Dear** means 'loved' or 'expensive'. **! deer**.

decode *verb*
decodes
decoding
decoded

decompose *verb*
decomposes
decomposing
decomposed

decorate *verb*
decorates
decorating
decorated

decoration *noun*
decorations

decorative

decorator *noun*
decorators

decoy *noun*
decoys

decrease *verb*
decreases
decreasing
decreased

decrease *noun*
decreases

decree *noun*
decrees

decree *verb*
decrees
decreeing
decreed

decrepit

dedicate *verb*
dedicates
dedicating
dedicated

dedication

deduce *verb*
deduces
deducing
deduced

deduct *verb*
deducts
deducting
deducted

deductible

deduction *noun*
deductions

deed *noun*
deeds

deep *adjective*
deeper
deepest
deeply

deepen *verb*
deepens
deepening
deepened

deep-freeze *noun*
deep-freezes

deer★ *noun*
deer

deface *verb*
defaces
defacing
defaced

default *noun*
defaults

defeat *verb*
defeats
defeating
defeated

defeat *noun*
defeats

defect *noun*
defects

defect *verb*
defects
defecting
defected

defective *adjective*
defectively

defence *noun*
defences

defenceless

defend *verb*
defends
defending
defended

defendant *noun*
defendants

defender *noun*
defenders

defensible

defensive *adjective*
defensively

defer *verb*
defers
deferring
deferred

deferment

defiance

defiant *adjective*
defiantly

deficiency *noun*
deficiencies

deficient

deficit *noun*
deficits

defile *verb*
defiles
defiling
defiled

define *verb*
defines
defining
defined

definite *adjective*
definitely

definition *noun*
definitions

deflate *verb*
deflates
deflating
deflated

★ A **deer** is an animal. **! dear**.

a b c **d** e f g h i j k l m n o p q r s t u v w x y z

deflect *verb*
deflects
deflecting
deflected
deflection
deforestation
deformed
deformity *noun*
deformities
defrost *verb*
defrosts
defrosting
defrosted
deft *adjective*
defter
deftest
deftly
defuse *verb*
defuses
defusing
defused
defy *verb*
defies
defying
defied
degenerate *verb*
degenerates
degenerating
degenerated
degeneration
degradation
degrade *verb*
degrades
degrading
degraded
degree *noun*
degrees
dehydrated
dehydration
de-ice *verb*
de-ices
de-icing
de-iced
de-icer
deity *noun*
deities
dejected
dejection
delay *verb*
delays
delaying
delayed
delay *noun*
delays
delegate *noun*
delegates
delegate *verb*
delegates
delegating
delegated
delegation
delete *verb*
deletes
deleting
deleted
deletion
deliberate *adjective*
deliberately
deliberate *verb*
deliberates
deliberating
deliberated
deliberation
delicacy *noun*
delicacies
delicate *adjective*
delicately
delicatessen *noun*
delicatessens
delicious *adjective*
deliciously
delight *verb*
delights
delighting
delighted
delight *noun*
delights
delightful *adjective*
delightfully
delinquency
delinquent *noun*
delinquents
delirious *adjective*
deliriously
delirium *noun*
deliver *verb*
delivers
delivering
delivered
delivery *noun*
deliveries
delta *noun*
deltas
delude *verb*
deludes
deluding
deluded
deluge *noun*
deluges
deluge *verb*
deluges
deluging
deluged
delusion *noun*
delusions
de luxe
demand *verb*
demands
demanding
demanded
demand *noun*
demands
demanding
demerara
demist *verb*
demists
demisting
demisted
demo *noun*
demos
democracy *noun*
democracies
democrat *noun*
democrats

democratic *adjective*
democratically

demolish *verb*
demolishes
demolishing
demolished

demolition

demon *noun*
demons

demonstrate *verb*
demonstrates
demonstrating
demonstrated

demonstration *noun*
demonstrations

demonstrator *noun*
demonstrators

demoralize *verb*
demoralizes
demoralizing
demoralized

demote *verb*
demotes
demoting
demoted

den *noun*
dens

denial *noun*
denials

denim

denominator *noun*
denominators

denote *verb*
denotes
denoting
denoted

denounce *verb*
denounces
denouncing
denounced

denunciation

dense *adjective*
denser
densest
densely

density *noun*

dent *noun*
dents

dental

dentist *noun*
dentists

dentistry

denture *noun*
dentures

deny *verb*
denies
denying
denied

deodorant *noun*
deodorants

depart *verb*
departs
departing
departed

department *noun*
departments

departure *noun*
departures

depend *verb*
depends
depending
depended

dependable

dependant★ *noun*
dependants

dependence

dependent☆ *adjective*

depict *verb*
depicts
depicting
depicted

deplorable *adjective*
deplorably

deplore *verb*
deplores
deploring
deplored

deport *verb*
deports
deporting
deported

deposit *verb*
deposits
depositing
deposited

deposit *noun*
deposits

depot *noun*
depots

depress *verb*
depresses
depressing
depressed

depression *noun*
depressions

deprivation

deprive *verb*
deprives
depriving
deprived

depth *noun*
depths

deputize *verb*
deputizes
deputizing
deputized

deputy *noun*
deputies

derail *verb*
derails
derailing
derailed

★ **Dependant** is a noun: *She has three dependants.* **! dependent**.
☆ **Dependent** is an adjective: *She has three dependent children.* **! dependant**.

a b c d e f g h i j k l m n o p q r s t u v w x y z

derby *noun*
derbies
derelict
deride *verb*
derides
deriding
derided
derision
derive *verb*
derives
deriving
derived
derrick *noun*
derricks
derv
descant★ *noun*
descants
descend *verb*
descends
descending
descended
descendant *noun*
descendants
descent☆
describe *verb*
describes
describing
described
description *noun*
descriptions
descriptive *adjective*
descriptively
desert✪ *noun*
deserts
desert *verb*
deserts
deserting
deserted
deserter *noun*
deserters
desertion
deserve *verb*
deserves
deserving
deserved
design *verb*
designs
designing
designed
design *noun*
designs
designate *verb*
designates
designating
designated
designer *noun*
designers
desirable
desire *verb*
desires
desiring
desired
desire *noun*
desires
desk *noun*
desks
desktop
desolate
desolation
despair *verb*
despairs
despairing
despaired
despair *noun*
despatch *verb* use **dispatch**
desperate *adjective*
desperately
desperation
despicable *adjective*
despicably
despise *verb*
despises
despising
despised
despite
dessert✣ *noun*
desserts
dessertspoon *noun*
dessertspoons
destination *noun*
destinations
destined
destiny *noun*
destinies
destroy *verb*
destroys
destroying
destroyed
destroyer *noun*
destroyers
destruction
destructive
detach *verb*
detaches
detaching
detached
detachable
detached
detachment *noun*
detachments
detail *noun*
details
detain *verb*
detains
detaining
detained

★ **Descant** is a term in music. **! descent**.
☆ **Descent** is a way down. **! descant**.
✪ A **desert** is a very dry area of land. **! dessert**.
✣ A **dessert** is a sweet pudding. **! desert**.

detect *verb*
detects
detecting
detected
detection
detector
detective *noun*
detectives
detention *noun*
detentions
deter *verb*
deters
deterring
deterred
detergent *noun*
detergents
deteriorate *verb*
deteriorates
deteriorating
deteriorated
deterioration
determination
determine *verb*
determines
determining
determined
determined
deterrence
deterrent *noun*
deterrents
detest *verb*
detests
detesting
detested
detestable
detonate *verb*
detonates
detonating
detonated
detonation

detonator
detour *noun*
detours
deuce★
devastate *verb*
devastates
devastating
devastated
devastation
develop *verb*
develops
developing
developed
development *noun*
developments
device *noun*
devices
devil *noun*
devils
devilish
devilment
devious *adjective*
deviously
devise *verb*
devises
devising
devised
devolution
devote *verb*
devotes
devoting
devoted
devotee
devotion
devour *verb*
devours
devouring
devoured
devout
dew☆

dewy
dhoti✪ *noun*
dhotis
diabetes
diabetic
diabolical *adjective*
diabolically
diagnose *verb*
diagnoses
diagnosing
diagnosed
diagnosis *noun*
diagnoses
diagonal *adjective*
diagonally
diagonal *noun*
diagonals
diagram *noun*
diagrams
dial *noun*
dials
dial *verb*
dials
dialling
dialled
dialect *noun*
dialects
dialogue *noun*
dialogues
diameter *noun*
diameters
diamond *noun*
diamonds
diaphragm *noun*
diaphragms
diarrhoea
diary *noun*
diaries
dice *noun*
dice

★ **Deuce** is a score in tennis. **! juice**.
☆ **Dew** is moisture on grass and plants. **! due**.
✪ A **dhoti** is a piece of clothing worn by Hindus.

a b c **d** e f g h i j k l m n o p q r s t u v w x y z

dictate *verb*
dictates
dictating
dictated
dictation
dictator *noun*
dictators
dictatorial *adjective*
dictatorially
dictionary *noun*
dictionaries
did see **do**
diddle *verb*
diddles
diddling
diddled
didn't *verb*
die *verb*
dies
dying
died
diesel *noun*
diesels
diet *noun*
diets
diet *verb*
diets
dieting
dieted
differ *verb*
differs
differing
differed
difference *noun*
differences
different *adjective*
differently
difficult
difficulty *noun*
difficulties

dig *verb*
digs
digging
dug
dig *noun*
digs
digest *verb*
digests
digesting
digested
digestible
digestion
digestive
digger
digit *noun*
digits
digital *adjective*
digitally
dignified
dignity
dike *noun* use **dyke**
dilemma *noun*
dilemmas
dilute *verb*
dilutes
diluting
diluted
dilution
dim *adjective*
dimmer
dimmest
dimly
dimension *noun*
dimensions
diminish *verb*
diminishes
diminishing
diminished

dimple *noun*
dimples
din *noun*
dins
dine *verb*
dines
dining
dined
diner★ *noun*
diners
dinghy☆ *noun*
dinghies
dingy✪ *adjective*
dingier
dingiest
dinner✣ *noun*
dinners
dinosaur *noun*
dinosaurs
dioxide *noun*
dioxides
dip *verb*
dips
dipping
dipped
dip *noun*
dips
diphtheria
diploma *noun*
diplomas
diplomacy
diplomat
diplomatic *adjective*
diplomatically
dire *adjective*
direr
direst
direct *adjective*
directly

★ A **diner** is someone who eats dinner. **! dinner**.
☆ A **dinghy** is a small sailing boat. **! dingy**.
✪ **Dingy** means 'dirty-looking, drab, dull-coloured'. **! dinghy**.
✣ **Dinner** is a meal. **! diner**.

direct *verb*
directs
directing
directed

direction *noun*
directions

director *noun*
directors

directory *noun*
directories

dirt

dirtiness

dirty *adjective*
dirtier
dirtiest
dirtily

dis-
dis- makes a word with an opposite meaning, e.g. **disobey** means 'to refuse to obey' and **disloyal** means 'not loyal'. These words are spelt joined up.

disability *noun*
disabilities

disabled

disadvantage *noun*
disadvantages

disagree *verb*
disagrees
disagreeing
disagreed

disagreeable *adjective*
disagreeably

disagreement *noun*
disagreements

disappear *verb*
disappears
disappearing
disappeared

disappearance *noun*
disappearances

disappoint *verb*
disappoints
disappointing
disappointed

disappointing

disappointment *noun*
disappointments

disapproval

disapprove *verb*
disapproves
disapproving
disapproved

disarm *verb*
disarms
disarming
disarmed

disarmament

disaster *noun*
disasters

disastrous *adjective*
disastrously

disc★ *noun*
discs

discard *verb*
discards
discarding
discarded

discharge *verb*
discharges
discharging
discharged

disciple *noun*
disciples

discipline

disc jockey *noun*
disc jockeys

disclose *verb*
discloses
disclosing
disclosed

disclosure

disco *noun*
discos

discomfort

disconnect *verb*
disconnects
disconnecting
disconnected

disconnection

discontent

discontented

discotheque *noun*
discotheques

discount *noun*
discounts

discourage *verb*
discourages
discouraging
discouraged

discouragement

discover *verb*
discovers
discovering
discovered

discovery *noun*
discoveries

discreet *adjective*
discreetly

discriminate *verb*
discriminates
discriminating
discriminated

discrimination

discus *noun*
discuses

discuss *verb*
discusses
discussing
discussed

★ A **disc** is a flat round object. **!** **disk**.

discussion *noun*
discussions

disease *noun*
diseases

diseased

disgrace *verb*
disgraces
disgracing
disgraced

disgrace *noun*

disgraceful *adjective*
disgracefully

disguise *verb*
disguises
disguising
disguised

disguise *noun*
disguises

disgust *verb*
disgusts
disgusting
disgusted

disgust *noun*

disgusting

dish *noun*
dishes

dish *verb*
dishes
dishing
dished

dishcloth *noun*
dishcloths

dishevelled

dishonest *adjective*
dishonestly

dishonesty

dishwasher *noun*
dishwashers

disinfect *verb*
disinfects
disinfecting
disinfected

disinfectant *noun*
disinfectants

disintegrate *verb*
disintegrates
disintegrating
disintegrated

disintegration

disinterested

disk★ *noun*
disks

dislike *verb*
dislikes
disliking
disliked

dislike *noun*
dislikes

dislocate *verb*
dislocates
dislocating
dislocated

dislodge *verb*
dislodges
dislodging
dislodged

disloyal *adjective*
disloyally

disloyalty

dismal *adjective*
dismally

dismantle *verb*
dismantles
dismantling
dismantled

dismay

dismayed

dismiss *verb*
dismisses
dismissing
dismissed

dismissal

dismount *verb*
dismounts
dismounting
dismounted

disobedience

disobedient

disobey *verb*
disobeys
disobeying
disobeyed

disorder *noun*
disorders

disorderly

dispatch *verb*
dispatches
dispatching
dispatched

dispense *verb*
dispenses
dispensing
dispensed

dispenser *noun*
dispensers

dispersal

disperse *verb*
disperses
dispersing
dispersed

display *verb*
displays
displaying
displayed

display *noun*
displays

displease *verb*
displeases
displeasing
displeased

disposable

disposal

★ A **disk** is what you put in a computer. **! disc**.

dispose *verb*
disposes
disposing
disposed

disprove *verb*
disproves
disproving
disproved

dispute *noun*
disputes

disqualification

disqualify *verb*
disqualifies
disqualifying
disqualified

disregard *verb*
disregards
disregarding
disregarded

disrespect

disrespectful
adjective
disrespectfully

disrupt *verb*
disrupts
disrupting
disrupted

disruption

disruptive

dissatisfaction

dissatisfied

dissect *verb*
dissects
dissecting
dissected

dissection

dissolve *verb*
dissolves
dissolving
dissolved

dissuade *verb*
dissuades
dissuading
dissuaded

distance *noun*
distances

distant *adjective*
distantly

distil *verb*
distils
distilling
distilled

distillery *noun*
distilleries

distinct *adjective*
distinctly

distinction *noun*
distinctions

distinctive

distinguish *verb*
distinguishes
distinguishing
distinguished

distinguished

distort *verb*
distorts
distorting
distorted

distortion *noun*
distortions

distract *verb*
distracts
distracting
distracted

distraction *noun*
distractions

distress *verb*
distresses
distressing
distressed

distress *noun*

distribute *verb*
distributes
distributing
distributed

distribution

distributor

district *noun*
districts

distrust

distrustful

disturb *verb*
disturbs
disturbing
disturbed

disturbance *noun*
disturbances

disused

ditch *noun*
ditches

dither *verb*
dithers
dithering
dithered

divan *noun*
divans

dive *verb*
dives
diving
dived

diver *noun*
divers

diverse

diversify *verb*
diversifies
diversifying
diversified

diversion *noun*
diversions

diversity

divert *verb*
diverts
diverting
diverted

divide *verb*
divides
dividing
divided

dividend *noun*
dividends

dividers *plural noun*

divine *adjective*
divinely

a b c **d** e f g h i j k l m n o p q r s t u v w x y z

divine *verb*
divines
divining
divined

divinity

divisible

division *noun*
divisions

divorce *verb*
divorces
divorcing
divorced

divorce *noun*
divorces

Diwali★

dizziness

dizzy *adjective*
dizzier
dizziest
dizzily

do *verb*
does
doing
did
done

docile *adjective*
docilely

dock *noun*
docks

dock *verb*
docks
docking
docked

dock *noun*
docks

docker *noun*
dockers

dockyard *noun*
dockyards

doctor *noun*
doctors

doctrine *noun*
doctrines

document *noun*
documents

documentary *noun*
documentaries

doddery

dodge *verb*
dodges
dodging
dodged

dodge *noun*
dodges

dodgem *noun*
dodgems

dodgy *adjective*
dodgier
dodgiest

doe☆ *noun*
does

doesn't *abbreviation*

dog *noun*
dogs

dog-eared

dogged *adjective*
doggedly

doldrums *plural noun*

dole *verb*
doles
doling
doled

dole *noun*

doll *noun*
dolls

dollar *noun*
dollars

dolly *noun*
dollies

dolphin *noun*
dolphins

> **-dom**
> *-dom* makes nouns, e.g. **kingdom**. Other noun suffixes are **-hood**, **-ment**, **-ness**, and **-ship**.

domain *noun*
domains

dome *noun*
domes

domestic *adjective*
domestically

domesticated

dominance

dominant *adjective*
dominantly

dominate *verb*
dominates
dominating
dominated

domination

dominion *noun*
dominions

domino *noun*
dominoes

donate *verb*
donates
donating
donated

donation *noun*
donations

done see **do**

donkey *noun*
donkeys

donor *noun*
donors

don't *abbreviation*

★ **Diwali** is a Hindu festival.
☆ A **doe** is a female deer. **! dough**.

doodle *verb*
doodles
doodling
doodled

doodle *noun*
doodles

doom *verb*
dooms
dooming
doomed

doom *noun*

door *noun*
doors

doorstep *noun*
doorsteps

doorway *noun*
doorways

dope *noun*
dopes

dopey *adjective*
dopier
dopiest

dormitory *noun*
dormitories

dose *noun*
doses

dossier *noun*
dossiers

dot *verb*
dots
dotting
dotted

dot *noun*
dots

dottiness

dotty *adjective*
dottier
dottiest
dottily

double *adjective*
doubly

double *noun*
doubles

double *verb*
doubles
doubling
doubled

double-cross *verb*
double-crosses
double-crossing
double-crossed

double-decker *noun*
double-deckers

doubt *verb*
doubts
doubting
doubted

doubt *noun*
doubts

doubtful *adjective*
doubtfully

doubtless

dough★

doughnut *noun*
doughnuts

doughy *adjective*
doughier
doughiest

dove *noun*
doves

dowel *noun*
dowels

down

downcast

downfall *noun*
downfalls

downhill

downpour *noun*
downpours

downright *adjective*

downs *plural noun*

downstairs

downstream

downward *adjective*
and *adverb*

downwards *adverb*

downy *adjective*
downier
downiest

doze *verb*
dozes
dozing
dozed

dozen *noun*
dozens

dozy *adjective*
dozier
doziest

drab *adjective*
drabber
drabbest

draft *verb*
drafts
drafting
drafted

draft *noun*
drafts

drag *verb*
drags
dragging
dragged

drag *noun*

dragon *noun*
dragons

dragonfly *noun*
dragonflies

drain *verb*
drains
draining
drained

drain *noun*
drains

drainage

drake *noun*
drakes

drama *noun*
dramas

★ **Dough** is a mixture of flour and water used for baking. **! doe**.

a b c d e f g h i j k l m n o p q r s t u v w x y z

dramatic *adjective*
dramatically

dramatist *noun*
dramatists

dramatization

dramatize *verb*
dramatizes
dramatizing
dramatized

drank see **drink**

drape *verb*
drapes
draping
draped

drastic *adjective*
drastically

draught *noun*
draughts

draughty *adjective*
draughtier
draughtiest

draughts *noun*

draughtsman *noun*
draughtsmen

draw★ *verb*
draws
drawing
drew
drawn

draw *noun*
draws

drawback *noun*
drawbacks

drawbridge *noun*
drawbridges

drawer☆ *noun*
drawers

drawing *noun*
drawings

drawl *verb*
drawls
drawling
drawled

dread *verb*
dreads
dreading
dreaded

dread *noun*

dreadful *adjective*
dreadfully

dreadlocks

dream *noun*
dreams

dream *verb*
dreams
dreaming
dreamt *or* dreamed

dreamy *adjective*
dreamier
dreamiest

dreariness

dreary *adjective*
drearier
dreariest
drearily

dredge *verb*
dredges
dredging
dredged

dredger

drench *verb*
drenches
drenching
drenched

dress *verb*
dresses
dressing
dressed

dress *noun*
dresses

dresser *noun*
dressers

dressing *noun*
dressings

dressmaker *noun*
dressmakers

drew see **draw**

dribble *verb*
dribbles
dribbling
dribbled

dried see **dry**

drier *noun*
driers

drift *verb*
drifts
drifting
drifted

drift *noun*
drifts

driftwood

drill *verb*
drills
drilling
drilled

drill *noun*
drills

drink *verb*
drinks
drinking
drank
drunk

drink *noun*
drinks

drinker *noun*
drinkers

drip *noun*
drips

★ To **draw** is to make a picture with a pencil, pen, or crayon. **! drawer**.

☆ A **drawer** is part of a cupboard. **! draw**.

drip *verb*
drips
dripping
dripped

dripping

drive *verb*
drives
driving
drove
driven

drive *noun*
drives

driver *noun*
drivers

drizzle *verb*
drizzles
drizzling
drizzled

drizzle *noun*

drone *verb*
drones
droning
droned

drone *noun*
drones

drool *verb*
drools
drooling
drooled

droop *verb*
droops
drooping
drooped

drop *verb*
drops
dropping
dropped

drop *noun*
drops

droplet *noun*
droplets

drought *noun*
droughts

drove see **drive**

drown *verb*
drowns
drowning
drowned

drowsiness

drowsy *adjective*
drowsier
drowsiest
drowsily

drug *noun*
drugs

drug *verb*
drugs
drugging
drugged

Druid *noun*
Druids

drum *noun*
drums

drum *verb*
drums
drumming
drummed

drummer *noun*
drummers

drumstick *noun*
drumsticks

drunk see **drink**

drunk *adjective* and *noun*
drunks

drunkard *noun*
drunkards

dry *adjective*
drier
driest
drily

dry *verb*
dries
drying
dried

dryness

dual★ *adjective*
dually

dub *verb*
dubs
dubbing
dubbed

duchess *noun*
duchesses

duck *noun*
ducks

duck *verb*
ducks
ducking
ducked

duckling *noun*
ducklings

duct *noun*
ducts

dud *noun*
duds

due☆

duel✪ *noun*
duels

duet *noun*
duets

duff

duffel coat *noun*
duffel coats

dug see **dig**

dugout *noun*
dugouts

duke *noun*
dukes

★ **Dual** means 'having two parts'. **! duel**.
☆ **Due** means 'expected'. **! dew**.
✪ A **duel** is a fight between two people. **! dual**.

a b c d e f g h i j k l m n o p q r s t u v w x y z

dull *adjective*
duller
dullest
dully

dullness

duly

dumb *adjective*
dumber
dumbest

dumbfounded

dummy *noun*
dummies

dump *verb*
dumps
dumping
dumped

dump *noun*
dumps

dumpling *noun*
dumplings

dumpy *adjective*
dumpier
dumpiest

dune *noun*
dunes

dung

dungarees

dungeon *noun*
dungeons

duo *noun*
duos

duplicate *noun*
duplicates

duplicate *verb*
duplicates
duplicating
duplicated

duplication

durability

durable

duration

during

dusk

dust

dust *verb*
dusts
dusting
dusted

dustbin *noun*
dustbins

duster *noun*
dusters

dustman *noun*
dustmen

dustpan *noun*
dustpans

dusty *adjective*
dustier
dustiest

dutiful *adjective*
dutifully

duty *noun*
duties

duvet *noun*
duvets

dwarf *noun*
dwarfs *or* dwarves

dwarf *verb*
dwarfs
dwarfing
dwarfed

dwell *verb*
dwells
dwelling
dwelt

dwelling *noun*
dwellings

dwindle *verb*
dwindles
dwindling
dwindled

dye★ *verb*
dyes
dyeing
dyed

dye *noun*
dyes

dying see **die**

dyke *noun*
dykes

dynamic *adjective*
dynamically

dynamite

dynamo *noun*
dynamos

dynasty *noun*
dynasties

dyslexia

dyslexic

dystrophy *noun*

Ee

e-
e- stands for 'electronic' and makes words about computers and the Internet, e.g. **email** (spelt joined up), **e-commerce** and **e-shopping** (spelt with hyphens).

each

eager *adjective*
eagerly

eagerness

eagle *noun*
eagles

ear *noun*
ears

earache

★ **Dye** means 'to change the colour of something'. **! die**.

eardrum *noun*
eardrums

earl *noun*
earls

early *adjective* and *adverb*
earlier
earliest

earmark *verb*
earmarks
earmarking
earmarked

earn *verb*
earns
earning
earned

earnest *adjective*
earnestly

earnings *plural noun*

earphones

earring *noun*
earrings

earth *noun*
earths

earthenware

earthly

earthquake *noun*
earthquakes

earthworm *noun*
earthworms

earthy *adjective*
earthier
earthiest

earwig *noun*
earwigs

ease *verb*
eases
easing
eased

ease *noun*

easel *noun*
easels

east *adjective* and *adverb*

east★ *noun*

Easter

easterly *adjective* and *noun*
easterlies

eastern

eastward *adjective* and *adverb*

eastwards *adverb*

easy *adjective* and *adverb*
easier
easiest
easily

eat *verb*
eats
eating
ate
eaten

eatable

eaves

ebb *verb*
ebbs
ebbing
ebbed

ebb

ebony

eccentric

eccentricity *noun*
eccentricities

echo *verb*
echoes
echoing
echoed

echo *noun*
echoes

éclair *noun*
éclairs

eclipse *noun*
eclipses

ecological

ecology

economic

economical *adjective*
economically

economics

economist *noun*
economists

economize *verb*
economizes
economizing
economized

economy *noun*
economies

ecstasy *noun*
ecstasies

ecstatic *adjective*
ecstatically

eczema

> **-ed** and **-t**
> Some verbs ending in *l*, *m*, *n*, and *p* have past forms and past participles ending in *-ed* and *-t*, e.g. **burned/burnt**, **leaped/leapt**. Both forms are correct, and the *-t* form is especially common when it comes before a noun, e.g. *burnt cakes*.

edge *noun*
edges

edge *verb*
edges
edging
edged

edgeways

★ You use a capital E in **the East**, meaning China, Japan, etc.

a b c d **e** f g h i j k l m n o p q r s t u v w x y z

edgy *adjective*
edgier
edgiest

edible

edit *verb*
edits
editing
edited

edition *noun*
editions

editor *noun*
editors

editorial *noun*
editorials

educate *verb*
educates
educating
educated

education

educational

educator

eel *noun*
eels

eerie *adjective*
eerier
eeriest
eerily

eeriness

effect★ *noun*
effects

effective *adjective*
effectively

effectiveness

effeminate

effervescence

effervescent

efficiency

efficient *adjective*
efficiently

effort *noun*
efforts

effortless *adjective*
effortlessly

egg *noun*
eggs

egg *verb*
eggs
egging
egged

> **-ei-** and **-ie-**
> The rule 'i before e except after c' is true when it is pronounced -ee-, e.g. **thief**, **ceiling**. There are a few exceptions, of which the most important are **seize** and **protein**.

Eid☆

eiderdown *noun*
eiderdowns

eight✪

eighteen

eighteenth

eighth✣ *adjective* and *noun*
eighthly

eightieth

eighty *noun*
eighties

either

eject *verb*
ejects
ejecting
ejected

ejection

elaborate *adjective*
elaborately

elaborate *verb*
elaborates
elaborating
elaborated

elaboration

elastic

elated

elation

elbow *noun*
elbows

elbow *verb*
elbows
elbowing
elbowed

elder *adjective* and *noun*
elders

elderberry *noun*
elderberries

elderly

eldest

elect *verb*
elects
electing
elected

election *noun*
elections

electorate

electric

electrical *adjective*
electrically

electrician *noun*
electricians

electricity

electrification

★ An **effect** is something that is caused by something else. **! affect**.
☆ **Eid** is a Muslim festival.
✪ **Eight** is the number. **! ate**.
✣ Note that there are two h's in **eighth**.

electrify *verb*
electrifies
electrifying
electrified

electrocute *verb*
electrocutes
electrocuting
electrocuted

electrocution

electromagnet *noun*
electromagnets

electron *noun*
electrons

electronic *adjective*
electronically

electronics

elegance

elegant *adjective*
elegantly

element *noun*
elements

elementary

elephant *noun*
elephants

elevate *verb*
elevates
elevating
elevated

elevation *noun*
elevations

eleven

eleventh

elf *noun*
elves

eligibility

eligible

eliminate *verb*
eliminates
eliminating
eliminated

elimination

élite *noun*
élites

elk *noun*
elk *or* elks

ellipse *noun*
ellipses

elliptical *adjective*
elliptically

elm *noun*
elms

elocution

eloquence

eloquent

else

elsewhere

elude *verb*
eludes
eluding
eluded

elusive *adjective*
elusively

elves see **elf**

email★ *noun*
emails

email *verb*
emails
emailing
emailed

emancipate *verb*
emancipates
emancipating
emancipated

emancipation

embankment *noun*
embankments

embark *verb*
embarks
embarking
embarked

embarkation

embarrass☆ *verb*
embarrasses
embarrassing
embarrassed

embarrassment

embassy *noun*
embassies

embedded

embers *plural noun*

emblem *noun*
emblems

embrace *verb*
embraces
embracing
embraced

embroider *verb*
embroiders
embroidering
embroidered

embroidery *noun*
embroideries

embryo *noun*
embryos

emerald *noun*
emeralds

emerge *verb*
emerges
emerging
emerged

emergence

emergency *noun*
emergencies

emery paper

emigrant *noun*
emigrants

emigrate *verb*
emigrates
emigrating
emigrated

★ **Email** is short for **electronic mail**.
☆ Note that there are two rs in **embarrass** and **embarrassment**.

a b c d **e** f g h i j k l m n o p q r s t u v w x y z

emigration

eminence

eminent

emission★ *noun*
emissions

emit *verb*
emits
emitting
emitted

emotion *noun*
emotions

emotional *adjective*
emotionally

emperor *noun*
emperors

emphasis *noun*
emphases

emphasize *verb*
emphasizes
emphasizing
emphasized

emphatic *adjective*
emphatically

empire *noun*
empires

employ *verb*
employs
employing
employed

employee *noun*
employees

employer *noun*
employers

employment

empress *noun*
empresses

empties *plural noun*

emptiness

empty *adjective*
emptier
emptiest

empty *verb*
empties
emptying
emptied

emu *noun*
emus

emulsion *noun*
emulsions

enable *verb*
enables
enabling
enabled

enamel *noun*
enamels

encampment *noun*
encampments

-ence
See the note at **-ance**.

enchant *verb*
enchants
enchanting
enchanted

enchantment

encircle *verb*
encircles
encircling
encircled

enclose *verb*
encloses
enclosing
enclosed

enclosure

encore *noun*
encores

encounter *verb*
encounters
encountering
encountered

encourage *verb*
encourages
encouraging
encouraged

encouragement

encyclopedia *noun*
encyclopedias

encyclopedic

end *verb*
ends
ending
ended

end *noun*
ends

endanger *verb*
endangers
endangering
endangered

endeavour *verb*
endeavours
endeavouring
endeavoured

ending *noun*
endings

endless *adjective*
endlessly

endurance

endure *verb*
endures
enduring
endured

enemy *noun*
enemies

energetic *adjective*
energetically

energy *noun*
energies

enforce *verb*
enforces
enforcing
enforced

★ An **emission** is something that escapes, like fumes. **! omission**.

enforceable

enforcement

engage *verb*
engages
engaging
engaged

engagement *noun*
engagements

engine *noun*
engines

engineer *noun*
engineers

engineering

engrave *verb*
engraves
engraving
engraved

engraver

engrossed

engulf *verb*
engulfs
engulfing
engulfed

enhance *verb*
enhances
enhancing
enhanced

enhancement

enjoy *verb*
enjoys
enjoying
enjoyed

enjoyable

enjoyment

enlarge *verb*
enlarges
enlarging
enlarged

enlargement *noun*
enlargements

enlist *verb*
enlists
enlisting
enlisted

enmity *noun*
enmities

enormity★ *noun*
enormities

enormous *adjective*
enormously

enormousness

enough

enquire *verb*
enquires
enquiring
enquired

enquiry☆ *noun*
enquiries

enrage *verb*
enrages
enraging
enraged

enrich *verb*
enriches
enriching
enriched

enrichment

enrol *verb*
enrols
enrolling
enrolled

enrolment

ensemble *noun*
ensembles

ensue *verb*
ensues
ensuing
ensued

ensure *verb*
ensures
ensuring
ensured

-ent
See the note at **-ant**.

entangle *verb*
entangles
entangling
entangled

entanglement

enter *verb*
enters
entering
entered

enterprise *noun*
enterprises

enterprising

entertain *verb*
entertains
entertaining
entertained

entertainer *noun*
entertainers

entertainment *noun*
entertainments

enthusiasm *noun*
enthusiasms

enthusiast *noun*
enthusiasts

enthusiastic *adjective*
enthusiastically

entire *adjective*
entirely

entirety

entitle *verb*
entitles
entitling
entitled

★ An **enormity** is a wicked act. If you mean 'large size', use **enormousness**.

☆ An **enquiry** is a question. **! inquiry**.

a b c d e f g h i j k l m n o p q r s t u v w x y z

entrance *noun*
entrances
entrance *verb*
entrances
entrancing
entranced
entrant *noun*
entrants
entreat *verb*
entreats
entreating
entreated
entreaty *noun*
entreaties
entrust *verb*
entrusts
entrusting
entrusted
entry *noun*
entries
envelop *verb*
envelops
enveloping
enveloped
envelope *noun*
envelopes
envious *adjective*
enviously
environment *noun*
environments
environmental
environmentalist *noun*
environmentalists
envy *verb*
envies
envying
envied
envy *noun*
enzyme *noun*
enzymes
epic *noun*
epics
epidemic *noun*
epidemics
epilepsy
epileptic *adjective* and *noun*
epileptics
epilogue *noun*
epilogues
episode *noun*
episodes
epistle *noun*
epistles
epitaph *noun*
epitaphs
epoch *noun*
epochs
equal *adjective*
equally
equal *verb*
equals
equalling
equalled
equal *noun*
equals
equality
equalize *verb*
equalizes
equalizing
equalized
equalizer *noun*
equalizers
equation *noun*
equations
equator
equatorial
equestrian
equilateral
equilibrium *noun*
equilibria
equinox *noun*
equinoxes
equip *verb*
equips
equipping
equipped
equipment
equivalence
equivalent

-er and **-est**
-er and *-est* make adjectives and adverbs meaning 'more' or 'most', e.g. **faster**, **slowest**. You can do this when the word has one syllable, and when a consonant comes at the end of the word after a single vowel you double it, e.g. **fatter**, **bigger**. You can use *-er* and *-est* with some two-syllable adjectives, e.g. **commoner**, **pleasantest**, and words ending in *y*, which change to *-ier* and *-iest*, e.g. **angrier**, **happiest**.

-er and **-or**
-er makes nouns meaning 'a person or thing that does something', e.g. a **helper** is a person who helps and an **opener** is a tool that opens things. You can make new words this way, e.g. **complainer**, **repairer**. Some words end in *-or*, e.g. **actor**, **visitor**, but you can't use *-or* to make new words.

era *noun*
eras

erase *verb*
erases
erasing
erased

eraser

erect *adjective*

erect *verb*
erects
erecting
erected

erection *noun*
erections

ermine *noun*
ermine

erode *verb*
erodes
eroding
eroded

erosion

errand *noun*
errands

erratic *adjective*
erratically

erroneous *adjective*
erroneously

error *noun*
errors

erupt *verb*
erupts
erupting
erupted

eruption

escalate *verb*
escalates
escalating
escalated

escalation

escalator *noun*
escalators

escape *verb*
escapes
escaping
escaped

escape *noun*
escapes

escort *verb*
escorts
escorting
escorted

escort *noun*
escorts

Eskimo *noun*
Eskimos *or* Eskimo

especially

espionage

esplanade *noun*
esplanades

> **-ess**
> *-ess* makes nouns for female people and animals, e.g. **manageress**, **lioness**.

essay *noun*
essays

essence *noun*
essences

essential *adjective*
essentially

essential *noun*
essentials

establish *verb*
establishes
establishing
established

establishment *noun*
establishments

estate *noun*
estates

esteem *verb*
esteems
esteeming
esteemed

estimate *noun*
estimates

estimate *verb*
estimates
estimating
estimated

estuary *noun*
estuaries

etch *verb*
etches
etching
etched

etching *noun*
etchings

eternal *adjective*
eternally

eternity

ether

ethnic

etymology *noun*
etymologies

eucalyptus *noun*
eucalyptuses

euphemism *noun*
euphemisms

euphemistic *adjective*
euphemistically

Eurasian

euro *noun*
euro *or* euros

European *adjective* and *noun*
Europeans

euthanasia

evacuate *verb*
evacuates
evacuating
evacuated

evacuation

evacuee

evade *verb*
evades
evading
evaded

evaluate *verb*
evaluates
evaluating
evaluated

a b c d e f g h i j k l m n o p q r s t u v w x y z

evaluation

evangelical

evangelism

evangelist *noun*
evangelists

evaporate *verb*
evaporates
evaporating
evaporated

evaporation

evasion *noun*
evasions

evasive

eve *noun*
eves

even *adjective*
evenly

even *adverb*

even *verb*
evens
evening
evened

evening *noun*
evenings

evenness

event *noun*
events

eventful *adjective*
eventfully

eventual *adjective*
eventually

ever

evergreen *adjective and noun*
evergreens

everlasting

every

everybody

everyday

everyone

everything

everywhere

evict *verb*
evicts
evicting
evicted

eviction

evidence

evident *adjective*
evidently

evil *adjective*
evilly

evil *noun*
evils

evolution

evolutionary

evolve *verb*
evolves
evolving
evolved

ewe★ *noun*
ewes

> **ex-**
> *ex-* makes nouns with the meaning 'former' or 'who used to be', e.g. **ex-president**, **ex-wife**. You use a hyphen to make these words.

exact *adjective*
exactly

exactness

exaggerate *verb*
exaggerates
exaggerating
exaggerated

exaggeration

exalt *verb*
exalts
exalting
exalted

exam *noun*
exams

examination *noun*
examinations

examine *verb*
examines
examining
examined

examiner *noun*
examiners

example *noun*
examples

exasperate *verb*
exasperates
exasperating
exasperated

exasperation

excavate *verb*
excavates
excavating
excavated

excavation *noun*
excavations

excavator *noun*
excavators

exceed *verb*
exceeds
exceeding
exceeded

exceedingly

excel *verb*
excels
excelling
excelled

excellence

excellent *adjective*
excellently

★ A **ewe** is a female sheep. **! yew**, **you**.

except★

exception *noun*
exceptions

exceptional *adjective*
exceptionally

excerpt *noun*
excerpts

excess *noun*
excesses

excessive *adjective*
excessively

exchange *verb*
exchanges
exchanging
exchanged

exchange *noun*
exchanges

excitable *adjective*
excitably

excite *verb*
excites
exciting
excited

excitedly

excitement *noun*
excitements

exclaim *verb*
exclaims
exclaiming
exclaimed

exclamation *noun*
exclamations

exclude *verb*
excludes
excluding
excluded

exclusion

exclusive *adjective*
exclusively

excrement

excrete *verb*
excretes
excreting
excreted

excretion

excursion *noun*
excursions

excusable

excuse *verb*
excuses
excusing
excused

excuse *noun*
excuses

execute *verb*
executes
executing
executed

execution *noun*
executions

executioner *noun*
executioners

executive *noun*
executives

exempt *adjective*

exemption *noun*

exercise *noun*
exercises

exercise☆ *verb*
exercises
exercising
exercised

exert *verb*
exerts
exerting
exerted

exertion *noun*
exertions

exhale *verb*
exhales
exhaling
exhaled

exhalation

exhaust *verb*
exhausts
exhausting
exhausted

exhaust *noun*
exhausts

exhaustion

exhibit *verb*
exhibits
exhibiting
exhibited

exhibit *noun*
exhibits

exhibition *noun*
exhibitions

exhibitor *noun*
exhibitors

exile *verb*
exiles
exiling
exiled

exile *noun*
exiles

exist *verb*
exists
existing
existed

existence *noun*
existences

exit *verb*
exits
exiting
exited

exit *noun*
exits

exorcism

exorcist

★ You use **except** in e.g. *everyone except me*. **! accept**.
☆ To **exercise** is to keep your body fit. **! exorcise**.

a b c d e f g h i j k l m n o p q r s t u v w x y z

exorcize★ *verb*
exorcizes
exorcizing
exorcized

exotic *adjective*
exotically

expand *verb*
expands
expanding
expanded

expanse *noun*
expanses

expansion

expect *verb*
expects
expecting
expected

expectant *adjective*
expectantly

expectation *noun*
expectations

expedition *noun*
expeditions

expel *verb*
expels
expelling
expelled

expenditure

expense *noun*
expenses

expensive

experience *verb*
experiences
experiencing
experienced

experience *noun*
experiences

experienced

experiment *verb*
experiments
experimenting
experimented

experiment *noun*
experiments

experimental *adjective*
experimentally

experimentation

expert *adjective* and *noun*
experts

expertise

expire *verb*
expires
expiring
expired

expiry

explain *verb*
explains
explaining
explained

explanation *noun*
explanations

explanatory

explode *verb*
explodes
exploding
exploded

exploit *noun*
exploits

exploit *verb*
exploits
exploiting
exploited

exploitation

exploration *noun*
explorations

exploratory

explore *verb*
explores
exploring
explored

explorer *noun*
explorers

explosion *noun*
explosions

explosive *adjective* and *noun*
explosives

export *verb*
exports
exporting
exported

export *noun*
exports

exporter *noun*
exporters

expose *verb*
exposes
exposing
exposed

exposure *noun*
exposures

express *adjective* and *noun*
expresses

express *verb*
expresses
expressing
expressed

expression *noun*
expressions

expressive *adjective*
expressively

expulsion *noun*
expulsions

exquisite *adjective*
exquisitely

extend *verb*
extends
extending
extended

extension *noun*
extensions

extensive *adjective*
extensively

extent *noun*
extents

★ To **exorcise** is to get rid of evil spirits. **!** **exercise**.

exterior *noun*
exteriors
exterminate *verb*
exterminates
exterminating
exterminated
extermination
external *adjective*
externally
extinct
extinction
extinguish *verb*
extinguishes
extinguishing
extinguished
extinguisher *noun*
extinguishers
extra *adjective* and *noun*
extras
extract *verb*
extracts
extracting
extracted
extract *noun*
extracts
extraction *noun*
extractions
extraordinary *adjective*
extraordinarily
extrasensory
extraterrestrial *adjective* and *noun*
extraterrestrials
extravagance
extravagant *adjective*
extravagantly
extreme *adjective*
extremely
extreme *noun*
extremes
extremity *noun*
extremities
exuberance
exuberant *adjective*
exuberantly
exult *verb*
exults
exulting
exulted
exultant
exultation
eye *noun*
eyes
eye *verb*
eyes
eyeing
eyed
eyeball *noun*
eyeballs
eyebrow *noun*
eyebrows
eyelash *noun*
eyelashes
eyelid *noun*
eyelids
eyepiece *noun*
eyepieces
eyesight
eyesore *noun*
eyesores
eyewitness *noun*
eyewitnesses

Ff

-f
Most nouns ending in *-f* have plurals ending in *-ves*, e.g. **shelf** - **shelves**, but some have plurals ending in *-fs*, e.g. **chiefs**. Nouns ending in *-ff* have plurals ending in *-ffs*, e.g. **cuffs**.

fable *noun*
fables
fabric *noun*
fabrics
fabricate *verb*
fabricates
fabricating
fabricated
fabulous *adjective*
fabulously
face *noun*
faces
face *verb*
faces
facing
faced
facet *noun*
facets
facetious *adjective*
facetiously
facial *adjective*
facially
facilitate *verb*
facilitates
facilitating
facilitated
facility *noun*
facilities
fact *noun*
facts
factor *noun*
factors
factory *noun*
factories
factual *adjective*
factually
fad *noun*
fads
fade *verb*
fades
fading
faded
faeces
fag *noun*
fags

a b c d e f g h i j k l m n o p q r s t u v w x y z

fagged
faggot *noun*
faggots
Fahrenheit
fail *verb*
fails
failing
failed
fail *noun*
fails
failing *noun*
failings
failure *noun*
failures
faint *adjective*
fainter
faintest
faintly
faint *verb*
faints
fainting
fainted
faint-hearted
faintness
fair *adjective*
fairer
fairest
fair★ *noun*
fairs
fairground *noun*
fairgrounds
fairly
fairness
fairy *noun*
fairies
fairyland
faith *noun*
faiths
faithful *adjective*
faithfully
faithfulness
fake *noun*
fakes
fake *verb*
fakes
faking
faked
faker
falcon *noun*
falcons
falconry
fall *verb*
falls
falling
fell
fallen
fall *noun*
falls
fallacious *adjective*
fallaciously
fallacy *noun*
fallacies
fallen see **fall**
fallout
fallow
falls *plural noun*
false *adjective*
falser
falsest
falsely
falsehood *noun*
falsehoods
falseness
falter *verb*
falters
faltering
faltered
fame
famed
familiar *adjective*
familiarly
familiarity
family *noun*
families
famine *noun*
famines
famished
famous *adjective*
famously
fan *verb*
fans
fanning
fanned
fan *noun*
fans
fanatic *noun*
fanatics
fanatical *adjective*
fanatically
fanciful *adjective*
fancifully
fancy *adjective*
fancier
fanciest
fancy *verb*
fancies
fancying
fancied
fancy *noun*
fancies
fanfare *noun*
fanfares
fang *noun*
fangs
fantastic *adjective*
fantastically
fantasy *noun*
fantasies
far *adjective* and *adverb*
farther
farthest
far-away
farce *noun*
farces

★ A **fair** is a group of outdoor entertainments or an exhibition. **! fare**.

farcical *adjective*
farcically

fare *verb*
fares
faring
fared

fare★ *noun*
fares

farewell

far-fetched

farm *noun*
farms

farm *verb*
farms
farming
farmed

farmer *noun*
farmers

farmhouse *noun*
farmhouses

farmyard *noun*
farmyards

farther☆

farthest✪

farthing *noun*
farthings

fascinate *verb*
fascinates
fascinating
fascinated

fascination

fascism

fascist *noun*
fascists

fashion *noun*
fashions

fashion *verb*
fashions
fashioning
fashioned

fashionable

fast *adjective* and *adverb*
faster
fastest

fast *verb*
fasts
fasting
fasted

fasten *verb*
fastens
fastening
fastened

fastener

fastening

fat *adjective*
fatter
fattest

fat *noun*
fats

fatal *adjective*
fatally

fatality *noun*
fatalities

fate✣ *noun*
fates

father *noun*
fathers

father-in-law *noun*
fathers-in-law

fathom *noun*
fathoms

fathom *verb*
fathoms
fathoming
fathomed

fatigue

fatigued

fatten *verb*
fattens
fattening
fattened

fattening

fatty *adjective*
fattier
fattiest

fault *noun*
faults

fault *verb*
faults
faulting
faulted

faultless *adjective*
faultlessly

faulty *adjective*
faultier
faultiest

fauna

favour *noun*
favours

favour *verb*
favours
favouring
favoured

favourable *adjective*
favourably

favourite *adjective* and *noun*
favourites

favouritism

★ A **fare** is money you pay, for example on a bus. **! fair**.

☆ You can use **farther** or **further** in e.g. *farther up the road*. See **further**.

✪ You can use **farthest** or **furthest** in e.g. *the place farthest from here*. See **furthest**.

✣ **Fate** is a power that is thought to make things happen. **! fête**.

a b c d e **f** g h i j k l m n o p q r s t u v w x y z

fawn *noun*
fawns

fax *noun*
faxes

fax *verb*
faxes
faxing
faxed

> **-fe**
> Most nouns ending in *-fe* have plurals ending in *-ves*, e.g. **life** - **lives**.

fear *noun*
fears

fear *verb*
fears
fearing
feared

fearful *adjective*
fearfully

fearless *adjective*
fearlessly

fearsome

feasible

feast *noun*
feasts

feast *verb*
feasts
feasting
feasted

feat★ *noun*
feats

feather *noun*
feathers

feathery

feature *noun*
features

feature *verb*
features
featuring
featured

February☆ *noun*
Februaries

fed see **feed**

federal

federation

fee *noun*
fees

feeble *adjective*
feebler
feeblest
feebly

feed *verb*
feeds
feeding
fed

feed *noun*
feeds

feedback

feel *verb*
feels
feeling
felt

feel *noun*

feeler *noun*
feelers

feeling *noun*
feelings

feet✪ see **foot**

feline

fell see **fall**

fell *verb*
fells
felling
felled

fell *noun*
fells

fellow *noun*
fellows

fellowship *noun*
fellowships

felt see **feel**

felt *noun*

felt-tip pen or **felt-tipped pen** *noun*
felt-tip pens *or* felt-tipped pens

female *adjective* and *noun*
females

feminine

femininity

feminism

feminist *noun*
feminists

fen *noun*
fens

fence *noun*
fences

fence *verb*
fences
fencing
fenced

fencer *adjective*
fencers

fencing

fend *verb*
fends
fending
fended

fender *noun*
fenders

ferment *verb*
ferments
fermenting
fermented

fermentation

★ A **feat** is an achievement. **! feet**.
☆ Note that **February** has two rs.
✪ **Feet** is the plural of foot. **! feat**.

ferment
fern *noun*
ferns
ferocious *adjective*
ferociously
ferocity
ferret *noun*
ferrets
ferret *verb*
ferrets
ferreting
ferreted
ferry *noun*
ferries
ferry *verb*
ferries
ferrying
ferried
fertile
fertility
fertilization
fertilize *verb*
fertilizes
fertilizing
fertilized
fertilizer *noun*
fertilizers
fervent *adjective*
fervently
fervour
festival *noun*
festivals
festive
festivity
festoon *verb*
festoons
festooning
festooned
fetal

fetch *verb*
fetches
fetching
fetched
fête★ *noun*
fêtes
fetlock *noun*
fetlocks
fetters *plural noun*
fetus☆ *noun*
fetuses
feud *noun*
feuds
feudal
feudalism
fever *noun*
fevers
fevered
feverish *adjective*
feverishly
few *adjective*
fewer
fewest
fez *noun*
fezzes
fiancé✪ *noun*
fiancés
fiancée✢ *noun*
fiancées
fiasco *noun*
fiascos
fib *noun*
fibs
fibber *noun*
fibbers
fibre *noun*
fibres
fibreglass
fibrous

fickle
fiction *noun*
fictions
fictional *adjective*
fictionally
fictitious *adjective*
fictitiously
fiddle *verb*
fiddles
fiddling
fiddled
fiddle *noun*
fiddles
fiddler *noun*
fiddlers
fiddling
fiddly
fidelity
fidget *verb*
fidgets
fidgeting
fidgeted
fidgety
field *noun*
fields
field *verb*
fields
fielding
fielded
fielder *noun*
fielders
field marshal *noun*
field marshals
fieldwork
fiend *noun*
fiends
fiendish *adjective*
fiendishly

★ A **fête** is an outdoor entertainment with stalls. **! fate**.
☆ You will also see this word spelt **foetus**.
✪ A woman's **fiancé** is the man who is going to marry her.
✢ A man's **fiancée** is the woman who is going to marry him.

a b c d e f g h i j k l m n o p q r s t u v w x y z

fierce *adjective*
fiercer
fiercest
fiercely

fierceness

fiery *adjective*
fierier
fieriest

fife *noun*
fifes

fifteen

fifteenth

fifth

fifthly

fiftieth

fifty *noun*
fifties

fig *noun*
figs

fight *verb*
fights
fighting
fought

fight *noun*
fights

fighter *noun*
fighters

figurative *adjective*
figuratively

figure *noun*
figures

figure *verb*
figures
figuring
figured

filament *noun*
filaments

file *verb*
files
filing
filed

file *noun*
files

filings *plural noun*

fill *verb*
fills
filling
filled

fill *noun*
fills

filler *noun*
fillers

fillet *noun*
fillets

filling *noun*
fillings

filly *noun*
fillies

film *noun*
films

film *verb*
films
filming
filmed

filter *noun*
filters

filter *verb*
filters
filtering
filtered

filth

filthy *adjective*
filthier
filthiest

fin *noun*
fins

final *adjective*
finally

final *noun*
finals

finale *noun*
finales

finalist *noun*
finalists

finality

finance

finance *verb*
finances
financing
financed

finances *plural noun*

financial *adjective*
financially

financier *noun*
financiers

finch *noun*
finches

find *verb*
finds
finding
found

finder *noun*
finders

findings *plural noun*

fine *adjective*
finer
finest
finely

fine *noun*
fines

fine *verb*
fines
fining
fined

finger *noun*
fingers

finger *verb*
fingers
fingering
fingered

fingernail *noun*
fingernails

fingerprint *noun*
fingerprints

finicky

finish *verb*
finishes
finishing
finished

finish *noun*
finishes

fir★ *noun*
firs

fire *noun*
fires

fire *verb*
fires
firing
fired

firearm *noun*
firearms

firefighter *noun*
firefighters

fireman *noun*
firemen

fireplace *noun*
fireplaces

fireproof

fireside *noun*
firesides

firewood

firework *noun*
fireworks

firm *adjective*
firmer
firmest
firmly

firm *noun*
firms

firmness

first *adjective* and *adverb*
firstly

first class

first floor *noun*
first floors

first-hand *adjective*

first-rate

fish *noun*
fish *or* fishes

fish *verb*
fishes
fishing
fished

fisherman *noun*
fishermen

fishmonger *noun*
fishmongers

fishy *adjective*
fishier
fishiest

fission

fist *noun*
fists

fit *adjective*
fitter
fittest

fit *verb*
fits
fitting
fitted

fit *noun*
fits

fitness

fitter *noun*
fitters

fitting *adjective*

fitting *noun*
fittings

five

fiver *noun*
fivers

fix *verb*
fixes
fixing
fixed

fix *noun*
fixes

fixture *noun*
fixtures

fizz *verb*
fizzes
fizzing
fizzed

fizzy *adjective*
fizzier
fizziest

fizzle *verb*
fizzles
fizzling
fizzled

fjord *noun*
fjords

flabbergasted

flabby *adjective*
flabbier
flabbiest

flag *noun*
flags

flag *verb*
flags
flagging
flagged

flagpole *noun*
flagpoles

flagship *noun*
flagships

flagstaff *noun*
flagstaffs

flagstone *noun*
flagstones

flair☆ *noun*

flake *noun*
flakes

flake *verb*
flakes
flaking
flaked

flaky *adjective*
flakier
flakiest

★ A **fir** is a tree. **! fur**.
☆ **Flair** is a special talent. **! flare**.

a b c d e **f** g h i j k l m n o p q r s t u v w x y z

a b c d e **f** g h i j k l m n o p q r s t u v w x y z

flame *noun*
flames

flame *verb*
flames
flaming
flamed

flamingo *noun*
flamingos

flan *noun*
flans

flank *noun*
flanks

flannel *noun*
flannels

flap *noun*
flaps

flap *verb*
flaps
flapping
flapped

flapjack *noun*
flapjacks

flare★ *noun*
flares

flare *verb*
flares
flaring
flared

flash *noun*
flashes

flash *verb*
flashes
flashing
flashed

flashback *noun*
flashbacks

flashy *adjective*
flashier
flashiest

flask *noun*
flasks

flat *adjective*
flatter
flattest
flatly

flat *noun*
flats

flatness

flatten *verb*
flattens
flattening
flattened

flatter *verb*
flatters
flattering
flattered

flatterer *noun*
flatterers

flattery

flaunt *verb*
flaunts
flaunting
flaunted

flavour *noun*
flavours

flavour *verb*
flavours
flavouring
flavoured

flavouring

flaw *noun*
flaws

flawed

flawless *adjective*
flawlessly

flax

flea☆ *noun*
fleas

fleck *noun*
flecks

flee✪ *verb*
flees
fleeing
fled

fleece *noun*
fleeces

fleece *verb*
fleeces
fleecing
fleeced

fleecy *adjective*
fleecier
fleeciest

fleet *noun*
fleets

fleeting

flesh

fleshy *adjective*
fleshier
fleshiest

flew✣ see **fly**

flex *noun*
flexes

flex *verb*
flexes
flexing
flexed

flexibility

flexible *adjective*
flexibly

flick *verb*
flicks
flicking
flicked

flick *noun*
flicks

★ A **flare** is a bright light. **! flair**.
☆ A **flea** is an insect. **! flee**.
✪ To **flee** is to run away. **! flea**.
✣ **Flew** is the past of **fly**. **! flu**, **flue**.

flicker *verb*
flickers
flickering
flickered

flight *noun*
flights

flimsy *adjective*
flimsier
flimsiest

flinch *verb*
flinches
flinching
flinched

fling *verb*
flings
flinging
flung

flint *noun*
flints

flinty *adjective*
flintier
flintiest

flip *verb*
flips
flipping
flipped

flippancy

flippant *adjective*
flippantly

flipper *noun*
flippers

flirt *verb*
flirts
flirting
flirted

flirtation

flit *verb*
flits
flitting
flitted

float *verb*
floats
floating
floated

float *noun*
floats

flock *verb*
flocks
flocking
flocked

flock *noun*
flocks

flog *verb*
flogs
flogging
flogged

flood *verb*
floods
flooding
flooded

flood *noun*
floods

floodlight *noun*
floodlights

floodlit

floor *noun*
floors

floor *verb*
floors
flooring
floored

floorboard *noun*
floorboards

flop *verb*
flops
flopping
flopped

flop *noun*
flops

floppy *adjective*
floppier
floppiest

floppy disk *noun*
floppy disks

flora

floral

florist *noun*
florists

floss

flounder *verb*
flounders
floundering
floundered

flour★

flourish *verb*
flourishes
flourishing
flourished

floury *adjective*
flourier
flouriest

flow *verb*
flows
flowing
flowed

flow *noun*
flows

flower☆ *noun*
flowers

flower *verb*
flowers
flowering
flowered

flowerpot *noun*
flowerpots

flowery

flown

flu✪

★ **Flour** is powder used in making bread. **! flower**.
☆ A **flower** is a part of a plant. **! flour**.
✪ **Flu** is an illness. **! flew**, **flue**.

a b c d e **f** g h i j k l m n o p q r s t u v w x y z

fluctuate *verb*
fluctuates
fluctuating
fluctuated

fluctuation

flue★ *noun*
flues

fluency

fluent *adjective*
fluently

fluff

fluffy *adjective*
fluffier
fluffiest

fluid *noun*
fluids

fluke *noun*
flukes

flung see **fling**

fluorescent

fluoridation

fluoride

flurry *noun*
flurries

flush *verb*
flushes
flushing
flushed

flush *noun*
flushes

flush *adjective*

flustered

flute *noun*
flutes

flutter *verb*
flutters
fluttering
fluttered

flutter *noun*
flutters

fly *verb*
flies
flying
flew
flown

fly *noun*
flies

flyleaf *noun*
flyleaves

flyover *noun*
flyovers

flywheel *noun*
flywheels

foal *noun*
foals

foam *noun*

foam *verb*
foams
foaming
foamed

foamy *adjective*
foamier
foamiest

focal

focus *verb*
focuses
focusing
focused

focus *noun*
focuses *or* foci

fodder

foe *noun*
foes

foetus *noun* see **fetus**

fog *noun*
fogs

foggy☆ *adjective*
foggier
foggiest

foghorn *noun*
foghorns

fogy✪ *noun*
fogies

foil *verb*
foils
foiling
foiled

foil *noun*
foils

fold *verb*
folds
folding
folded

fold *noun*
folds

folder *noun*
folders

foliage

folk

folklore

follow *verb*
follows
following
followed

follower *noun*
followers

fond *adjective*
fonder
fondest
fondly

fondness

font *noun*
fonts

food *noun*
foods

fool *noun*
fools

★ A **flue** is a pipe for smoke and fumes. **! flew, flu**.
☆ **Foggy** means 'covered in fog'. **! fogy**.
✪ A **fogy** is someone with old-fashioned ideas. **! foggy**.

fool *verb*
fools
fooling
fooled

foolhardiness

foolhardy *adjective*
foolhardier
foolhardiest

foolish *adjective*
foolishly

foolishness

foolproof

foot★ *noun*
feet

football *noun*
footballs

footballer *noun*
footballers

foothill *noun*
foothills

foothold *noun*
footholds

footing

footlights

footnote *noun*
footnotes

footpath *noun*
footpaths

footprint *noun*
footprints

footstep *noun*
footsteps

for☆ *preposition* and *conjunction*

forbid *verb*
forbids
forbidding
forbade
forbidden

force *verb*
forces
forcing
forced

force *noun*
forces

forceful *adjective*
forcefully

forceps *plural noun*

forcible *adjective*
forcibly

ford *verb*
fords
fording
forded

ford *noun*
fords

fore✪ *adjective* and *noun*

forecast *verb*
forecasts
forecasting
forecast
forecasted

forecast *noun*
forecasts

forecourt *noun*
forecourts

forefathers *plural noun*

forefinger *noun*
forefingers

foregone✢ *adjective*

foreground *noun*
foregrounds

forehead *noun*
foreheads

foreign

foreigner *noun*
foreigners

foreman *noun*
foremen

foremost

forename *noun*
forenames

foresee *verb*
foresees
foreseeing
foresaw
foreseen

foreseeable

foresight

forest *noun*
forests

forester *noun*
foresters

forestry

foretell *verb*
foretells
foretelling
foretold

forever✹ *adverb*

forfeit *verb*
forfeits
forfeiting
forfeited

forfeit *noun*
forfeits

forgave see **forgive**

★ The plural is **foot** in e.g. *a six-foot pole*.
☆ You use **for** in phrases like *a present for you*. **! fore**.
✪ You use **fore** in phrases like *come to the fore*. **! for**.
✢ You can use **foregone** in *a foregone conclusion*.
✹ You use **forever** in e.g. *They are forever complaining*. You can also use **for ever** in e.g. *The rain seemed to go on for ever*.

a b c d e f g h i j k l m n o p q r s t u v w x y z

freeze★ *verb*
freezes
freezing
froze
frozen

freezer *noun*
freezers

freight

freighter *noun*
freighters

frenzied

frenzy *noun*
frenzies

frequency *noun*
frequencies

frequent *adjective*
frequently

frequent *verb*
frequents
frequenting
frequented

fresh *adjective*
fresher
freshest
freshly

freshness

freshen *verb*
freshens
freshening
freshened

freshwater

fret *verb*
frets
fretting
fretted

fretful *adjective*
fretfully

fretsaw *noun*
fretsaws

fretwork

friar *noun*
friars

friary *noun*
friaries

friction

Friday *noun*
Fridays

fridge *noun*
fridges

friend *noun*
friends

friendless

friendliness

friendly *adjective*
friendlier
friendliest

friendship *noun*
friendships

frieze☆ *noun*
friezes

frigate *noun*
frigates

fright *noun*
frights

frighten *verb*
frightens
frightening
frightened

frightful *adjective*
frightfully

frill *noun*
frills

frilled

frilly *adjective*
frillier
frilliest

fringe *noun*
fringes

fringed

frisk *verb*
frisks
frisking
frisked

friskiness

frisky *adjective*
friskier
friskiest
friskily

fritter *verb*
fritters
frittering
frittered

fritter *noun*
fritters

frivolous *adjective*
frivolously

frivolity *noun*
frivolities

frizzy *adjective*
frizzier
frizziest

fro✪

frock *noun*
frocks

frog *noun*
frogs

frogman *noun*
frogmen

frolic *noun*
frolics

frolicsome

frolic *verb*
frolics
frolicking
frolicked

front *noun*
fronts

frontier *noun*
frontiers

★ To **freeze** is to be very cold. **! frieze**.
☆ A **frieze** is a strip of designs along a wall. **! freeze**.
✪ You use **fro** in *to and fro*.

frost *noun*
frosts

frost *verb*
frosts
frosting
frosted

frostbite

frostbitten

frosty *adjective*
frostier
frostiest

froth *noun*

froth *verb*
froths
frothing
frothed

frothy *adjective*
frothier
frothiest

froth *verb*
froths
frothing
frothed

frown *verb*
frowns
frowning
frowned

frown *noun*
frowns

froze see **freeze**

frozen see **freeze**

frugal *adjective*
frugally

frugality

fruit *noun*
fruit *or* fruits

fruitful *adjective*
fruitfully

fruitless *adjective*
fruitlessly

fruity *adjective*
fruitier
fruitiest

frustrate *verb*
frustrates
frustrating
frustrated

frustration *noun*
frustrations

fry *verb*
fries
frying
fried

fudge

fuel *noun*
fuels

fuel *verb*
fuels
fuelling
fuelled

fug *noun*
fugs

fuggy *adjective*
fuggier
fuggiest

fugitive *noun*
fugitives

-ful
-ful makes nouns for amounts, e.g. **handful**, **spoonful**. The plural of these words ends in *-fuls*, e.g. **handfuls**. *-ful* also makes adjectives, e.g. **graceful**, and when the adjective ends in *-y* following a consonant, you change the *y* to *i*, e.g. **beauty - beautiful**.

fulcrum *noun*
fulcra *or* fulcrums

fulfil *verb*
fulfils
fulfilling
fulfilled

fulfilment

full *adjective*
fully

fullness

fumble *verb*
fumbles
fumbling
fumbled

fume *verb*
fumes
fuming
fumed

fumes *plural noun*

fun

function *verb*
functions
functioning
functioned

function *noun*
functions

functional *adjective*
functionally

fund *noun*
funds

fundamental *adjective*
fundamentally

funeral *noun*
funerals

fungus *noun*
fungi

funk *verb*
funks
funking
funked

funnel *noun*
funnels

funny *adjective*
funnier
funniest
funnily

a b c d e **f** g h i j k l m n o p q r s t u v w x y z

a b c d e **f** **g** h i j k l m n o p q r s t u v w x y z

fur★ *noun*
furs

furious *adjective*
furiously

furl *verb*
furls
furling
furled

furlong *noun*
furlongs

furnace *noun*
furnaces

furnish *verb*
furnishes
furnishing
furnished

furniture

furrow *noun*
furrows

furry *adjective*
furrier
furriest

further☆ *adjective*

further✪ *verb*
furthers
furthering
furthered

furthermore

furthest✣

furtive *adjective*
furtively

fury *noun*
furies

fuse *verb*
fuses
fusing
fused

fuse *noun*
fuses

fuselage *noun*
fuselages

fusion *noun*
fusions

fuss *verb*
fusses
fussing
fussed

fuss *noun*
fusses

fussiness

fussy *adjective*
fussier
fussiest
fussily

futile *adjective*
futilely

futility

futon *noun*
futons

future

fuzz

fuzziness *noun*

fuzzy *adjective*
fuzzier
fuzziest
fuzzily

Gg

gabardine *noun*
gabardines

gabble *verb*
gabbles
gabbling
gabbled

gable *noun*
gables

gabled

gadget *noun*
gadgets

Gaelic

gag *verb*
gags
gagging
gagged

gag *noun*
gags

gaiety

gaily

gain *verb*
gains
gaining
gained

gain *noun*
gains

gala *noun*
galas

galactic

galaxy *noun*
galaxies

gale *noun*
gales

gallant *adjective*
gallantly

gallantry

galleon✹ *noun*
galleons

gallery *noun*
galleries

galley *noun*
galleys

★ **Fur** is the hair of animals. **! fir**.
☆ You use **further** in e.g. *We need further information*. See **farther**.
✪ To **further** something is to make it progress.
✣ You use **furthest** in e.g. *Who has read the furthest?* See **farthest**.
✹ A **galleon** is a type of ship. **! gallon**.

gallon★ *noun*
gallons
gallop *verb*
gallops
galloping
galloped
gallop *noun*
gallops
gallows
galore
galvanize *verb*
galvanizes
galvanizing
galvanized
gamble *verb*
gambles
gambling
gambled
gamble *noun*
gambles
gambler *noun*
gamblers
game *noun*
games
gamekeeper *noun*
gamekeepers
gammon
gander *noun*
ganders
gang *noun*
gangs
gang *verb*
gangs
ganging
ganged
gangplank *noun*
gangplanks
gangster *noun*
gangsters
gangway *noun*
gangways

gaol *noun* see **jail**
gaoler *noun* see **jailer**
gap *noun*
gaps
gape *verb*
gapes
gaping
gaped
garage *noun*
garages
garbage
garden *noun*
gardens
gardener *noun*
gardeners
gardening
gargle *verb*
gargles
gargling
gargled
gargoyle *noun*
gargoyles
garland *noun*
garlands
garlic
garment *noun*
garments
garnish *verb*
garnishes
garnishing
garnished
garrison *noun*
garrisons
garter *noun*
garters
gas *noun*
gases
gas *verb*
gasses
gassing
gassed

gaseous
gash *noun*
gashes
gasket *noun*
gaskets
gasoline
gasometer *noun*
gasometers
gasp *verb*
gasps
gasping
gasped
gasp *noun*
gasps
gastric
gate *noun*
gates
gateau☆ *noun*
gateaux
gateway *noun*
gateways
gather *verb*
gathers
gathering
gathered
gathering *noun*
gatherings
gaudy *adjective*
gaudier
gaudiest
gauge *verb*
gauges
gauging
gauged
gauge *noun*
gauges
gaunt
gauntlet *noun*
gauntlets
gauze
gave see **give**

★ A **gallon** is a measurement of liquid. **! galleon**.
☆ **Gateau** is a French word used in English. It means 'a rich cream cake'.

a b c d e f **g** h i j k l m n o p q r s t u v w x y z

gay *adjective*
gayer
gayest
gaze *verb*
gazes
gazing
gazed
gaze *noun*
gazes
gazetteer *noun*
gazetteers
gear *noun*
gears
geese see **goose**
Geiger counter *noun*
Geiger counters
gel *noun*
gels
gelatine
gelding *noun*
geldings
gem *noun*
gems
gender *noun*
genders
gene *noun*
genes
genealogy *noun*
genealogies
general *adjective*
generally
general *noun*
generals
generalization *noun*
generalizations
generalize *verb*
generalizes
generalizing
generalized
generate *verb*
generates
generating
generated
generation *noun*
generations
generator *noun*
generators
generosity
generous *adjective*
generously
genetic *adjective*
genetically
genetics *plural noun*
genial *adjective*
genially
genie *noun*
genies
genitals *plural noun*
genius *noun*
geniuses
gent *noun*
gents
gentle *adjective*
gentler
gentlest
gently
gentleman *noun*
gentlemen
gentlemanly
gentleness
genuine *adjective*
genuinely
genus *noun*
genera

> **geo-**
> *geo-* means 'earth', e.g. **geography** (the study of the earth).

geographer
geographical *adjective*
geographically
geography
geological *adjective*
geologically
geologist
geology
geometric *adjective*
geometrically
geometrical *adjective*
geometrically
geometry
geranium *noun*
geraniums
gerbil *noun*
gerbils
germ *noun*
germs
germinate *verb*
germinates
germinating
germinated
germination
gesticulate *verb*
gesticulates
gesticulating
gesticulated
gesture *noun*
gestures
get *verb*
gets
getting
got
getaway *noun*
getaways
geyser *noun*
geysers
ghastly *adjective*
ghastlier
ghastliest
ghetto *noun*
ghettos
ghost *noun*
ghosts
ghostly *adjective*
ghostlier
ghostliest
ghoulish *adjective*
ghoulishly
giant *noun*
giants
giddiness

giddy *adjective*
giddier
giddiest
giddily
gift *noun*
gifts
gifted
gigantic *adjective*
gigantically
giggle *verb*
giggles
giggling
giggled
giggle *noun*
giggles
gild★ *verb*
gilds
gilding
gilded
gills *plural noun*
gimmick *noun*
gimmicks
gin
ginger
gingerbread
gingerly
gingery
gipsy *noun* see **gypsy**
giraffe *noun*
giraffes
girder *noun*
girders
girdle *noun*
girdles
girl *noun*
girls
girlfriend *noun*
girlfriends
girlhood
girlish
giro☆ *noun*
giros
girth *noun*
girths
gist
give *verb*
gives
giving
gave
given
given see **give**
giver *noun*
givers
glacial
glacier *noun*
glaciers
glad *adjective*
gladder
gladdest
gladly
gladden *verb*
gladdens
gladdening
gladdened
gladiator *noun*
gladiators
gladness
glamorize *verb*
glamorizes
glamorizing
glamorized
glamorous *adjective*
glamorously
glamour
glance *verb*
glances
glancing
glanced
glance *noun*
glances
gland *noun*
glands
glandular
glare *verb*
glares
glaring
glared
glare *noun*
glares
glass *noun*
glasses
glassful *noun*
glassfuls
glassy *adjective*
glassier
glassiest
glaze *verb*
glazes
glazing
glazed
glaze *noun*
glazes
glazier *noun*
glaziers
gleam *noun*
gleams
gleam *verb*
gleams
gleaming
gleamed
glee
gleeful *adjective*
gleefully
glen *noun*
glens
glide *verb*
glides
gliding
glided
glider *noun*
gliders
glimmer *verb*
glimmers
glimmering
glimmered

★ To **gild** something is to cover it with gold. **! guild**.
☆ A **giro** is a system of paying money. **! gyro**.

a b c d e f **g** h i j k l m n o p q r s t u v w x y z

glimmer *noun*
glimmers
glimpse *verb*
glimpses
glimpsing
glimpsed
glimpse *noun*
glimpses
glint *verb*
glints
glinting
glinted
glint *noun*
glints
glisten *verb*
glistens
glistening
glistened
glitter *verb*
glitters
glittering
glittered
gloat *verb*
gloats
gloating
gloated
global *adjective*
globally
globe *noun*
globes
gloom
gloominess
gloomy *adjective*
gloomier
gloomiest
gloomily
glorification
glorify *verb*
glorifies
glorifying
glorified
glorious *adjective*
gloriously
glory *noun*
glories
gloss *noun*
glosses
glossary *noun*
glossaries
glossy *adjective*
glossier
glossiest
glove *noun*
gloves
glow *verb*
glows
glowing
glowed
glow *noun*
glows
glower *verb*
glowers
glowering
glowered
glow-worm *noun*
glow-worms
glucose
glue *noun*
glues
glue *verb*
glues
gluing
glued
gluey *adjective*
gluier
gluiest
glum *adjective*
glummer
glummest
glumly
glutton *noun*
gluttons
gluttonous
gluttony
gnarled
gnash★ *verb*
gnashes
gnashing
gnashed
gnat★ *noun*
gnats
gnaw★ *verb*
gnaws
gnawing
gnawed
gnome★ *noun*
gnomes
go *verb*
goes
going
went
gone
go *noun*
goes
goal *noun*
goals
goalie *noun*
goalies
goalkeeper *noun*
goalkeepers
goalpost *noun*
goalposts
goat *noun*
goats
gobble *verb*
gobbles
gobbling
gobbled
gobbledegook
goblet *noun*
goblets
goblin *noun*
goblins
God☆

★ In these words beginning with **gn-** the 'g' is silent.
☆ You use a capital G when you mean the Christian, Jewish, and Muslim creator.

god★ *noun*
gods
godchild *noun*
godchildren
goddess *noun*
goddesses
godparent *noun*
godparents
goggles *plural noun*
gold
golden
goldfinch *noun*
goldfinches
goldfish *noun*
goldfish
golf
golfer *noun*
golfers
golfing
gondola *noun*
gondolas
gondolier *noun*
gondoliers
gone see **go**
gong *noun*
gongs
good *adjective*
better
best
goodbye *interjection*
Good Friday
good-looking
good-natured
goodness
goods *plural noun*
goodwill
gooey *adjective*
gooier
gooiest

goose *noun*
geese
gooseberry *noun*
gooseberries
gore *verb*
gores
goring
gored
gorge *noun*
gorges
gorgeous *adjective*
gorgeously
gorilla☆ *noun*
gorillas
gorse
gory *adjective*
gorier
goriest
gosling *noun*
goslings
gospel *noun*
gospels
gossip *verb*
gossips
gossiping
gossiped
gossip *noun*
gossips
got see **get**
gouge *verb*
gouges
gouging
gouged
gourd *noun*
gourds
govern *verb*
governs
governing
governed
government *noun*
governments

governor *noun*
governors
gown *noun*
gowns
grab *verb*
grabs
grabbing
grabbed
grace *noun*
graces
graceful *adjective*
gracefully
gracefulness
gracious *adjective*
graciously
grade *noun*
grades
grade *verb*
grades
grading
graded
gradient *noun*
gradients
gradual *adjective*
gradually
graduate *noun*
graduates
graduate *verb*
graduates
graduating
graduated
graduation
graffiti *plural noun*
grain *noun*
grains
grainy *adjective*
grainier
grainiest
gram *noun*
grams

★ You use a small g when you mean any male divine being.
☆ A **gorilla** is a large ape. **! guerrilla**.

grammar *noun*
grammars

grammatical *adjective*
grammatically

gramophone *noun*
gramophones

grand *adjective*
grander
grandest
grandly

grandad *noun*
grandads

grandchild *noun*
grandchildren

grandeur

grandfather *noun*
grandfathers

grandma *noun*
grandmas

grandmother *noun*
grandmothers

grandpa *noun*
grandpas

grandparent *noun*
grandparents

grandstand *noun*
grandstands

granite

granny *noun*
grannies

grant *verb*
grants
granting
granted

grant *noun*
grants

granulated

grape *noun*
grapes

grapefruit *noun*
grapefruit

grapevine *noun*
grapevines

graph *noun*
graphs

graphic *adjective*
graphically

graphics *plural noun*

graphite

> **-graphy**
> *-graphy* makes words for subjects of study, e.g. **geography** (the study of the earth). A **bibliography** is a list of books on a subject, and the plural is **bibliographies**.

grapple *verb*
grapples
grappling
grappled

grasp *verb*
grasps
grasping
grasped

grasp *noun*
grasps

grass *noun*
grasses

grasshopper *noun*
grasshoppers

grassy *adjective*
grassier
grassiest

grate★ *verb*
grates
grating
grated

grate☆ *noun*
grates

grateful *adjective*
gratefully

grating *noun*
gratings

gratitude

grave *noun*
graves

grave *adjective*
graver
gravest
gravely

gravel

gravelled

gravestone *noun*
gravestones

graveyard *noun*
graveyards

gravitation

gravitational

gravity

gravy

graze *verb*
grazes
grazing
grazed

graze *noun*
grazes

grease

greasy *adjective*
greasier
greasiest

great *adjective*
greater
greatest
greatly

greatness

greed

greediness

★ To **grate** something is to shred it. **! great**.
☆ A **grate** is a fireplace. **! great**.

greedy *adjective*
greedier
greediest
greedily

green *adjective* and *noun*
greener
greenest

greenery

greengage *noun*
greengages

greengrocer *noun*
greengrocers

greengrocery *noun*
greengroceries

greenhouse *noun*
greenhouses

greens *plural noun*

greet *verb*
greets
greeting
greeted

greeting *noun*
greetings

grenade *noun*
grenades

grew see **grow**

grey *adjective* and *noun*
greyer
greyest

greyhound *noun*
greyhounds

grid *noun*
grids

grief

grievance *noun*
grievances

grieve *verb*
grieves
grieving
grieved

grievous★ *adjective*
grievously

grill *verb*
grills
grilling
grilled

grill *noun*
grills

grim *adjective*
grimmer
grimmest
grimly

grimace *noun*
grimaces

grime

grimness

grimy *adjective*
grimier
grimiest

grin *noun*
grins

grin *verb*
grins
grinning
grinned

grind *verb*
grinds
grinding
ground

grinder *noun*
grinders

grindstone *noun*
grindstones

grip *verb*
grips
gripping
gripped

grip *noun*
grips

grisly☆ *adjective*
grislier
grisliest

gristle

gristly *adjective*
gristlier
gristliest

grit *verb*
grits
gritting
gritted

grit *noun*

gritty *adjective*
grittlier
grittliest

grizzly✪ *adjective*

groan *verb*
groans
groaning
groaned

groan *noun*
groans

grocer *noun*
grocers

grocery *noun*
groceries

groggy *adjective*
groggier
groggiest

groin *noun*
groins

groom *verb*
grooms
grooming
groomed

groom *noun*
grooms

groove *noun*
grooves

★ Note that this word does not end *-ious*.
☆ **Grisly** means 'revolting' or 'horrible'. **! grizzly**.
✪ You use **grizzly** in *grizzly bear*. **! grisly**.

a b c d e f **g** h i j k l m n o p q r s t u v w x y z

grope *verb*
gropes
groping
groped

gross *adjective*
grosser
grossest
grossly

gross *noun*
gross

grossness

grotesque★ *adjective*
grotesquely

grotty *adjective*
grottier
grottiest

ground *noun*
grounds

ground see **grind**

grounded

grounds *plural noun*

groundsheet *noun*
groundsheets

groundsman *noun*
groundsmen

group *noun*
groups

group *verb*
groups
grouping
grouped

grouse *verb*
grouses
grousing
groused

grouse *noun*
grouse

grove *noun*
groves

grovel *verb*
grovels
grovelling
grovelled

grow *verb*
grows
growing
grew
grown

grower *noun*
growers

growl *verb*
growls
growling
growled

growl *noun*
growls

grown-up *noun*
grown-ups

growth *noun*
growths

grub *noun*
grubs

grubby *adjective*
grubbier
grubbiest

grudge *verb*
grudges
grudging
grudged

grudge *noun*
grudges

grudgingly

gruelling

gruesome

gruff *adjective*
gruffer
gruffest
gruffly

grumble *verb*
grumbles
grumbling
grumbled

grumbler *noun*
grumblers

grumpiness

grumpy *adjective*
grumpier
grumpiest
grumpily

grunt *verb*
grunts
grunting
grunted

grunt *noun*
grunts

guarantee *noun*
guarantees

guarantee *verb*
guarantees
guaranteeing
guaranteed

guard *verb*
guards
guarding
guarded

guard *noun*
guards

guardian *noun*
guardians

guardianship

guerrilla☆ *noun*
guerrillas

guess *verb*
guesses
guessing
guessed

guess *noun*
guesses

guesswork

★ **Grotesque** means 'strange' and 'ugly'. It sounds like 'grotesk'.
☆ A **guerrilla** is a member of a small army. **! gorilla**.

guest *noun*
guests

guidance

guide *verb*
guides
guiding
guided

guide *noun*
guides

guidelines *plural noun*

guild★ *noun*
guilds

guillotine *noun*
guillotines

guilt

guilty *adjective*
guiltier
guiltiest

guinea *noun*
guineas

guinea pig *noun*
guinea pigs

guitar *noun*
guitars

guitarist

gulf *noun*
gulfs

gull *noun*
gulls

gullet *noun*
gullets

gullible

gully *noun*
gullies

gulp *verb*
gulps
gulping
gulped

gulp *noun*
gulps

gum *noun*
gums

gum *verb*
gums
gumming
gummed

gummy *adjective*
gummier
gummiest

gun *noun*
guns

gun *verb*
guns
gunning
gunned

gunboat *noun*
gunboats

gunfire

gunman *noun*
gunmen

gunner *noun*
gunners

gunnery

gunpowder

gunshot *noun*
gunshots

gurdwara☆ *noun*
gurdwaras

gurgle *verb*
gurgles
gurgling
gurgled

guru *noun*
gurus

Guru Granth Sahib✪

gush *verb*
gushes
gushing
gushed

gust *noun*
gusts

gusty *adjective*
gustier
gustiest

gut *noun*
guts

gut *verb*
guts
gutting
gutted

gutter *noun*
gutters

guy *noun*
guys

guzzle *verb*
guzzles
guzzling
guzzled

gym *noun*
gyms

gymkhana *noun*
gymkhanas

gymnasium *noun*
gymnasiums

gymnast *noun*
gymnasts

gymnastics *plural noun*

gypsy *noun*
gypsies

gyro✣ *noun*
gyros

gyroscope *noun*
gyroscopes

★ A **guild** is an organization of people. **! gild**.
☆ A Sikh place of worship.
✪ The holy book of Sikhs.
✣ A **gyro** is type of compass. **! giro**.

a b c d e f **g** h i j k l m n o p q r s t u v w x y z

Hh

habit *noun*
habits

habitat *noun*
habitats

habitual *adjective*
habitually

hack *verb*
hacks
hacking
hacked

hacker *noun*
hackers

hacksaw *noun*
hacksaws

had see **has**

haddock *noun*
haddock

hadn't *verb*

hag *noun*
hags

haggard

haggis *noun*
haggises

haggle *verb*
haggles
haggling
haggled

haiku★ *noun*
haiku

hail *verb*
hails
hailing
hailed

hail

hailstone *noun*
hailstones

hair☆ *noun*
hairs

hairbrush *noun*
hairbrushes

haircut *noun*
haircuts

hairdresser *noun*
hairdressers

hairpin *noun*
hairpins

hair-raising

hairstyle *noun*
hairstyles

hairy *adjective*
hairier
hairiest

hake *noun*
hake

halal

half *adjective* and *noun*
halves

half-baked

half-hearted *adjective*
half-heartedly

half-life *noun*
half-lives

half-mast

halfpenny✪ *noun*
halfpennies *or*
halfpence

half-term *noun*
half-terms

half-time *noun*
half-times

halfway

halibut *noun*
halibut

hall✣ *noun*
halls

hallo

Halloween✹

hallucination *noun*
hallucinations

halo *noun*
haloes

halt *verb*
halts
halting
halted

halt *noun*
halts

halter *noun*
halters

halting *adjective*
haltingly

halve *verb*
halves
halving
halved

halves see **half**

ham *noun*
hams

hamburger *noun*
hamburgers

hammer *noun*
hammers

hammer *verb*
hammers
hammering
hammered

hammock *noun*
hammocks

★ A Japanese poem.
☆ **Hair** is the covering on the head. **! hare**.
✪ You use **halfpennies** when you mean several coins and **halfpence** for a sum of money.
✣ A **hall** is a large space in a building. **! haul**.
✹ You will also see this word spelt *Hallowe´en*.

hamper *verb*
hampers
hampering
hampered

hamper *noun*
hampers

hamster *noun*
hamsters

hand *noun*
hands

hand *verb*
hands
handing
handed

handbag *noun*
handbags

handbook *noun*
handbooks

handcuffs *plural noun*

handful *noun*
handfuls

handicap *noun*
handicaps

handicapped

handicraft *noun*
handicrafts

handiwork

handkerchief *noun*
handkerchiefs

handle *noun*
handles

handle *verb*
handles
handling
handled

handlebars *plural noun*

handrail *noun*
handrails

handsome *adjective*
handsomer
handsomest
handsomely

hands-on

handstand *noun*
handstands

handwriting

handwritten

handy *adjective*
handier
handiest

handyman *noun*
handymen

hang *verb*
hangs
hanging
hung

hangar★ *noun*
hangars

hanger☆ *noun*
hangers

hang-glider *noun*
hang-gliders

hang-gliding

hangman *noun*
hangmen

hangover *noun*
hangovers

hank *noun*
hanks

hanker *verb*
hankers
hankering
hankered

hanky *noun*
hankies

Hanukkah✪

haphazard *adjective*
haphazardly

happen *verb*
happens
happening
happened

happening *noun*
happenings

happiness

happy *adjective*
happier
happiest
happily

happy-go-lucky

harass✣ *verb*
harasses
harassing
harassed

harassment

harbour *noun*
harbours

harbour *verb*
harbours
harbouring
harboured

hard *adjective*
harder
hardest

hard *adverb*
harder
hardest

hardboard

hard-boiled

hard disk *noun*
hard disks

harden *verb*
hardens
hardening
hardened

hardly

★ A **hangar** is a shed for aircraft. **! hanger**.
☆ A **hanger** is a thing for hanging clothes on. **! hangar**.
✪ A Jewish festival.
✣ Note that there is only one r in **harass** and **harassment**.

a b c d e f g **h** i j k l m n o p q r s t u v w x y z

hardness
hardship *noun*
hardships
hardware
hardwood *noun*
hardwoods
hardy *adjective*
hardier
hardiest
hare★ *noun*
hares
hark *verb*
harks
harking
harked
harm *verb*
harms
harming
harmed
harm *noun*
harmful *adjective*
harmfully
harmless *adjective*
harmlessly
harmonic
harmonica *noun*
harmonicas
harmonious *adjective*
harmoniously
harmonization
harmonize *verb*
harmonizes
harmonizing
harmonized
harmony *noun*
harmonies
harness *verb*
harnesses
harnessing
harnessed
harness *noun*
harnesses
harp *noun*
harps
harp *verb*
harps
harping
harped
harpist *noun*
harpists
harpoon *noun*
harpoons
harpsichord *noun*
harpsichords
harrow *noun*
harrows
harsh *adjective*
harsher
harshest
harshly
harshness
harvest *noun*
harvests
harvest *verb*
harvests
harvesting
harvested
hash *noun*
hashes
hasn't *verb*
hassle *noun*
hassles
haste
hasten *verb*
hastens
hastening
hastened
hastiness
hasty *adjective*
hastier
hastiest
hastily
hatch *verb*
hatches
hatching
hatched
hatch *noun*
hatches
hatchback *noun*
hatchbacks
hatchet *noun*
hatchets
hate *verb*
hates
hating
hated
hate *noun*
hates
hateful *adjective*
hatefully
hatred
hat trick *noun*
hat tricks
haughtiness
haughty *adjective*
haughtier
haughtiest
haughtily
haul☆ *verb*
hauls
hauling
hauled
haul *noun*
hauls
haunt *verb*
haunts
haunting
haunted
have *verb*
has
having
had
haven *noun*
havens

★ A **hare** is an animal like a large rabbit. **! hair**.
☆ To **haul** is to pull something heavy. **! hall**.

haven't *verb*
haversack *noun*
haversacks
hawk *noun*
hawks
hawk *verb*
hawks
hawking
hawked
hawker *noun*
hawkers
hawthorn *noun*
hawthorns
hay fever
haymaking
haystack *noun*
haystacks
hazard *noun*
hazards
hazardous
haze *noun*
hazes
hazel *noun*
hazels
haziness
hazy *adjective*
hazier
haziest
hazily
H-bomb *noun*
H-bombs
head *noun*
heads
head *verb*
heads
heading
headed
headache *noun*
headaches
headdress *noun*
headdresses

header *noun*
headers
heading *noun*
headings
headland *noun*
headlands
headlight *noun*
headlights
headline *noun*
headlines
headlong
headmaster *noun*
headmasters
headmistress *noun*
headmistresses
head-on
headphones
headquarters *noun*
headquarters
headteacher *noun*
headteachers
headway
heal *verb*
heals
healing
healed
healer *noun*
healers
health
healthiness
healthy *adjective*
healthier
healthiest
healthily
heap *verb*
heaps
heaping
heaped
heap *noun*
heaps

hear★ *verb*
hears
hearing
heard
hearing *noun*
hearings
hearse *noun*
hearses
heart *noun*
hearts
hearth *noun*
hearths
heartiness
heartless
hearty *adjective*
heartier
heartiest
heartily
heat *verb*
heats
heating
heated
heat *noun*
heats
heater *noun*
heaters
heath *noun*
heaths
heathen *noun*
heathens
heather
heatwave *noun*
heatwaves
heave☆ *verb*
heaves
heaving
heaved
hove
heaven
heavenly
heaviness

★ You use **hear** in e.g. *I can't hear you.* **! here**.
☆ You use **hove** in e.g. *the ship hove to.*

a b c d e f g **h** i j k l m n o p q r s t u v w x y z

heavy *adjective*
heavier
heaviest
heavily

heavyweight *noun*
heavyweights

Hebrew

hectare *noun*
hectares

hectic *adjective*
hectically

he'd *verb*

hedge *noun*
hedges

hedge *verb*
hedges
hedging
hedged

hedgehog *noun*
hedgehogs

hedgerow *noun*
hedgerows

heed *verb*
heeds
heeding
heeded

heed *noun*

heedless

heel *noun*
heels

heel *verb*
heels
heeling
heeled

hefty *adjective*
heftier
heftiest

heifer *noun*
heifers

height *noun*
heights

heighten *verb*
heightens
heightening
heightened

heir★ *noun*
heirs

heiress *noun*
heiresses

held see **hold**

helicopter *noun*
helicopters

helium

helix *noun*
helices

hell

he'll *verb*

hellish *adjective*
hellishly

hello

helm *noun*
helms

helmsman *noun*
helmsmen

helmet *noun*
helmets

helmeted

help *verb*
helps
helping
helped

help *noun*
helps

helper *noun*
helpers

helpful *adjective*
helpfully

helping *noun*
helpings

helpless *adjective*
helplessly

helter-skelter *noun*
helter-skelters

hem *noun*
hems

hem *verb*
hems
hemming
hemmed

hemisphere *noun*
hemispheres

hemp

hence

henceforth

herald *noun*
heralds

herald *verb*
heralds
heralding
heralded

heraldic

heraldry

herb *noun*
herbs

herbal

herbivore *noun*
herbivores

herd *noun*
herds

herd☆ *verb*
herds
herding
herded

here✪

hereditary

heredity

heritage *noun*
heritages

hermit *noun*
hermits

hermitage

★ You do not pronounce the 'h' in **heir** (sounds like *air*).
☆ A **herd** is a group of sheep. **! heard**.
✪ You use **here** in e.g. *come here*. **! hear**.

hero *noun*
heroes
heroic *adjective*
heroically
heroin★ *noun*
heroine☆ *noun*
heroines
heroism
heron *noun*
herons
herring *noun*
herring
herrings
hers✪
herself
he`s *verb*
hesitant *adjective*
hesitantly
hesitate *verb*
hesitates
hesitating
hesitated
hesitation
hexagon *noun*
hexagons
hexagonal
hibernate *verb*
hibernates
hibernating
hibernated
hibernation
hiccup *noun*
hiccups
hide *verb*
hides
hiding
hidden
hid
hidden
hide-and-seek
hideous *adjective*
hideously
hideout *noun*
hideouts
hiding *noun*
hidings
hieroglyphics *plural noun*
hi-fi *noun*
hi-fis
higgledy-piggledy
high *adjective*
higher
highest
highland *adjective*
highlands *plural noun*
highlander *noun*
highlanders
highlight *noun*
highlights
highlighter *noun*
highlighters
highly
Highness *noun*
Highnesses
high-rise
highway *noun*
highways
highwayman *noun*
highwaymen
hijack *verb*
hijacks
hijacking
hijacked
hijacker *noun*
hijackers
hike *verb*
hikes
hiking
hiked
hike *noun*
hikes
hiker *noun*
hikers
hilarious *adjective*
hilariously
hilarity
hill *noun*
hills
hillside *noun*
hillsides
hilly *adjective*
hillier
hilliest
hilt *noun*
hilts
himself
hind *adjective*
hind *noun*
hinds
hinder *verb*
hinders
hindering
hindered
Hindi
hindrance *noun*
hindrances
Hindu *noun*
Hindus
hinge *noun*
hinges
hinge *verb*
hinges
hinging
hinged

★ **Heroin** is a drug. **! heroine**.
☆ A **heroine** is a woman or girl in a story. **! heroin**.
✪ You use **hers** in e.g. *the book is hers*. Note that there is no apostrophe in this word.

a b c d e f g **h** i j k l m n o p q r s t u v w x y z

hint *noun*
hints
hint *verb*
hints
hinting
hinted
hip *noun*
hips
hippo *noun*
hippos
hippopotamus *noun*
hippopotamuses
hire *verb*
hires
hiring
hired
hiss *verb*
hisses
hissing
hissed
histogram *noun*
histograms
historian *noun*
historians
historic
historical *adjective*
historically
history *noun*
histories
hit *verb*
hits
hitting
hit
hit *noun*
hits
hitch *verb*
hitches
hitching
hitched
hitch *noun*
hitches
hitch-hike *verb*
hitch-hikes
hitch-hiking
hitch-hiked
hitch-hiker *noun*
hitch-hikers
hi-tech
hither
hitherto
hive *noun*
hives
hoard *verb*
hoards
hoarding
hoarded
hoard★ *noun*
hoards
hoarder *noun*
hoarders
hoarding *noun*
hoardings
hoar frost
hoarse☆ *adjective*
hoarser
hoarsest
hoax *verb*
hoaxes
hoaxing
hoaxed
hoax *noun*
hoaxes
hobble *verb*
hobbles
hobbling
hobbled
hobby *noun*
hobbies
hockey
hoe *noun*
hoes
hoe *verb*
hoes
hoeing
hoed
hog *noun*
hogs
hog *verb*
hogs
hogging
hogged
Hogmanay
hoist *verb*
hoists
hoisting
hoisted
hold *verb*
holds
holding
held
hold *noun*
holds
holdall *noun*
holdalls
holder *noun*
holders
hold-up *noun*
hold-ups
hole✪ *noun*
holes
holey✣ *adjective*
Holi✸
holiday *noun*
holidays
holiness
hollow *adjective* and *adverb*

★ A **hoard** is a secret store. **! horde**.
☆ A **hoarse** voice is rough or croaking. **! horse**.
✪ A **hole** is a gap or opening. **! whole**.
✣ **Holey** means 'full of holes'. **! holy**.
✸ A Hindu festival.

hollow *verb*
hollows
hollowing
hollowed

hollow *noun*
hollows

holly

holocaust *noun*
holocausts

hologram *noun*
holograms

holster *noun*
holsters

holy★ *adjective*
holier
holiest

home *noun*
homes

home *verb*
homes
homing
homed

homeless

homely

home-made

homesick

homesickness

homestead *noun*
homesteads

homeward *adjective*

homewards *adjective* and *adverb*

homework

homing

homosexual *adjective* and *noun*
homosexuals

honest *adjective*
honestly

honesty

honey *noun*
honeys

honeycomb *noun*
honeycombs

honeymoon *noun*
honeymoons

honeysuckle

honk *verb*
honks
honking
honked

honk *noun*
honks

honour *verb*
honours
honouring
honoured

honour *noun*
honours

honourable *adjective*
honourably

hood *noun*
hoods

> **-hood**
> *-hood* makes nouns, e.g. **childhood**. Other noun suffixes are **-dom**, **-ment**, **-ness**, and **-ship**.

hooded

hoof *noun*
hoofs

hook *noun*
hooks

hook *verb*
hooks
hooking
hooked

hooligan *noun*
hooligans

hoop *noun*
hoops

hoopla

hooray

hoot *verb*
hoots
hooting
hooted

hoot *noun*
hoots

hooter *noun*
hooters

hop *verb*
hops
hopping
hopped

hop *noun*
hops

hope *verb*
hopes
hoping
hoped

hope *noun*
hopes

hopeful *adjective*
hopefully

hopeless *adjective*
hopelessly

hopscotch

horde☆ *noun*
hordes

horizon *noun*
horizons

horizontal *adjective*
horizontally

hormone *noun*
hormones

horn *noun*
horns

hornet *noun*
hornets

★ You use **holy** in e.g. *a holy man.* **! holey**.
☆ A **horde** is a large crowd. **! hoard**.

a b c d e f g **h** i j k l m n o p q r s t u v w x y z

horoscope *noun*
horoscopes
horrible *adjective*
horribly
horrid
horrific *adjective*
horrifically
horrify *verb*
horrifies
horrifying
horrified
horror *noun*
horrors
horse *noun*
horses
horseback
horseman *noun*
horsemen
horsemanship
horsepower *noun*
horsepower
horseshoe *noun*
horseshoes
horsewoman *noun*
horsewomen
horticulture
hose *noun*
hoses
hospitable *adjective*
hospitably
hospital *noun*
hospitals
hospitality
host *noun*
hosts
hostage *noun*
hostages
hostel *noun*
hostels
hostess *noun*
hostesses
hostile
hostility *noun*
hostilities
hot *adjective*
hotter
hottest
hotly
hot *verb*
hots
hotting
hotted
hotel *noun*
hotels
hothouse *noun*
hothouses
hotpot *noun*
hotpots
hound *noun*
hounds
hound *verb*
hounds
hounding
hounded
hour★ *noun*
hours
hourglass *noun*
hourglasses
hourly *adjective* and *adverb*
house *noun*
houses
house *verb*
houses
housing
housed
houseboat *noun*
houseboats
household *noun*
households
householder *noun*
householders
housekeeper *noun*
housekeepers
housekeeping
housewife *noun*
housewives
housework
housing *noun*
housings
hove see **heave**
hover *verb*
hovers
hovering
hovered
hovercraft *noun*
hovercraft
however
howl *verb*
howls
howling
howled
howl *noun*
howls
howler *noun*
howlers
hub *noun*
hubs
huddle *verb*
huddles
huddling
huddled
hue *noun*
hues
huff
hug *verb*
hugs
hugging
hugged
hug *noun*
hugs
huge *adjective*
huger
hugest
hugely
hugeness
hulk *noun*
hulks

★ An **hour** is a measure of time. **! our**.

hulking
hull *noun*
hulls
hullabaloo *noun*
hullabaloos
hullo
hum *verb*
hums
humming
hummed
hum *noun*
hums
human *adjective* and *noun*
humans
humane *adjective*
humanely
humanitarian
humanity *noun*
humanities
humble *adjective*
humbler
humblest
humbly
humid
humidity
humiliate *verb*
humiliates
humiliating
humiliated
humiliation
humility
hummingbird *noun*
hummingbirds
humorous *adjective*
humorously
humour *noun*
humour *verb*
humours
humouring
humoured
hump *noun*
humps

hump *verb*
humps
humping
humped
humpback
humus
hunch *verb*
hunches
hunching
hunched
hunch *noun*
hunches
hunchback *noun*
hunchbacks
hunchbacked
hundred *noun*
hundreds
hundredth
hundredweight *noun*
hundredweights
hung see **hang**
hunger
hungry *adjective*
hungrier
hungriest
hungrily
hunk *noun*
hunks
hunt *verb*
hunts
hunting
hunted
hunt *noun*
hunts
hunter *noun*
hunters
hurdle *noun*
hurdles
hurdler *noun*
hurdlers
hurdling
hurl *verb*
hurls
hurling
hurled

hurrah or **hurray**
hurricane *noun*
hurricanes
hurriedly
hurry *verb*
hurries
hurrying
hurried
hurry *noun*
hurries
hurt *verb*
hurts
hurting
hurt
hurt *noun*
hurtle *verb*
hurtles
hurtling
hurtled
husband *noun*
husbands
hush *verb*
hushes
hushing
hushed
hush *noun*
husk *noun*
husks
huskiness
husky *adjective*
huskier
huskiest
huskily
husky *noun*
huskies
hustle *verb*
hustles
hustling
hustled
hutch *noun*
hutches
hyacinth *noun*
hyacinths
hybrid *noun*
hybrids

hydrangea *noun*
hydrangeas
hydrant *noun*
hydrants
hydraulic *adjective*
hydraulically
hydroelectric
hydrofoil *noun*
hydrofoils
hydrogen
hydrophobia
hyena *noun*
hyenas
hygiene
hygienic *adjective*
hygienically
hymn *noun*
hymns
hyperactive
hypermarket *noun*
hypermarkets
hyphen *noun*
hyphens
hyphenated
hypnosis
hypnotism
hypnotist
hypnotize *verb*
hypnotizes
hypnotizing
hypnotized
hypocrisy
hypocrite *noun*
hypocrites
hypocritical *adjective*
hypocritically
hypodermic
hypotenuse *noun*
hypotenuses
hypothermia
hypothesis *noun*
hypotheses
hypothetical *adjective*
hypothetically
hysteria
hysterical *adjective*
hysterically
hysterics *plural noun*

Ii

-i
Most nouns ending in *-i*, e.g. **ski**, **taxi**, have plurals ending in *-is*, e.g. **skis**, **taxis**.

-ible
See the note at **-able**.

-ic and **-ically**
Most adjectives ending in *-ic* have adverbs ending in *-ically*, e.g. **heroic** - **heroically**, **scientific** - **scientifically**. An exception is **public**, which has an adverb - **publicly**.

ice *noun*
ices
ice *verb*
ices
icing
iced
iceberg *noun*
icebergs
ice cream *noun*
ice creams
icicle *noun*
icicles
icing
icon *noun*
icons
icy *adjective*
icier
iciest
icily
I'd *verb*
idea *noun*
ideas
ideal *adjective*
ideally
ideal *noun*
ideals
identical *adjective*
identically
identification
identify *verb*
identifies
identifying
identified
identity *noun*
identities
idiocy *noun*
idiocies
idiom *noun*
idioms
idiomatic
idiot *noun*
idiots
idiotic *adjective*
idiotically
idle★ *adjective*
idler
idlest
idly

★ **Idle** means 'lazy'. **! idol**.

idle *verb*
idles
idling
idled
idol★ *noun*
idols
idolatry
idolize *verb*
idolizes
idolizing
idolized

> **-ie-**
> See the note at **-ei-**.

igloo *noun*
igloos
igneous
ignite *verb*
ignites
igniting
ignited
ignition
ignorance
ignorant
ignore *verb*
ignores
ignoring
ignored
I'll *verb*
ill
illegal *adjective*
illegally
illegible *adjective*
illegibly
illegitimate
illiteracy
illiterate
illness *noun*
illnesses
illogical *adjective*
illogically

illuminate *verb*
illuminates
illuminating
illuminated
illumination *noun*
illuminations
illusion *noun*
illusions
illustrate *verb*
illustrates
illustrating
illustrated
illustration *noun*
illustrations
illustrious
I'm *verb*
image *noun*
images
imagery
imaginable
imaginary
imagination *noun*
imaginations
imaginative *adjective*
imaginatively
imagine *verb*
imagines
imagining
imagined
imam☆ *noun*
imams
imbecile *noun*
imbeciles
imitate *verb*
imitates
imitating
imitated
imitation *noun*
imitations
imitator *noun*
imitators

immature
immaturity
immediate *adjective*
immediately
immense *adjective*
immensely
immensity
immerse *verb*
immerses
immersing
immersed
immersion
immigrant *noun*
immigrants
immigrate *verb*
immigrates
immigrating
immigrated
immigration
immobile
immobility
immobilize *verb*
immobilizes
immobilizing
immobilized
immoral *adjective*
immorally
immorality
immortal
immortality
immune
immunity *noun*
immunities
immunization
immunize *verb*
immunizes
immunizing
immunized
imp *noun*
imps
impish

★ An **idol** is someone people admire. **! idle**.
☆ A Muslim religious leader.

a b c d e f g h i j k l m n o p q r s t u v w x y z

impact *noun*
impacts

impair *verb*
impairs
impairing
impaired

impale *verb*
impales
impaling
impaled

impartial *adjective*
impartially

impartiality

impassable

impatience

impatient *adjective*
impatiently

impede *verb*
impedes
impeding
impeded

imperative

imperceptible *adjective*
imperceptibly

imperfect *adjective*
imperfectly

imperfection *noun*
imperfections

imperial

impersonal *adjective*
impersonally

impersonate *verb*
impersonates
impersonating
impersonated

impersonation *noun*
impersonations

impersonator *noun*
impersonators

impertinence

impertinent *adjective*
impertinently

implement *verb*
implements
implementing
implemented

implement *noun*
implements

implication *noun*
implications

implore *verb*
implores
imploring
implored

imply *verb*
implies
implying
implied

impolite *adjective*
impolitely

import *verb*
imports
importing
imported

import *noun*
imports

importance

important *adjective*
importantly

importer *noun*
importers

impose *verb*
imposes
imposing
imposed

imposition *noun*
impositions

impossibility

impossible *adjective*
impossibly

impostor *noun*
impostors

impracticable

impractical

impress *verb*
impresses
impressing
impressed

impression *noun*
impressions

impressive *adjective*
impressively

imprison *verb*
imprisons
imprisoning
imprisoned

imprisonment

improbability

improbable *adjective*
improbably

impromptu

improper *adjective*
improperly

impropriety *noun*
improprieties

improve *verb*
improves
improving
improved

improvement *noun*
improvements

improvisation *noun*
improvisations

improvise *verb*
improvises
improvising
improvised

impudence

impudent *adjective*
impudently

impulse *noun*
impulses

impulsive *adjective*
impulsively

impure
impurity *adjective*
impurities

in-
in- makes words with the meaning 'not', e.g. **inedible**, **infertile**. There is a fixed number of these, and you cannot freely add *in-* as you can with *un-*. *in-* changes to *il-* or *im-* before certain sounds, e.g. **illogical**, **impossible**.

inability
inaccessible
inaccuracy *noun*
inaccuracies
inaccurate *adjective*
inaccurately
inaction
inactive
inactivity
inadequacy
inadequate *adjective*
inadequately
inanimate
inappropriate *adjective*
inappropriately
inattention
inattentive
inaudible *adjective*
inaudibly
incapable
incapacity
incendiary
incense *noun*
incense *verb*
incenses
incensing
incensed
incentive *noun*
incentives
incessant *adjective*
incessantly
inch *noun*
inches
incident *noun*
incidents
incidental *adjective*
incidentally
incinerator *noun*
incinerators
inclination *noun*
inclinations
incline *verb*
inclines
inclining
inclined
incline *noun*
inclines
include *verb*
includes
including
included
inclusion
inclusive
income *noun*
incomes
incompatible
incompetence
incompetent *adjective*
incompetently
incomplete *adjective*
incompletely
incomprehensible *adjective*
incomprehensibly
incongruity
incongruous *adjective*
incongruously
inconsiderate *adjective*
inconsiderately
inconsistency *noun*
inconsistencies
inconsistent *adjective*
inconsistently
inconspicuous *adjective*
inconspicuously
inconvenience
inconvenient *adjective*
inconveniently
incorporate *verb*
incorporates
incorporating
incorporated
incorporation
incorrect *adjective*
incorrectly
increase *verb*
increases
increasing
increased
increase *noun*
increases
increasingly
incredible *adjective*
incredibly
incredulity
incredulous
incubate *verb*
incubates
incubating
incubated
incubation
incubator *noun*
incubators
indebted

a b c d e f g h i j k l m n o p q r s t u v w x y z

indecency

indecent *adjective*
indecently

indeed

indefinite *adjective*
indefinitely

indelible *adjective*
indelibly

indent *verb*
indents
indenting
indented

indentation

independence

independent *adjective*
independently

index *noun*
indexes

Indian *adjective* and *noun*
Indians

indicate *verb*
indicates
indicating
indicated

indication *noun*
indications

indicative

indicator *noun*
indicators

indifference

indifferent *adjective*
indifferently

indigestible

indigestion

indignant *adjective*
indignantly

indignation

indigo

indirect *adjective*
indirectly

indispensable *adjective*
indispensably

indistinct *adjective*
indistinctly

indistinguishable

individual *adjective*
individually

individual *noun*
individuals

individuality

indoctrinate *verb*
indoctrinates
indoctrinating
indoctrinated

indoctrination

indoor *adjective*

indoors *adverb*

induce *verb*
induces
inducing
induced

inducement *noun*
inducements

indulge *verb*
indulges
indulging
indulged

indulgence *noun*
indulgences

indulgent

industrial

industrialist *noun*
industrialists

industrialization

industrialize *verb*
industrializes
industrializing
industrialized

industrious *adjective*
industriously

industry *noun*
industries

ineffective *adjective*
ineffectively

ineffectual *adjective*
ineffectually

inefficiency *noun*
inefficiencies

inefficient *adjective*
inefficiently

inequality *noun*
inequalities

inert

inertia

inevitability

inevitable *adjective*
inevitably

inexhaustible

inexpensive *adjective*
inexpensively

inexperience

inexperienced

inexplicable *adjective*
inexplicably

infallibility

infallible *adjective*
infallibly

infamous *adjective*
infamously

infamy

infancy

infant *noun*
infants

infantile

infantry

infect *verb*
infects
infecting
infected

infection *noun*
infections

infectious *adjective*
infectiously

infer *verb*
infers
inferring
inferred

inference *noun*
inferences

inferior *adjective* and *noun*
inferiors

inferiority

infernal *adjective*
infernally

inferno *noun*
infernos

infested

infiltrate *verb*
infiltrates
infiltrating
infiltrated

infiltration

infinite *adjective*
infinitely

infinitive *noun*
infinitives

infinity

infirm

infirmary *noun*
infirmaries

infirmity

inflame *verb*
inflames
inflaming
inflamed

inflammable

inflammation *noun*
inflammations

inflammatory

inflatable

inflate *verb*
inflates
inflating
inflated

inflation

inflect *verb*
inflects
inflecting
inflected

inflection *noun*
inflections

inflexibility

inflexible *adjective*
inflexibly

inflict *verb*
inflicts
inflicting
inflicted

influence *verb*
influences
influencing
influenced

influence *noun*
influences

influential *adjective*
influentially

influenza

inform *verb*
informs
informing
informed

informal *adjective*
informally

informality

informant *noun*
informants

information

informative

informed

informer *noun*
informers

infrequency

infrequent *adjective*
infrequently

infuriate *verb*
infuriates
infuriating
infuriated

-ing
-ing makes present participles and nouns, e.g. **hunt** - **hunting**. You normally drop an *e* at the end, e.g. **change** - **changing**, **smoke** - **smoking**. An exception is **ageing**. Words ending in a consonant following a single vowel double the consonant, e.g. **run** - **running**.

ingenious *adjective*
ingeniously

ingenuity

ingot *noun*
ingots

ingrained

ingredient *noun*
ingredients

inhabit *verb*
inhabits
inhabiting
inhabited

inhabitant *noun*
inhabitants

inhale *verb*
inhales
inhaling
inhaled

inhaler *noun*
inhalers

inherent *adjective*
inherently

inherit *verb*
inherits
inheriting
inherited

inheritance

inhibited

inhospitable
adjective
inhospitably

inhuman

inhumanity

initial *adjective*
initially

initial *noun*
initials

initiate *verb*
initiates
initiating
initiated

initiation

initiative *noun*
initiatives

inject *verb*
injects
injecting
injected

injection *noun*
injections

injure *verb*
injures
injuring
injured

injurious *adjective*
injuriously

injury *noun*
injuries

injustice *noun*
injustices

ink *noun*
inks

inkling *noun*
inklings

inky *adjective*
inkier
inkiest

inland

inlet *noun*
inlets

inn *noun*
inns

innkeeper *noun*
innkeepers

inner

innermost

innings *noun*
innings

innocence

innocent *adjective*
innocently

innocuous *adjective*
innocuously

innovation *noun*
innovations

innovative

innovator *noun*
innovators

innumerable

inoculate *verb*
inoculates
inoculating
inoculated

inoculation

input *verb*
inputs
inputting
input

input *noun*
inputs

inquest *noun*
inquests

inquire *verb*
inquires
inquiring
inquired

inquiry★ *noun*
inquiries

inquisitive *adjective*
inquisitively

insane *adjective*
insanely

insanitary

insanity

inscribe *verb*
inscribes
inscribing
inscribed

inscription *noun*
inscriptions

insect *noun*
insects

insecticide *noun*
insecticides

insecure *adjective*
insecurely

insecurity

insensitive *adjective*
insensitively

insensitivity

inseparable *adjective*
inseparably

insert *verb*
inserts
inserting
inserted

insertion *noun*
insertions

inshore *adjective* and
adverb

inside *noun*
insides

inside *adverb,*
adjective, and
preposition

insight *noun*
insights

insignificance

insignificant
adjective
insignificantly

insincere *adjective*
insincerely

insincerity

★ An **inquiry** is an official investigation. **! enquiry**.

insist *verb*
insists
insisting
insisted

insistence

insistent *adjective*
insistently

insolence

insolent *adjective*
insolently

insolubility

insoluble *adjective*
insolubly

insomnia

inspect *verb*
inspects
inspecting
inspected

inspection *noun*
inspections

inspector *noun*
inspectors

inspiration

inspire *verb*
inspires
inspiring
inspired

install *verb*
installs
installing
installed

installation *noun*
installations

instalment *noun*
instalments

instance *noun*
instances

instant *adjective*
instantly

instant *noun*
instants

instantaneous *adjective*
instantaneously

instead

instep *noun*
insteps

instinct *noun*
instincts

instinctive *adjective*
instinctively

institute *verb*
institutes
instituting
instituted

institute *noun*
institutes

institution *noun*
institutions

instruct *verb*
instructs
instructing
instructed

instruction *noun*
instructions

instrument *noun*
instruments

instrumental

insufficient *adjective*
insufficiently

insulate *verb*
insulates
insulating
insulated

insulation

insulin

insult *verb*
insults
insulting
insulted

insult *noun*
insults

insurance

insure *verb*
insures
insuring
insured

intact

intake *noun*
intakes

integer *noun*
integers

integral *adjective*
integrally

integrate *verb*
integrates
integrating
integrated

integration

integrity

intellect *noun*
intellects

intellectual *adjective*
intellectually

intellectual *noun*
intellectuals

intelligence

intelligent *adjective*
intelligently

intelligibility

intelligible *adjective*
intelligibly

intend *verb*
intends
intending
intended

intense *adjective*
intensely

intensification

intensify *verb*
intensifies
intensifying
intensified

intensity *noun*
intensities

intensive *adjective*
intensively

intent *adjective*
intently

intent *noun*
intents

intention *noun*
intentions

a b c d e f g h i j k l m n o p q r s t u v w x y z

intentional *adjective*
intentionally

interact *verb*
interacts
interacting
interacted

interaction

interactive

intercept *verb*
intercepts
intercepting
intercepted

interception

interchange *noun*
interchanges

interchangeable *adjective*
interchangeably

intercom *noun*
intercoms

intercourse

interest *verb*
interests
interesting
interested

interest *noun*
interests

interface *noun*
interfaces

interfere *verb*
interferes
interfering
interfered

interference

interior *noun*
interiors

interjection *noun*
interjections

interlock *verb*
interlocks
interlocking
interlocked

interlude *noun*
interludes

intermediate

interminable *adjective*
interminably

intermission *noun*
intermissions

intermittent *adjective*
intermittently

intern *verb*
interns
interning
interned

internal *adjective*
internally

international *adjective*
internationally

internee

internment

internet

interplanetary

interpret *verb*
interprets
interpreting
interpreted

interpretation *noun*
interpretations

interpreter *noun*
interpreters

interrogate *verb*
interrogates
interrogating
interrogated

interrogation

interrogative

interrogator *noun*
interrogators

interrupt *verb*
interrupts
interrupting
interrupted

interruption *noun*
interruptions

intersect *verb*
intersects
intersecting
intersected

intersection *noun*
intersections

interval *noun*
intervals

intervene *verb*
intervenes
intervening
intervened

intervention *noun*
interventions

interview *noun*
interviews

interview *verb*
interviews
interviewing
interviewed

interviewer *noun*
interviewers

intestinal

intestine

intimacy

intimate *adjective*
intimately

intimate *verb*
intimates
intimating
intimated

intimation *noun*
intimations

intimidate *verb*
intimidates
intimidating
intimidated

intimidation

into *preposition*

intolerable *adjective*
intolerably

intolerance

intolerant *adjective*
intolerantly

intonation *noun*
intonations

intoxicate *verb*
intoxicates
intoxicating
intoxicated

intoxication

intransitive

intrepid *adjective*
intrepidly

intricacy *noun*
intricacies

intricate *adjective*
intricately

intrigue *verb*
intrigues
intriguing
intrigued

introduce *verb*
introduces
introducing
introduced

introduction *noun*
introductions

introductory

intrude *verb*
intrudes
intruding
intruded

intruder *noun*
intruders

intrusion *noun*
intrusions

intrusive *adjective*
intrusively

intuition

intuitive *adjective*
intuitively

Inuit *noun*
Inuit *or* Inuits

inundate *verb*
inundates
inundating
inundated

inundation *noun*
inundations

invade *verb*
invades
invading
invaded

invader *noun*
invaders

invalid *noun*
invalids

invalid *adjective*
invalidly

invaluable

invariable *adjective*
invariably

invasion *noun*
invasions

invent *verb*
invents
inventing
invented

invention *noun*
inventions

inventive *adjective*
inventively

inventor *noun*
inventors

inverse *noun* and *adjective*
inversely

inversion *noun*
inversions

invert *verb*
inverts
inverting
inverted

invertebrate *noun*
invertebrates

invest *verb*
invests
investing
invested

investigate *verb*
investigates
investigating
investigated

investigation *noun*
investigations

investigator *noun*
investigators

investiture *noun*
investitures

investment *noun*
investments

investor *noun*
investors

invigilate *verb*
invigilates
invigilating
invigilated

invigilation

invigilator *noun*
invigilators

invigorate *verb*
invigorates
invigorating
invigorated

invincible

invisibility

invisible *adjective*
invisibly

invitation *noun*
invitations

invite *verb*
invites
inviting
invited

invoice *noun*
invoices

involuntary

involve *verb*
involves
involving
involved

a b c d e f g h **i** j k l m n o p q r s t u v w x y z

involvement
inward *adjective*
inwardly
inwards *adverb*
iodine
ion *noun*
ions
iris *noun*
irises
iron *noun*
irons
iron *verb*
irons
ironing
ironed
ironic *adjective*
ironically
ironmonger *noun*
ironmongers
ironmongery
irony *noun*
ironies
irrational *adjective*
irrationally
irregular *adjective*
irregularly
irregularity *noun*
irregularities
irrelevance
irrelevant *adjective*
irrelevantly
irresistible *adjective*
irresistibly
irresponsible *adjective*
irresponsibly
irresponsibility
irreverence
irreverent *adjective*
irreverently
irrigate *verb*
irrigates
irrigating
irrigated
irrigation
irritability
irritable *adjective*
irritably
irritant
irritate *verb*
irritates
irritating
irritated
irritation *noun*
irritations

-ish
-ish makes words meaning 'rather' or 'fairly', e.g. **soft** - **softish**. You normally drop an *e* at the end, e.g. **blue** - **bluish**. Words ending in a consonant following a single vowel double the consonant, e.g. **fat** - **fattish**.

Islam
Islamic
island *noun*
islands
islander *noun*
islanders
isle★ *noun*
isles
isn't *verb*
isobar *noun*
isobars
isolate *verb*
isolates
isolating
isolated
isolation
isosceles *adjective*
isotope *noun*
isotopes
issue *verb*
issues
issuing
issued
issue *noun*
issues
isthmus *noun*
isthmuses
italics
itch *verb*
itches
itching
itched
itch *noun*
itches
itchy *adjective*
itchier
itchiest
item *noun*
items
itinerary *noun*
itineraries
it'll *verb*
its☆
it's✪ *verb*
itself
I've *verb*
ivory *adjective* and *noun*
ivories
ivy

★ An **isle** is a small island. **! aisle**.
☆ You use **its** in e.g. *the cat licked its paw*. **! it´s**.
✪ You use **it´s** in *it´s* (it is) *raining* and *it´s* (it has) *been raining*. **! its**.

> **-ize** and **-ise**
> You can use *-ize* or *-ise* at the end of many verbs, e.g. **realize** or **realise**, **privatize** or **privatise**. This book prefers *-ize*, but some words have to be spelt *-ise*, e.g. **advertise**, **exercise**, **supervise**. Check each spelling if you are not sure.

Jj

jab *verb*
jabs
jabbing
jabbed

jab *noun*
jabs

jabber *verb*
jabbers
jabbering
jabbered

jack *noun*
jacks

jack *verb*
jacks
jacking
jacked

jackal *noun*
jackals

jackass *noun*
jackasses

jackdaw *noun*
jackdaws

jacket *noun*
jackets

jack-in-the-box *noun*
jack-in-the-boxes

jackknife *verb*
jackknifes
jackknifing
jackknifed

jackpot *noun*
jackpots

jacuzzi *noun*
jacuzzis

jade

jaded

jagged

jaguar *noun*
jaguars

jail *noun*
jails

jail *verb*
jails
jailing
jailed

jailer *noun*
jailers

Jain★ *noun*
Jains

jam *noun*
jams

jam *verb*
jams
jamming
jammed

jamboree *noun*
jamborees

jammy *adjective*
jammier
jammiest

jangle *verb*
jangles
jangling
jangled

January *noun*
Januaries

jar *noun*
jars

jar *verb*
jars
jarring
jarred

jaundice

jaunt *noun*
jaunts

jauntiness

jaunty *adjective*
jauntier
jauntiest
jauntily

javelin *noun*
javelins

jaw *noun*
jaws

jay *noun*
jays

jazz

jazzy *adjective*
jazzier
jazziest

jealous *adjective*
jealously

jealousy

jeans

Jeep *noun*
Jeeps

jeer *verb*
jeers
jeering
jeered

jellied

jelly *noun*
jellies

jellyfish *noun*
jellyfish

★★ A member of an Indian religion.

a b c d e f g h i j **k** l m n o p q r s t u v w x y z

kayak *noun*
kayaks
kebab *noun*
kebabs
keel *noun*
keels
keel *verb*
keels
keeling
keeled
keen *adjective*
keener
keenest
keenly
keenness
keep *verb*
keeps
keeping
kept
keep *noun*
keeps
keeper *noun*
keepers
keg *noun*
kegs
kennel *noun*
kennels
kept see **keep**
kerb★ *noun*
kerbs
kerbstone *noun*
kerbstones
kernel☆ *noun*
kernels
kestrel *noun*
kestrels
ketchup
kettle *noun*
kettles
kettledrum *noun*
kettledrums
key✪ *noun*
keys
keyboard *noun*
keyboards
keyhole *noun*
keyholes
keynote *noun*
keynotes
khaki
kibbutz *noun*
kibbutzim
kick *verb*
kicks
kicking
kicked
kick *noun*
kicks
kick-off *noun*
kick-offs
kid *noun*
kids
kid *verb*
kids
kidding
kidded
kidnap *verb*
kidnaps
kidnapping
kidnapped
kidnapper *noun*
kidnappers
kidney *noun*
kidneys
kill *verb*
kills
killing
killed
killer *noun*
killers
kiln *noun*
kilns
kilo *noun*
kilos
kilogram *noun*
kilograms
kilometre *noun*
kilometres
kilowatt *noun*
kilowatts
kilt *noun*
kilts
kin
kind *adjective*
kinder
kindest
kindly
kind *noun*
kinds
kindergarten *noun*
kindergartens
kind-hearted
kindle *verb*
kindles
kindling
kindled
kindliness
kindling
kindly *adjective*
kindlier
kindliest
kindness
kinetic
king *noun*
kings
kingdom *noun*
kingdoms
kingfisher *noun*
kingfishers
kingly

★ A **kerb** is the edge of a pavement. **! curb**.
☆ **Kernel** is part of a nut. **! colonel**.
✪ A **key** is a device for opening a lock. **! quay**.

kink *noun*
kinks
kinky *adjective*
kinkier
kinkiest
kiosk *noun*
kiosks
kipper *noun*
kippers
kiss *verb*
kisses
kissing
kissed
kiss *noun*
kisses
kit *noun*
kits
kitchen *noun*
kitchens
kite *noun*
kites
kitten *noun*
kittens
kitty *noun*
kitties
kiwi *noun*
kiwis
knack
knapsack *noun*
knapsacks
knave *noun*
knaves
knead★ *verb*
kneads
kneading
kneaded
knee *noun*
knees
kneecap *noun*
kneecaps

kneel *verb*
kneels
kneeling
knelt
knew☆ see **know**
knickers *plural noun*
knife *noun*
knives
knife *verb*
knifes
knifing
knifed
knight✪ *noun*
knights
knight *verb*
knights
knighting
knighted
knighthood *noun*
knighthoods
knit *verb*
knits
knitting
knitted
knives see **knife**
knob *noun*
knobs
knobbly *adjective*
knobblier
knobbliest
knock *verb*
knocks
knocking
knocked
knock *noun*
knocks
knocker *noun*
knockers
knockout *noun*
knockouts

knot *noun*
knots
knot *verb*
knots
knotting
knotted
knotty *adjective*
knottier
knottiest
know *verb*
knows
knowing
knew
known
know-all *noun*
know-alls
know-how
knowing *adjective*
knowingly
knowledge
knowledgeable *adjective*
knowledgeably
knuckle *noun*
knuckles
koala *noun*
koalas
kookaburra *noun*
kookaburras
Koran
kosher
kung fu

Ll

label *noun*
labels

★ To **knead** is to work a mixture into a dough. **! need**.
☆ **Knew** is the past tense of know. **! new**.
✪ A **knight** is a soldier in old times. **! night**.

a b c d e f g h i j k l m n o p q r s t u v w x y z

label *verb*
labels
labelling
labelled
laboratory *noun*
laboratories
laborious *adjective*
laboriously
labour *noun*
labours
labourer *noun*
labourers
Labrador *noun*
Labradors
laburnum *noun*
laburnums
labyrinth *noun*
labyrinths
lace *noun*
laces
lace *verb*
laces
lacing
laced
lack *verb*
lacks
lacking
lacked
lack *noun*
lacquer
lacrosse
lad *noun*
lads
ladder *noun*
ladders
laden
ladle *noun*
ladles
lady *noun*
ladies
ladybird *noun*
ladybirds
ladylike
ladyship *noun*
ladyships
lag *verb*
lags
lagging
lagged
lager *noun*
lagers
lagoon *noun*
lagoons
laid see **lay**
lain see **lie**
lair *noun*
lairs
lake *noun*
lakes
lama *noun*
lamas
lamb *noun*
lambs
lame *adjective*
lamer
lamest
lamely
lameness
lament *verb*
laments
lamenting
lamented
lament *noun*
laments
lamentation *noun*
lamentations
laminated
lamp *noun*
lamps
lamp-post *noun*
lamp-posts
lampshade *noun*
lampshades
lance *noun*
lances
lance corporal *noun*
lance corporals
land *noun*
lands
land *verb*
lands
landing
landed
landing *noun*
landings
landlady *noun*
landladies
landlord *noun*
landlords
landmark *noun*
landmarks
landowner *noun*
landowners
landscape *noun*
landscapes
landslide *noun*
landslides
lane *noun*
lanes
language *noun*
languages
lankiness
lanky *adjective*
lankier
lankiest
lantern *noun*
lanterns
lap *verb*
laps
lapping
lapped
lap *noun*
laps
lapel *noun*
lapels
lapse *verb*
lapses
lapsing
lapsed
lapse *noun*
lapses

laptop *noun*
laptops

lapwing *noun*
lapwings

larch *noun*
larches

lard

larder *noun*
larders

large *adjective*
larger
largest
largely

largeness

lark *noun*
larks

lark *verb*
larks
larking
larked

larva *noun*
larvae

lasagne *noun*
lasagnes

laser *noun*
lasers

lash *verb*
lashes
lashing
lashed

lash *noun*
lashes

lass *noun*
lasses

lasso *noun*
lassos

lasso *verb*
lassoes
lassoing
lassoed

last *adjective* and *adverb*
lastly

last *verb*
lasts
lasting
lasted

last *noun*

latch *noun*
latches

late *adjective* and *adverb*
later
latest

lately

lateness

latent

lateral *adjective*
laterally

lathe *noun*
lathes

lather *noun*
lathers

Latin

latitude *noun*
latitudes

latter *adjective*
latterly

lattice *noun*
lattices

laugh *verb*
laughs
laughing
laughed

laugh *noun*
laughs

laughable *adjective*
laughably

laughter

launch *verb*
launches
launching
launched

launch *noun*
launches

launder *verb*
launders
laundering
laundered

launderette *noun*
launderettes

laundry *noun*
laundries

laurel *noun*
laurels

lava

lavatory *noun*
lavatories

lavender

lavish *adjective*
lavishly

law *noun*
laws

lawcourt *noun*
lawcourts

lawful *adjective*
lawfully

lawless *adjective*
lawlessly

lawn *noun*
lawns

lawnmower *noun*
lawnmowers

lawsuit *noun*
lawsuits

lawyer *noun*
lawyers

lax *adjective*
laxly

laxative *noun*
laxatives

lay *verb*
lays
laying
laid

lay see **lie**

layabout *noun*
layabouts

a b c d e f g h i j k l m n o p q r s t u v w x y z

layer *noun*
layers

layman *noun*
laymen

layout *noun*
layouts

laze *verb*
lazes
lazing
lazed

laziness

lazy *adjective*
lazier
laziest
lazily

lead *verb*
leads
leading
led

lead★ *noun*
leads

leader *noun*
leaders

leadership

leaf *noun*
leaves

leaflet *noun*
leaflets

leafy *adjective*
leafier
leafiest

league *noun*
leagues

leak *verb*
leaks
leaking
leaked

leak☆ *noun*
leaks

leakage *noun*
leakages

leaky *adjective*
leakier
leakiest

lean *verb*
leans
leaning
leaned *or* leant

lean *adjective*
leaner
leanest

leap *verb*
leaps
leaping
leapt
leaped

leap *noun*
leaps

leapfrog

leap year *noun*
leap years

learn *verb*
learns
learning
learnt *or* learned

learned✪ *adjective*

learner *noun*
learners

lease *noun*
leases

leash *noun*
leashes

least *adjective* and *noun*

leather *noun*
leathers

leathery

leave *verb*
leaves
leaving
left

leave *noun*

leaves see **leaf**

lectern *noun*
lecterns

lecture *verb*
lectures
lecturing
lectured

lecture *noun*
lectures

lecturer *noun*
lecturers

led see **lead**

ledge *noun*
ledges

lee

leek✣ *noun*
leeks

leer *verb*
leers
leering
leered

leeward

left *adjective* and *noun*

left see **leave**

left-handed

leftovers *plural noun*

leg *noun*
legs

legacy *noun*
legacies

★ A **lead** (pronounced *leed*) is a cord for leading a dog. **Lead** (pronounced *led*) is a metal.
☆ A **leak** is a hole or crack that liquid or gas can get through. **! leek**.
✪ Pronounced *ler-nid*.
✣ A **leek** is a vegetable. **! leak**.

legal *adjective*
legally

legality

legalize *verb*
legalizes
legalizing
legalized

legend *noun*
legends

legendary

legibility

legible *adjective*
legibly

legion *noun*
legions

legislate *verb*
legislates
legislating
legislated

legislation

legislator *noun*
legislators

legitimacy

legitimate *adjective*
legitimately

leisure

leisurely

lemon *noun*
lemons

lemonade *noun*
lemonades

lend *verb*
lends
lending
lent

length *noun*
lengths

lengthen *verb*
lengthens
lengthening
lengthened

lengthways *adverb*

lengthwise *adverb*

lengthy *adjective*
lengthier
lengthiest
lengthily

lenience

lenient *adjective*
leniently

lens *noun*
lenses

Lent★

lent see **lend**

lentil *noun*
lentils

leopard *noun*
leopards

leotard *noun*
leotards

leper *noun*
lepers

leprosy

less

lessen☆ *verb*
lessens
lessening
lessened

lesser

lesson✪ *noun*
lessons

lest *conjunction*

let *verb*
lets
letting
let

> **-let**
> *-let* makes nouns meaning 'a small version of', e.g. **booklet**, **piglet**. It also makes words for pieces of jewellery, e.g. **anklet** (worn on the ankle), **bracelet** (from a French word *bras* meaning 'arm')

lethal *adjective*
lethally

let's *verb*

letter *noun*
letters

letter box *noun*
letter boxes

lettering

lettuce *noun*
lettuces

leukaemia

level *verb*
levels
levelling
levelled

level *adjective* and *noun*
levels

lever *noun*
levers

leverage

liability *noun*
liabilities

liable

liar *noun*
liars

liberal *adjective*
liberally

★ **Lent** is the Christian time of fasting. **! lent**.
☆ To **lessen** something is to make it less. **! lesson**.
✪ A **lesson** is a period of learning. **! lessen**.

a b c d e f g h i j k l m n o p q r s t u v w x y z

liberate *verb*
liberates
liberating
liberated

liberation

liberty *noun*
liberties

librarian *noun*
librarians

librarianship

library *noun*
libraries

licence *noun*
licences

license *verb*
licenses
licensing
licensed

lichen *noun*
lichens

lick *verb*
licks
licking
licked

lick *noun*
licks

lid *noun*
lids

lie★ *verb*
lies
lying
lay
lain

lie☆ *verb*
lies
lying
lied

lie *noun*
lies

lieutenant *noun*
lieutenants

life *noun*
lives

lifebelt *noun*
lifebelts

lifeboat *noun*
lifeboats

life cycle *noun*
life cycles

lifeguard *noun*
lifeguards

lifeless *adjective*
lifelessly

lifelike

lifelong

lifestyle *noun*
lifestyles

lifetime *noun*
lifetimes

lift *verb*
lifts
lifting
lifted

lift *noun*
lifts

lift-off *noun*
lift-offs

light *adjective*
lighter
lightest
lightly

light *verb*
lights
lighting
lit *or* lighted

light *noun*
lights

lighten *verb*
lightens
lightening
lightened

lighter *noun*
lighters

lighthouse *noun*
lighthouses

lighting

lightning

lightweight

like *verb*
likes
liking
liked

like *preposition*

likeable

likely *adjective*
likelier
likeliest

liken *verb*
likens
likening
likened

likeness *noun*
likenesses

likewise

liking *noun*
likings

lilac *noun*
lilacs

lily *noun*
lilies

limb *noun*
limbs

limber *verb*
limbers
limbering
limbered

lime *noun*
limes

limelight

limerick *noun*
limericks

limestone

★ As in *to lie on the bed.*
☆ Meaning 'to say something untrue'.

limit *noun*
limits
limit *verb*
limits
limiting
limited
limitation *noun*
limitations
limited
limitless
limp *adjective*
limper
limpest
limply
limp *verb*
limps
limping
limped
limp *noun*
limps
limpet *noun*
limpets
line *noun*
lines
line *verb*
lines
lining
lined
linen
liner *noun*
liners
linesman *noun*
linesmen

> **-ling**
> *-ling* makes words for small things, e.g. **duckling**.

linger *verb*
lingers
lingering
lingered
lingerie
linguist *noun*
linguists
linguistic
linguistics
lining *noun*
linings
link *verb*
links
linking
linked
link *noun*
links
lino
linoleum
lint
lion *noun*
lions
lioness *noun*
lionesses
lip *noun*
lips
lip-read *verb*
lip-reads
lip-reading
lip-read
lipstick *noun*
lipsticks
liquid *adjective* and *noun*
liquids
liquidizer *noun*
liquidizers
liquor *noun*
liquors
liquorice
lisp *noun*
lisps
lisp *verb*
lisps
lisping
lisped
list *noun*
lists
list *verb*
lists
listing
listed
listen *verb*
listens
listening
listened
listener *noun*
listeners
listless *adjective*
listlessly
lit see **light**
literacy
literal *adjective*
literally
literary
literate
literature
litmus
litre *noun*
litres
litter *noun*
litters
litter *verb*
litters
littering
littered
little★ *adjective* and *adverb*
less
least
live *verb*
lives
living
lived

★ You can also use **littler** and **littlest** when you are talking about size.

a b c d e f g h i j k l m n o p q r s t u v w x y z

live *adjective*

livelihood *noun*
livelihoods

liveliness

lively *adjective*
livelier
liveliest

liver *noun*
livers

livery *noun*
liveries

lives see **life**

livestock

livid

living *noun*
livings

lizard *noun*
lizards

llama *noun*
llamas

load *verb*
loads
loading
loaded

load *noun*
loads

loaf *noun*
loaves

loaf *verb*
loafs
loafing
loafed

loafer *noun*
loafers

loam

loamy *adjective*
loamier
loamiest

loan★ *noun*
loans

loan *verb*
loans
loaning
loaned

loath☆ *adjective*

loathe✪ *verb*
loathes
loathing
loathed

loathsome

loaves see **loaf**

lob *verb*
lobs
lobbing
lobbed

lobby *noun*
lobbies

lobby *verb*
lobbies
lobbying
lobbied

lobe *noun*
lobes

lobster *noun*
lobsters

local *adjective*
locally

local *noun*
locals

locality *noun*
localities

locate *verb*
locates
locating
located

location *noun*
locations

loch✣ *noun*
lochs

lock✹ *noun*
locks

lock *verb*
locks
locking
locked

locker *noun*
lockers

locket *noun*
lockets

locomotive *noun*
locomotives

locust *noun*
locusts

lodge *noun*
lodges

lodge *verb*
lodges
lodging
lodged

lodger *noun*
lodgers

lodgings *plural noun*

loft *noun*
lofts

lofty *adjective*
loftier
loftiest
loftily

log *noun*
logs

log *verb*
logs
logging
logged

logarithm *noun*
logarithms

★ A **loan** is a thing that is lent to someone. **! lone**.
☆ **Loath** means 'unwilling'. **! loathe**.
✪ To **loathe** is to dislike very much. **! loath**.
✣ A **loch** is a lake in Scotland. **! lock**.
✹ A **lock** is a mechanism for keeping something closed. **! loch**.

logbook *noun*
logbooks

logic

logical *adjective*
logically

logo *noun*
logos

> **-logy**
> *-logy* makes words for subjects of study, e.g. **archaeology** (the study of ancient remains). Most of these words end in *-ology*, but an important exception is **genealogy**. Some words have plurals, e.g. **genealogies**.

loiter *verb*
loiters
loitering
loitered

loiterer *noun*
loiterers

loll *verb*
lolls
lolling
lolled

lollipop *noun*
lollipops

lolly *noun*
lollies

lone★

loneliness

lonely *adjective*
lonelier
loneliest

long *adjective* and *adverb*
longer
longest

long *verb*
longs
longing
longed

longitude *noun*
longitudes

longitudinal *adjective*
longitudinally

loo *noun*
loos

look *verb*
looks
looking
looked

look *noun*
looks

lookout *noun*
lookouts

loom *noun*
looms

loom *verb*
looms
looming
loomed

loop *noun*
loops

loop *verb*
loops
looping
looped

loophole *noun*
loopholes

loose *adjective*
looser
loosest
loosely

loose *verb*
looses
loosing
loosed

loosen *verb*
loosens
loosening
loosened

looseness

loot *verb*
loots
looting
looted

loot *noun*

looter *noun*
looters

lopsided

lord *noun*
lords

lordly

lordship

lorry *noun*
lorries

lose *verb*
loses
losing
lost

loser *noun*
losers

loss *noun*
losses

lot *noun*
lots

lotion *noun*
lotions

lottery *noun*
lotteries

lotto

loud *adjective*
louder
loudest
loudly

loudness

loudspeaker *noun*
loudspeakers

lounge *noun*
lounges

★ **Lone** means 'alone'. **! loan**.

a b c d e f g h i j k l m n o p q r s t u v w x y z

lounge *verb*
lounges
lounging
lounged

louse *noun*
lice

lousy *adjective*
lousier
lousiest
lousily

lout *noun*
louts

lovable *adjective*
lovably

love *verb*
loves
loving
loved

love *noun*
loves

loveliness

lovely *adjective*
lovelier
loveliest

lover *noun*
lovers

loving *adjective*
lovingly

low *adjective*
lower
lowest

low *verb*
lows
lowing
lowed

lower *verb*
lowers
lowering
lowered

lowland *adjective*

lowlands *plural nouns*

lowlander *noun*
lowlanders

lowliness

lowly *adjective*
lowlier
lowliest

lowness

loyal *adjective*
loyally

loyalty *noun*
loyalties

lozenge *noun*
lozenges

lubricant *noun*
lubricants

lubricate *verb*
lubricates
lubricating
lubricated

lubrication

lucid *adjective*
lucidly

lucidity

luck

lucky *adjective*
luckier
luckiest
luckily

ludicrous *adjective*
ludicrously

ludo

lug *verb*
lugs
lugging
lugged

luggage

lukewarm

lull *verb*
lulls
lulling
lulled

lull *noun*
lulls

lullaby *noun*
lullabies

lumber *verb*
lumbers
lumbering
lumbered

lumber *noun*

lumberjack *noun*
lumberjacks

luminosity

luminous

lump *noun*
lumps

lump *verb*
lumps
lumping
lumped

lumpy *adjective*
lumpier
lumpiest

lunacy *noun*
lunacies

lunar

lunatic *noun*
lunatics

lunch *noun*
lunches

lung *noun*
lungs

lunge *verb*
lunges
lunging
lungeing *or* lunged

lupin *noun*
lupins

lurch *verb*
lurches
lurching
lurched

lurch *noun*
lurches

lure *verb*
lures
luring
lured

lurk *verb*
lurks
lurking
lurked
luscious *adjective*
lusciously
lush *adjective*
lusher
lushest
lushly
lushness
lust *noun*
lusts
lustful *adjective*
lustfully
lustre *noun*
lustres
lustrous
lute *noun*
lutes
luxury *noun*
luxuries
luxurious *adjective*
luxuriously
Lycra

> **-ly**
> *-ly* makes adverbs from adjectives, e.g. **slow** - **slowly**. When the adjective ends in *-y* following a consonant, you change the *y* to *i*, e.g. **happy** - **happily**. *-ly* is also used to make some adjectives, e.g. **lovely**, and some words that are adjectives and adverbs, e.g. **kindly**, **hourly**.

lying see **lie**
lynch *verb*
lynches
lynching
lynched
lyre *noun*
lyres
lyric *noun*
lyrics
lyrical *adjective*
lyrically
lyrics *plural noun*

Mm

ma *noun*
mas
mac *noun*
macs
macabre
macaroni
machine *noun*
machines
machinery
mackerel *noun*
mackerel
mackintosh *noun*
mackintoshes
mad *adjective*
madder
maddest
madly
madam
madden *verb*
maddens
maddening
maddened
made★ see **make**
madman *noun*
madmen
madness
magazine *noun*
magazines
maggot *noun*
maggots
magic *noun* and *adjective*
magical *adjective*
magically
magician *noun*
magicians
magistrate *noun*
magistrates
magma
magnesium
magnet *noun*
magnets
magnetism
magnetic *adjective*
magnetically
magnetize *verb*
magnetizes
magnetizing
magnetized
magnificent *adjective*
magnificently
magnificence
magnification
magnifier
magnify *verb*
magnifies
magnifying
magnified
magnitude *noun*
magnitudes
magnolia *noun*
magnolias
magpie *noun*
magpies
mahogany
maid☆ *noun*
maids

★ You use **made** in e.g. *I made a cake*. **! maid**.
☆ A **maid** is a female servant. **! made**.

a b c d e f g h i j k **l** **m** n o p q r s t u v w x y z

maiden *noun*
maidens
mail★ *noun*
mail *verb*
mails
mailing
mailed
maim *verb*
maims
maiming
maimed
main☆ *adjective*
mainly
mainland
mainly
mains *plural noun*
maintain *verb*
maintains
maintaining
maintained
maintenance
maisonette *noun*
maisonettes
maize
majestic *adjective*
majestically
majesty *noun*
majesties
major *adjective*
major *noun*
majors
majority *noun*
majorities
make *verb*
makes
making
made
make *noun*
makes
make-believe
maker *noun*
makers
make-up
maladjusted
malaria
male✪ *adjective* and *noun*
males
malevolence
malevolent *adjective*
malevolently
malice
malicious *adjective*
maliciously
mallet *noun*
mallets
malnourished
malnutrition
malt
malted
mammal *noun*
mammals
mammoth *adjective* and *noun*
mammoths
man *noun*
men
man *verb*
mans
manning
manned
manage *verb*
manages
managing
managed
manageable
management
manager *noun*
managers
manageress *noun*
manageresses
mane✣ *noun*
manes
manger *noun*
mangers
mangle *verb*
mangles
mangling
mangled
mango *noun*
mangoes
manhandle *verb*
manhandles
manhandling
manhandled
manhole *noun*
manholes
mania *noun*
manias
maniac *noun*
maniacs
manic *adjective*
manically
manifesto *noun*
manifestos
manipulate *verb*
manipulates
manipulating
manipulated
manipulation
manipulator
mankind
manliness
manly *adjective*
manlier
manliest

★ **Mail** is letters and parcels sent by post. **! male**.
☆ **Main** means 'most important'. **! mane**.
✪ A **male** is a man or an animal of the same gender as a man. **! mail**.
✣ A **mane** is the long piece of hair on a horse or lion. **! main**.

manner★ *noun*
manners

manoeuvrable

manoeuvre *verb*
manoeuvres
manoeuvring
manoeuvred

manoeuvre *noun*
manoeuvres

man-of-war *noun*
men-of-war

manor☆ *noun*
manors

mansion *noun*
mansions

manslaughter

mantelpiece *noun*
mantelpieces

mantle *noun*
mantles

manual *adjective*
manually

manual *noun*
manuals

manufacture *verb*
manufactures
manufacturing
manufactured

manufacture *noun*

manufacturer *noun*
manufacturers

manure

manuscript *noun*
manuscripts

Manx

many *adjective* and *noun*
more
most

Maori *noun*
Maoris

map *noun*
maps

map *verb*
maps
mapping
mapped

maple *noun*
maples

mar *verb*
mars
marring
marred

marathon *noun*
marathons

marauder *noun*
marauders

marauding

marble *noun*
marbles

March *noun*
Marches

march *verb*
marches
marching
marched

march *noun*
marches

marcher *noun*
marchers

mare✪ *noun*
mares

margarine

margin *noun*
margins

marginal *adjective*
marginally

marigold *noun*
marigolds

marijuana

marina *noun*
marinas

marine *adjective* and *noun*
marines

mariner *noun*
mariners

marionette *noun*
marionettes

mark *verb*
marks
marking
marked

mark *noun*
marks

market *noun*
markets

market *verb*
markets
marketing
marketed

marksman *noun*
marksmen

marksmanship

marmalade

maroon *verb*
maroons
marooning
marooned

maroon *adjective* and *noun*

marquee *noun*
marquees

marriage *noun*
marriages

★ You use **manner** in e.g. *a friendly manner*. **! manor**.
☆ A **manor** is a big house in the country. **! manner**.
✪ A **mare** is a female horse. **! mayor**.

marrow *noun*
marrows

marry *verb*
marries
marrying
married

marsh *noun*
marshes

marshal *noun*
marshals

marshmallow *noun*
marshmallows

marshy *adjective*
marshier
marshiest

marsupial *noun*
marsupials

martial

Martian *noun*
Martians

martin *noun*
martins

martyr *noun*
martyrs

martyrdom

marvel *verb*
marvels
marvelling
marvelled

marvel *noun*
marvels

marvellous *adjective*
marvellously

Marxism

Marxist

marzipan

mascot *noun*
mascots

masculine

masculinity

mash *verb*
mashes
mashing
mashed

mash *noun*

mask *noun*
masks

mask *verb*
masks
masking
masked

Mason★ *noun*
Masons

mason☆ *noun*
masons

masonry

Mass✪ *noun*
Masses

mass *noun*
masses

mass *verb*
masses
massing
massed

massacre *verb*
massacres
massacring
massacred

massacre *noun*
massacres

massage *verb*
massages
massaging
massaged

massage *noun*

massive *adjective*
massively

mast *noun*
masts

master *noun*
masters

master *verb*
masters
mastering
mastered

masterly

mastermind *noun*
masterminds

masterpiece *noun*
masterpieces

mastery

mat✣ *noun*
mats

matador *noun*
matadors

match *verb*
matches
matching
matched

match *noun*
matches

mate *noun*
mates

mate *verb*
mates
mating
mated

material *noun*
materials

materialistic

maternal *adjective*
maternally

maternity

mathematical *adjective*
mathematically

★ You use a capital M when you mean a member of the Freemasons.

☆ Use a small m when you mean someone who builds with stone.

✪ Use a capital M when you mean the Roman Catholic service.

✣ A **mat** is a covering for a floor. **! matt**.

mathematician *noun*
mathematicians
mathematics
maths
matinée *noun*
matinées
matrimonial
matrimony
matrix *noun*
matrices
matron *noun*
matrons
matt★
matted
matter *verb*
matters
mattering
mattered
matter *noun*
matters
matting
mattress *noun*
mattresses
mature
maturity
mauve
maximum *adjective*
and *noun*
maxima *or* maximums
May *noun*
Mays
may *verb*
might
may
maybe
May Day
mayday☆ *noun*
maydays
mayonnaise
mayor✪ *noun*
mayors
mayoress *noun*
mayoresses
maypole *noun*
maypoles
maze *noun*
mazes
meadow *noun*
meadows
meagre
meal *noun*
meals
mean *adjective*
meaner
meanest
meanly
mean *verb*
means
meaning
meant
meander *verb*
meanders
meandering
meandered
meaning *noun*
meanings
meaningful *adjective*
meaningfully
meaningless
adjective
meaninglessly
meanness
means *plural noun*
meantime
meanwhile
measles *plural noun*
measly *adjective*
measlier
measliest
measure *verb*
measures
measuring
measured
measure *noun*
measures
measurement *noun*
measurements
meat✣ *noun*
meats
meaty *adjective*
meatier
meatiest
mechanic *noun*
mechanics
mechanical *adjective*
mechanically
mechanics
mechanism *noun*
mechanisms
medal *noun*
medals
medallist *noun*
medallists
meddle *verb*
meddles
meddling
meddled
meddler *noun*
meddlers
meddlesome
media *plural noun*
median *noun*
medians
medical *adjective*
medically

★ **Matt** means 'not shiny'. **! mat**.
☆ An international radio signal.
✪ You use **mayor** in e.g. *the Mayor of London*. **! mare**.
✣ **Meat** is the flesh of an animal. **! meet**.

medicine *noun*
medicines
medicinal
medieval
mediocre
mediocrity
meditate *verb*
meditates
meditating
meditated
meditation
Mediterranean
medium *adjective*
medium *noun*
media *or* mediums
meek *adjective*
meeker
meekest
meekly
meekness
meet★ *verb*
meets
meeting
met
meeting *noun*
meetings
megaphone *noun*
megaphones
melancholy
mellow *adjective*
mellower
mellowest
melodious *adjective*
melodiously
melodrama *noun*
melodramas
melodramatic *adjective*
melodramatically
melody *noun*
melodies
melodic

melon *noun*
melons
melt *verb*
melts
melting
melted
member *noun*
members
membership
Member of Parliament *noun*
Members of Parliament
membrane *noun*
membranes
memoirs *plural noun*
memorable *adjective*
memorably
memorial *noun*
memorials
memorize *verb*
memorizes
memorizing
memorized
memory *noun*
memories
men see **man**
menace *verb*
menaces
menacing
menaced
menace *noun*
menaces
menagerie *noun*
menageries
mend *verb*
mends
mending
mended
mender *noun*
menders
menstrual
menstruation

> **-ment**
> *-ment* makes nouns from adjectives e.g. **contentment**. There is a fixed number of these, and you cannot freely add *-ment* as you can with *-ness*. When the adjective ends in *-y* following a consonant, you change the *y* to *i*, e.g. **merry** - **merriment**.

mental *adjective*
mentally
mention *verb*
mentions
mentioning
mentioned
mention *noun*
mentions
menu *noun*
menus
mercenary *adjective* and *noun*
mercenaries
merchandise
merchant *noun*
merchants
merciful *adjective*
mercifully
merciless *adjective*
mercilessly
mercury
mercy *noun*
mercies
mere *adjective*
mere *noun*
meres
merely *adverb*

★ People **meet** when they come together. **!** **meat**.

merge *verb*
merges
merging
merged

merger *noun*
mergers

meridian *noun*
meridians

meringue *noun*
meringues

merit *noun*
merits

merit *verb*
merits
meriting
merited

mermaid *noun*
mermaids

merriment

merry *adjective*
merrier
merriest
merrily

merry-go-round *noun*
merry-go-rounds

mesh *noun*
meshes

mess *noun*
messes

mess *verb*
messes
messing
messed

message *noun*
messages

messenger *noun*
messengers

Messiah

messiness

messy *adjective*
messier
messiest
messily

met see **meet**

metal★ *noun*
metals

metallic

metallurgical

metallurgist

metallurgy

metamorphosis *noun*
metamorphoses

metaphor *noun*
metaphors

metaphorical *adjective*
metaphorically

meteor *noun*
meteors

meteoric

meteorite *noun*
meteorites

meteorological

meteorologist

meteorology

meter☆ *noun*
meters

methane

method *noun*
methods

methodical *adjective*
methodically

Methodist *noun*
Methodists

meths

methylated spirit

meticulous *adjective*
meticulously

metre✪ *noun*
metres

metric *adjective*

metrical *adjective*
metrically

metronome *noun*
metronomes

mettle✣

mew *verb*
mews
mewing
mewed

miaow *verb*
miaows
miaowing
miaowed

mice see **mouse**

> **micro-**
> *micro-* makes words meaning 'small', e.g. **microwave**. When the word begins with a vowel you add a hyphen, e.g. **micro-organism**.

microbe *noun*
microbes

microchip *noun*
microchips

microcomputer *noun*
microcomputers

microfilm *noun*
microfilms

★ **Metal** is a hard substance used to make things. **! mettle**.
☆ A **meter** is a device that shows how much of something has been used. **! metre**.
✪ A **metre** is a unit of length. **! meter**.
✣ As in *to be on your mettle*. **! metal**.

a b c d e f g h i j k l m n o p q r s t u v w x y z

misjudge *verb*
misjudges
misjudging
misjudged

mislay *verb*
mislays
mislaying
mislaid

mislead *verb*
misleads
misleading
misled

misprint *noun*
misprints

miss *verb*
misses
missing
missed

miss *noun*
misses

missile *noun*
missiles

missing

mission *noun*
missions

missionary *noun*
missionaries

misspell *verb*
misspells
misspelling
misspelt *or* misspelled

mist★ *noun*
mists

mistake *noun*
mistakes

mistake *verb*
mistakes
mistaking
mistook
mistaken

mister

mistiness

mistletoe

mistreat *verb*
mistreats
mistreating
mistreated

mistreatment

mistress *noun*
mistresses

mistrust *verb*
mistrusts
mistrusting
mistrusted

misty *adjective*
mistier
mistiest
mistily

misunderstand *verb*
misunderstands
misunderstanding
misunderstood

misunderstanding *noun*
misunderstandings

misuse *verb*
misuses
misusing
misused

misuse *noun*
misuses

mite☆ *noun*
mites

mitre *noun*
mitres

mitten *noun*
mittens

mix *verb*
mixes
mixing
mixed

mixer *noun*
mixers

mixture *noun*
mixtures

mix-up *noun*
mix-ups

moan *verb*
moans
moaning
moaned

moan *noun*
moans

moat *noun*
moats

mob *noun*
mobs

mob *verb*
mobs
mobbing
mobbed

mobile *adjective* and *noun*
mobiles

mobility

mobilization

mobilize *verb*
mobilizes
mobilizing
mobilized

moccasin *noun*
moccasins

mock *adjective*

mock *verb*
mocks
mocking
mocked

mockery *noun*
mockeries

mock-up *noun*
mock-ups

mode *noun*
modes

model *noun*
models

★ **Mist** is damp air that is difficult to see through. **! missed**.
☆ A **mite** is a tiny insect. **! might**.

model *verb*
models
modelling
modelled

modem *noun*
modems

moderate *adjective*
moderately

moderate *verb*
moderates
moderating
moderated

moderation

modern

modernity

modernization

modernize *verb*
modernizes
modernizing
modernized

modest *adjective*
modestly

modesty

modification *noun*
modifications

modify *verb*
modifies
modifying
modified

module *noun*
modules

moist *adjective*
moister
moistest

moisture

moisten *verb*
moistens
moistening
moistened

molar *noun*
molars

mole *noun*
moles

molecular

molecule *noun*
molecules

molehill *noun*
molehills

molest *verb*
molests
molesting
molested

mollusc *noun*
molluscs

molten

moment *noun*
moments

momentary *adjective*
momentarily

momentous *adjective*
momentously

momentum

monarch *noun*
monarchs

monarchy *noun*
monarchies

monastery *noun*
monasteries

monastic

Monday *noun*
Mondays

money

mongoose *noun*
mongooses

mongrel *noun*
mongrels

monitor *verb*
monitors
monitoring
monitored

monitor *noun*
monitors

monk *noun*
monks

monkey *noun*
monkeys

monogram *noun*
monograms

monologue *noun*
monologues

monopolize *verb*
monopolizes
monopolizing
monopolized

monopoly *noun*
monopolies

monorail *noun*
monorails

monotonous *adjective*
monotonously

monotony

monsoon *noun*
monsoons

monster *noun*
monsters

monstrosity *noun*
monstrosities

monstrous *adjective*
monstrously

month *noun*
months

monthly *adjective* and *adverb*

monument *noun*
monuments

monumental *adjective*
monumentally

moo *verb*
moos
mooing
mooed

mood *noun*
moods

moodiness

moody *adjective*
moodier
moodiest
moodily

moon *noun*
moons

moonlight

a b c d e f g h i j k l m n o p q r s t u v w x y z

moonlit

moor★ *verb*
moors
mooring
moored

moor☆ *noun*
moors

moorhen *noun*
moorhens

mooring *noun*
moorings

moose✪ *noun*
moose

mop *noun*
mops

mop *verb*
mops
mopping
mopped

mope *verb*
mopes
moping
moped

moped *noun*
mopeds

moraine *noun*
moraines

moral *adjective*
morally

moral *noun*
morals

morale

morality

morals *plural noun*

morbid *adjective*
morbidly

more✣ *adjective, adverb,* and *noun*

moreover

Mormon *noun*
Mormons

morning *noun*
mornings

moron *noun*
morons

moronic *adjective*
moronically

morose *adjective*
morosely

morphine

morris dance *noun*
morris dances

Morse code

morsel *noun*
morsels

mortal *adjective*
mortally

mortality

mortar

mortgage *noun*
mortgages

mortuary *noun*
mortuaries

mosaic *noun*
mosaics

mosque *noun*
mosques

mosquito *noun*
mosquitoes

moss *noun*
mosses

mossy *adjective*
mossier
mossiest

most *adjective, adverb,* and *noun*

mostly *adverb*

motel *noun*
motels

moth *noun*
moths

mother *noun*
mothers

motherhood

mother-in-law *noun*
mothers-in-law

motherly

motion *noun*
motions

motionless

motivate *verb*
motivates
motivating
motivated

motive *noun*
motives

motor *noun*
motors

motorbike *noun*
motorbikes

motor boat *noun*
motor boats

motor car *noun*
motor cars

motorcycle *noun*
motorcycles

motorcyclist *noun*
motorcyclists

motorist *noun*
motorists

motorway *noun*
motorways

mottled

motto *noun*
mottoes

★ To **moor** a boat is to tie it up. **! more**.
☆ A **moor** is an area of rough land. **! more**.
✪ A **moose** is an American elk. **! mouse**, **mousse**.
✣ You use **more** in e.g. *I'd like more to eat*. **! moor**.

mould *verb*
moulds
moulding
moulded
mould *noun*
moulds
mouldy *adjective*
mouldier
mouldiest
moult *verb*
moults
moulting
moulted
mound *noun*
mounds
mount *verb*
mounts
mounting
mounted
mount *noun*
mounts
mountain *noun*
mountains
mountaineer *noun*
mountaineers
mountaineering
mountainous
mourn *verb*
mourns
mourning
mourned
mourner *noun*
mourners
mournful *adjective*
mournfully
mouse★ *noun*
mice
mousetrap *noun*
mousetraps
mousse☆ *noun*
mousses

moustache *noun*
moustaches
mousy *adjective*
mousier
mousiest
mouth *noun*
mouths
mouthful *noun*
mouthfuls
mouthpiece *noun*
mouthpieces
movable
move *verb*
moves
moving
moved
move *noun*
moves
movement *noun*
movements
movie *noun*
movies
mow *verb*
mows
mowing
mowed
mown
mower *noun*
mowers
much *adjective, adverb,* and *noun*
muck *noun*
muck *verb*
mucks
mucking
mucked
mucky *adjective*
muckier
muckiest
mud

muddle *verb*
muddles
muddling
muddled
muddle *noun*
muddles
muddler *noun*
muddlers
muddy *adjective*
muddier
muddiest
mudguard *noun*
mudguards
muesli
muezzin✪ *noun*
muezzins
muffle *verb*
muffles
muffling
muffled
mug *noun*
mugs
mug *verb*
mugs
mugging
mugged
mugger *noun*
muggers
muggy *adjective*
muggier
muggiest
mule *noun*
mules

multi-
multi- makes words with the meaning 'many', e.g. **multicultural**. You do not normally need a hyphen.

★ A **mouse** is a small animal. **! moose**, **mousse**.
☆ A **mousse** is a creamy pudding. **! moose**, **mouse**.
✪ A man who calls Muslims to prayer. Pronounced *moo-ezz-in*.

multiple *adjective* and *noun*
multiples

multiplication

multiply *verb*
multiplies
multiplying
multiplied

multiracial

multitude *noun*
multitudes

mumble *verb*
mumbles
mumbling
mumbled

mummify *verb*
mummifies
mummifying
mummified

mummy *noun*
mummies

mumps

munch *verb*
munches
munching
munched

mundane

municipal

mural *noun*
murals

murder *verb*
murders
murdering
murdered

murder *noun*
murders

murderer *noun*
murderers

murderous *adjective*
murderously

murky *adjective*
murkier
murkiest

murmur *verb*
murmurs
murmuring
murmured

murmur *noun*
murmurs

muscle★ *noun*
muscles

muscle *verb*
muscles
muscling
muscled

muscular

museum *noun*
museums

mushroom *noun*
mushrooms

mushroom *verb*
mushrooms
mushrooming
mushroomed

music

musical *adjective*
musically

musical *noun*
musicals

musician *noun*
musicians

musket *noun*
muskets

musketeer *noun*
musketeers

Muslim *noun*
Muslims

muslin

mussel☆ *noun*
mussels

must

mustard

muster *verb*
musters
mustering
mustered

mustiness

musty *adjective*
mustier
mustiest

mutation *noun*
mutations

mute *adjective*
mutely

mute *noun*
mutes

muted

mutilate *verb*
mutilates
mutilating
mutilated

mutilation

mutineer *noun*
mutineers

mutiny *noun*
mutinies

mutinous *adjective*
mutinously

mutiny *verb*
mutinies
mutinying
mutinied

mutter *verb*
mutters
muttering
muttered

mutton

mutual *adjective*
mutually

muzzle *verb*
muzzles
muzzling
muzzled

★ A **muscle** is a part of the body. **! mussel**.
☆ A **mussel** is a shellfish. **! muscle**.

muzzle *noun*
muzzles

myself

mysterious *adjective*
mysteriously

mystery *noun*
mysteries

mystification

mystify *verb*
mystifies
mystifying
mystified

myth *noun*
myths

mythical

mythological *adjective*

mythology

Nn

nab *verb*
nabs
nabbing
nabbed

nag *verb*
nags
nagging
nagged

nag *noun*
nags

nail *noun*
nails

nail *verb*
nails
nailing
nailed

naive *adjective*
naively

naivety

naked

nakedness

name *noun*
names

name *verb*
names
naming
named

nameless

namely

nanny *noun*
nannies

nap *noun*
naps

napkin *noun*
napkins

nappy *noun*
nappies

narcissus *noun*
narcissi

narcotic *noun*
narcotics

narrate *verb*
narrates
narrating
narrated

narration *noun*
narrations

narrative *noun*
narratives

narrator *noun*
narrators

narrow *adjective*
narrower
narrowest
narrowly

nasal *adjective*
nasally

nastiness

nasturtium *noun*
nasturtiums

nasty *adjective*
nastier
nastiest
nastily

nation *noun*
nations

national *adjective*
nationally

nationalism

nationalist

nationality *noun*
nationalities

nationalization

nationalize *verb*
nationalizes
nationalizing
nationalized

nationwide *adjective*

native *adjective* and *noun*
natives

Native American *noun*
Native Americans

nativity *noun*
nativities

natural *adjective*
naturally

natural *noun*
naturals

naturalist *noun*
naturalists

naturalization

naturalize *verb*
naturalizes
naturalizing
naturalized

nature *noun*
natures

naughtiness

naughty *adjective*
naughtier
naughtiest
naughtily

nausea

nautical

a b c d e f g h i j k l **m** **n** o p q r s t u v w x y z

a b c d e f g h i j k l m **n** o p q r s t u v w x y z

naval★ *adjective*

nave *noun*
naves

navel☆ *noun*
navels

navigable

navigate *verb*
navigates
navigating
navigated

navigation

navigator *noun*
navigators

navy *noun*
navies

Nazi *noun*
Nazis

Nazism

near *adjective* and *adverb*
nearer
nearest

near *preposition*

near *verb*
nears
nearing
neared

nearby

nearly

neat *adjective*
neater
neatest
neatly

neatness

necessarily

necessary

necessity *noun*
necessities

neck *noun*
necks

neckerchief *noun*
neckerchiefs

necklace *noun*
necklaces

nectar

nectarine *noun*
nectarines

need✪ *verb*
needs
needing
needed

need *noun*
needs

needle *noun*
needles

needless *adjective*
needlessly

needlework

needy *adjective*
needier
neediest

negative *adjective*
negatively

negative *noun*
negatives

neglect *verb*
neglects
neglecting
neglected

neglect *noun*

neglectful *adjective*
neglectfully

negligence

negligent *adjective*
negligently

negligible *adjective*
negligibly

negotiate *verb*
negotiates
negotiating
negotiated

negotiation *noun*
negotiations

negotiator *noun*
negotiators

neigh *verb*
neighs
neighing
neighed

neigh *noun*
neighs

neighbour *noun*
neighbours

neighbouring

neighbourhood *noun*
neighbourhoods

neighbourly

neither *adjective* and *conjunction*

neon

nephew *noun*
nephews

nerve *noun*
nerves

nerve-racking

nervous *adjective*
nervously

nervousness

> **-ness**
> *-ness* makes nouns from adjectives, e.g. **soft** - **softness**. When the adjective ends in *-y* following a consonant, you change the *y* to *i*, e.g. **lively** - **liveliness**.

nest *noun*
nests

★ **Naval** means 'to do with a navy'. **! navel**.
☆ A **navel** is a small hollow in your stomach. **! naval**.
✪ To **need** is to require something. **! knead**.

nest *verb*
nests
nesting
nested
nestle *verb*
nestles
nestling
nestled
nestling *noun*
nestlings
net *noun*
nets
net *adjective*
netball
nettle *noun*
nettles
network *noun*
networks
neuter *adjective*
neuter *verb*
neuters
neutering
neutered
neutral *adjective*
neutrally
neutrality
neutralize *verb*
neutralizes
neutralizing
neutralized
neutron *noun*
neutrons
never
nevertheless *conjunction*
new★ *adjective*
newer
newest
newly
newcomer *noun*
newcomers
newness
news
newsagent *noun*
newsagents
newsletter *noun*
newsletters
newspaper *noun*
newspapers
newt *noun*
newts
New Testament
newton *noun*
newtons
next *adjective* and *adverb*
next door
nib *noun*
nibs
nibble *verb*
nibbles
nibbling
nibbled
nice *adjective*
nicer
nicest
nicely
niceness
nicety *noun*
niceties
nick *verb*
nicks
nicking
nicked
nick *noun*
nicks
nickel *noun*
nickels
nickname *noun*
nicknames
nicotine
niece *noun*
nieces
night☆ *noun*
nights
nightclub *noun*
nightclubs
nightdress *noun*
nightdresses
nightfall
nightingale *noun*
nightingales
nightly
nightmare *noun*
nightmares
nightmarish
nil
nimble *adjective*
nimbler
nimblest
nimbly
nine *noun*
nines
nineteen *noun*
nineteens
nineteenth
ninetieth
ninety *noun*
nineties
ninth *adjective*
ninthly
nip *verb*
nips
nipping
nipped
nip *noun*
nips
nipple *noun*
nipples
nippy *adjective*
nippier
nippiest
nit *noun*
nits

★ You use **new** in e.g *She has a new bike*. **! knew**.
☆ **Night** is the opposite of day. **! knight**.

nitrate *noun*
nitrates

nitric acid

nitrogen

nitty-gritty

nitwit *noun*
nitwits

nobility

noble *adjective*
nobler
noblest
nobly

noble *noun*
nobles

nobleman *noun*
noblemen

noblewoman *noun*
noblewomen

nobody *noun*
nobodies

nocturnal *adjective*
nocturnally

nod *verb*
nods
nodding
nodded

noise *noun*
noises

noiseless *adjective*
noiselessly

noisiness

noisy *adjective*
noisier
noisiest
noisily

nomad *noun*
nomads

nomadic

no man's land

nominate *verb*
nominates
nominating
nominated

nomination *noun*
nominations

> **-nomy**
> *-nomy* makes words for subjects of study, e.g. **astronomy** (the study of the stars). Most of these words end in *-onomy*.

none★

> **non-**
> *non-* makes words meaning 'not', e.g. **non-existent**, **non-smoker**. You use a hyphen to make these words. When an *un-* word has a special meaning, e.g. **unprofessional**, you can use *non-* to make a word without the special meaning, e.g. **non-professional**.

non-existent

non-fiction

non-flammable

nonsense

nonsensical *adjective*
nonsensically

non-stop

noodle

noon

no one

noose *noun*
nooses

normal *adjective*
normally

normality

north *adjective* and *adverb*

north☆ *noun*

north-east *noun* and *adjective*

northerly *adjective* and *noun*
northerlies

northern

northerner *noun*
northerners

northward *adjective* and *adverb*

northwards *adverb*

north-west

nose *noun*
noses

nose *verb*
noses
nosing
nosed

nosedive *verb*
nosedives
nosediving
nosedived

nosedive *noun*
nosedives

nosiness

nostalgia

nostalgic *adjective*
nostalgically

nostril *noun*
nostrils

★ You use **none** in e.g. *none of us went.* **! nun**.
☆ You use a capital N in **the North**, when you mean a particular region.

nosy *adjective*
nosier
nosiest
nosily
notable *adjective*
notably
notch *noun*
notches
note *noun*
notes
note *verb*
notes
noting
noted
notebook *noun*
notebooks
notepaper
nothing
notice *verb*
notices
noticing
noticed
notice *noun*
notices
noticeable *adjective*
noticeably
noticeboard *noun*
noticeboards
notion *noun*
notions
notoriety
notorious *adjective*
notoriously
nougat
nought *noun*
noughts
noun *noun*
nouns
nourish *verb*
nourishes
nourishing
nourished
nourishment
novel *adjective*
novel *noun*
novels
novelist *noun*
novelists
novelty *noun*
novelties
November *noun*
Novembers
novice *noun*
novices
nowadays
nowhere
nozzle *noun*
nozzles
nuclear
nucleus *noun*
nuclei
nude *adjective* and *noun*
nudes
nudge *verb*
nudges
nudging
nudged
nudist *noun*
nudists
nudity
nugget *noun*
nuggets
nuisance *noun*
nuisances
numb *adjective*
numbly
number *noun*
numbers
number *verb*
numbers
numbering
numbered
numbness
numeracy
numeral *noun*
numerals
numerate
numerator *noun*
numerators
numerical *adjective*
numerically
numerous
nun★ *noun*
nuns
nunnery *noun*
nunneries
nurse *noun*
nurses
nurse *verb*
nurses
nursing
nursed
nursery *noun*
nurseries
nurture *verb*
nurtures
nurturing
nurtured
nut *noun*
nuts
nutcrackers *plural noun*
nutmeg *noun*
nutmegs
nutrient *noun*
nutrients
nutrition
nutritional *adjective*
nutritionally
nutritious
nutshell *noun*
nutshells
nutty *adjective*
nuttier
nuttiest

★ A **nun** is a member of a convent. **! none**.

a b c d e f g h i j k l m n p q r s t u v w x y z

nuzzle *verb*
nuzzles
nuzzling
nuzzled

nylon *adjective* and *noun*
nylons

nymph *noun*
nymphs

Oo

-o
Most nouns ending in -*o*, e.g. **hero**, **potato**, have plurals ending in -*oes*, e.g. **heroes**, **potatoes**, but a few end in -*os*. The most important are **kilos**, **photos**, **pianos**, **radios**, **ratios**, **solos**, **videos**, **zeros**. Verbs ending in -*o* usually have the forms -*oes* and -*oed*, e.g. **video** - **videoes** - **videoed**.

oak *noun*
oaks

oar★ *noun*
oars

oarsman *noun*
oarsmen

oarswoman *noun*
oarswomen

oasis *noun*
oases

oath *noun*
oaths

oatmeal

oats *plural noun*

obedience

obedient *adjective*
obediently

obey *verb*
obeys
obeying
obeyed

obituary *noun*
obituaries

object *noun*
objects

object *verb*
objects
objecting
objected

objection *noun*
objections

objectionable

objective *adjective*
objectively

objective *noun*
objectives

objector *noun*
objectors

obligation *noun*
obligations

obligatory

oblige *verb*
obliges
obliging
obliged

oblique *adjective*
obliquely

oblong *adjective* and *noun*
oblongs

oboe *noun*
oboes

oboist *noun*
oboists

obscene *adjective*
obscenely

obscenity *noun*
obscenities

obscure *adjective*
obscurer
obscurest
obscurely

obscurity

observance *noun*
observances

observant *adjective*
observantly

observation *noun*
observations

observatory *noun*
observatories

observe *verb*
observes
observing
observed

observer *noun*
observers

obsessed

obsession *noun*
obsessions

obsolete

obstacle *noun*
obstacles

obstinacy

obstinate *adjective*
obstinately

obstruct *verb*
obstructs
obstructing
obstructed

obstruction *noun*
obstructions

obstructive *adjective*
obstructively

★ An **oar** is used for rowing a boat. **! or**, **ore**.

obtain *verb*
obtains
obtaining
obtained

obtainable

obtuse *adjective*
obtuser
obtusest
obtusely

obvious *adjective*
obviously

occasion *noun*
occasions

occasional *adjective*
occasionally

occupant *noun*
occupants

occupation *noun*
occupations

occupy *verb*
occupies
occupying
occupied

occur *verb*
occurs
occurring
occurred

occurrence *noun*
occurrences

ocean *noun*
oceans

o'clock

octagon *noun*
octagons

octagonal *adjective*
octagonally

octave *noun*
octaves

October *noun*
Octobers

octopus *noun*
octopuses

odd *adjective*
odder
oddest
oddly

oddity *noun*
oddities

oddments *plural noun*

oddness

odds *plural noun*

odour *noun*
odours

odorous

oesophagus *noun*
oesophagi *or*
oesophaguses

of★

off☆

offence *noun*
offences

offend *verb*
offends
offending
offended

offender *noun*
offenders

offensive *adjective*
offensively

offer *verb*
offers
offering
offered

offer *noun*
offers

offhand

office *noun*
offices

officer *noun*
officers

official *adjective*
officially

official *noun*
officials

officious *adjective*
officiously

off-licence *noun*
off-licences

offset *verb*
offsets
offsetting
offset

offshore *adjective* and *adverb*

offside

offspring *noun*
offspring

often

ogre *noun*
ogres

ohm *noun*
ohms

oil *noun*
oils

oil *verb*
oils
oiling
oiled

oilfield *noun*
oilfields

oilskin *noun*
oilskins

oil well *noun*
oil wells

oily *adjective*
oilier
oiliest

ointment *noun*
ointments

old *adjective*
older
oldest

Old Testament

★ You use **of** in e.g. *a box of matches*. **! off**.
☆ You use **off** in e.g. *turn off the light*. **! of**.

a b c d e f g h i j k l m n **o** p q r s t u v w x y z

olive *noun*
olives
Olympic Games *plural noun*
Olympics *plural noun*
ombudsman *noun*
ombudsmen
omelette *noun*
omelettes
omen *noun*
omens
ominous *adjective*
ominously
omission★ *noun*
omissions
omit *verb*
omits
omitting
omitted
omnivorous
once
one☆ *adjective* and *noun*
ones
oneself
one-sided
one-way
ongoing
onion *noun*
onions
onlooker *noun*
onlookers
only
onshore *adjective* and *adverb*
onto *preposition*
onward *adjective* and *adverb*
onwards *adverb*
ooze *verb*
oozes
oozing
oozed
opaque
open *adjective*
openly
open *verb*
opens
opening
opened
opener *noun*
openers
opening *noun*
openings
opera *noun*
operas
operate *verb*
operates
operating
operated
operatic
operation *noun*
operations
operator *noun*
operators
opinion *noun*
opinions
opium
opponent *noun*
opponents
opportunity *noun*
opportunities
oppose *verb*
opposes
opposing
opposed
opposite *adjective*
opposite *noun*
opposites
opposition
oppress *verb*
oppresses
oppressing
oppressed
oppression
oppressive *adjective*
oppressively
oppressor *noun*
oppressors
opt *verb*
opts
opting
opted
optical *adjective*
optically
optician *noun*
opticians
optimism
optimist *noun*
optimists
optimistic *adjective*
optimistically
option *noun*
options
optional *adjective*
optionally
opulence
opulent *adjective*
opulently
or✪ *conjunction*
oral✣ *adjective*
orally
orange *adjective* and *noun*
oranges
orangeade *noun*
orangeades

★ An **omission** is something left out. **! emission**.
☆ You use **one** in e.g. *one more time*. **! won**.
✪ You use **or** in e.g. *Do you want a cake or a biscuit?* **! oar**, **ore**.
✣ **Oral** means spoken aloud. **! aural**.

orang-utan *noun*
orang-utans
oration *noun*
orations
orator *noun*
orators
oratorical
oratorio *noun*
oratorios
oratory
orbit *noun*
orbits
orbit *verb*
orbits
orbiting
orbited
orbital
orchard *noun*
orchards
orchestra *noun*
orchestras
orchestral
orchid *noun*
orchids
ordeal *noun*
ordeals
order *noun*
orders
order *verb*
orders
ordering
ordered
orderliness
orderly
ordinal number *noun*
ordinal numbers
ordinary *adjective*
ordinarily
ore★ *noun*
ores
organ *noun*
organs
organic *adjective*
organically
organism *noun*
organisms
organist *noun*
organists
organization *noun*
organizations
organize *verb*
organizes
organizing
organized
organizer *noun*
organizers
oriental
orienteering
origami
origin *noun*
origins
original *adjective*
originally
originality
originate *verb*
originates
originating
originated
origination
originator *noun*
originators
ornament *noun*
ornaments
ornamental *adjective*
ornamentally
ornamentation
ornithological
ornithologist
ornithology
orphan *noun*
orphans
orphanage *noun*
orphanages
orthodox
Orthodox Church
orthodoxy
oscillate *verb*
oscillates
oscillating
oscillated
oscillation *noun*
oscillations
ostrich *noun*
ostriches
other *adjective* and *noun*
others
otherwise
otter *noun*
otters
ought
ounce *noun*
ounces
ours
ourselves
outback
outboard motor *noun*
outboard motors
outbreak *noun*
outbreaks
outburst *noun*
outbursts
outcast *noun*
outcasts
outcome *noun*
outcomes
outcry *noun*
outcries
outdated
outdo *verb*
outdoes
outdoing
outdid
outdone
outdoor *adjective*
outdoors *adverb*

★ **Ore** is rock with metal in it. **! oar**, **or**.

a b c d e f g h i j k l m n o p q r s t u v w x y z

outer

outfit *noun*
outfits

outgrow *verb*
outgrows
outgrowing
outgrew
outgrown

outhouse *noun*
outhouses

outing *noun*
outings

outlast *verb*
outlasts
outlasting
outlasted

outlaw *noun*
outlaws

outlaw *verb*
outlaws
outlawing
outlawed

outlet *noun*
outlets

outline *noun*
outlines

outline *verb*
outlines
outlining
outlined

outlook *noun*
outlooks

outlying

outnumber *verb*
outnumbers
outnumbering
outnumbered

outpatient *noun*
outpatients

outpost *noun*
outposts

output *verb*
outputs
outputting
output

output *noun*
outputs

outrage *noun*
outrages

outrage *verb*
outrages
outraging
outraged

outrageous *adjective*
outrageously

outright

outset

outside *adverb* and *preposition*

outside *noun*
outsides

outsider *noun*
outsiders

outskirts *plural noun*

outspoken

outstanding *adjective*
outstandingly

outward *adjective*
outwardly

outwards *adverb*

outweigh *verb*
outweighs
outweighing
outweighed

outwit *verb*
outwits
outwitting
outwitted

oval *adjective* and *noun*
ovals

ovary *noun*
ovaries

oven *noun*
ovens

over *adverb* and *preposition*

over *noun*
overs

> **over-**
> *over-* makes words meaning 'too' or 'too much', e.g. **overactive** and **overcook**. You do not need a hyphen, except in some words beginning with *e*, e.g. **over-eager**.

overall *adjective*

overalls *plural noun*

overarm *adjective*

overboard

overcast

overcoat *noun*
overcoats

overcome *verb*
overcomes
overcoming
overcame
overcome

overdo *verb*
overdoes
overdoing
overdid
overdone

overdose *noun*
overdoses

overdue

overflow *verb*
overflows
overflowing
overflowed

overgrown

overhang *verb*
overhangs
overhanging
overhung

overhaul *verb*
overhauls
overhauling
overhauled

overhead *adjective*

overheads *plural noun*
overhear *verb*
overhears
overhearing
overheard
overland *adjective*
overlap *verb*
overlaps
overlapping
overlapped
overlook *verb*
overlooks
overlooking
overlooked
overnight
overpower *verb*
overpowers
overpowering
overpowered
overrun *verb*
overruns
overrunning
overran
overrun
overseas *adjective and adverb*
oversight *noun*
oversights
oversleep *verb*
oversleeps
oversleeping
overslept
overtake *verb*
overtakes
overtaking
overtook
overtaken
overthrow *verb*
overthrows
overthrowing
overthrew
overthrown
overthrow *noun*
overthrows
overtime
overture *noun*
overtures
overturn *verb*
overturns
overturning
overturned
overwhelm *verb*
overwhelms
overwhelming
overwhelmed
overwork *verb*
overworks
overworking
overworked
overwork *noun*
ovum *noun*
ova
owe *verb*
owes
owing
owed
owl *noun*
owls
own *adjective*
own *verb*
owns
owning
owned
owner *noun*
owners
ownership
ox *noun*
oxen
oxidation
oxide *noun*
oxides
oxidize *verb*
oxidizes
oxidizing
oxidized
oxygen
oyster *noun*
oysters
ozone

Pp

pa *noun*
pas
pace *noun*
paces
pace *verb*
paces
pacing
paced
pacemaker *noun*
pacemakers
pacification
pacifism
pacifist *noun*
pacifists
pacify *verb*
pacifies
pacifying
pacified
pack *verb*
packs
packing
packed
pack *noun*
packs
package *noun*
packages
packet *noun*
packets
pad *noun*
pads
pad *verb*
pads
padding
padded
padding
paddle *verb*
paddles
paddling
paddled
paddle *noun*
paddles

a b c d e f g h i j k l m n o p q r s t u v w x y z

paddock *noun*
paddocks

paddy *noun*
paddies

padlock *noun*
padlocks

pagan *adjective* and *noun*
pagans

page *noun*
pages

pageant *noun*
pageants

pageantry

pagoda *noun*
pagodas

paid see **pay**

pail★ *noun*
pails

pain☆ *noun*
pains

pain *verb*
pains
paining
pained

painful *adjective*
painfully

painkiller *noun*
painkillers

painless *adjective*
painlessly

painstaking

paint *noun*
paints

paint *verb*
paints
painting
painted

paintbox *noun*
paintboxes

paintbrush *noun*
paintbrushes

painter *noun*
painters

painting *noun*
paintings

pair✪ *noun*
pairs

pair *verb*
pairs
pairing
paired

pal *noun*
pals

palace *noun*
palaces

palate *noun*
palates

pale✣ *adjective*
paler
palest

paleness

palette *noun*
palettes

paling *noun*
palings

palisade *noun*
palisades

pall *verb*
palls
palling
palled

pallid

pallor

palm *noun*
palms

palm *verb*
palms
palming
palmed

palmistry

Palm Sunday

paltry *adjective*
paltrier
paltriest

pampas *plural noun*

pamper *verb*
pampers
pampering
pampered

pamphlet *noun*
pamphlets

pan *noun*
pans

pancake *noun*
pancakes

panda *noun*
pandas

pandemonium

pander *verb*
panders
pandering
pandered

pane✹ *noun*
panes

panel *noun*
panels

pang *noun*
pangs

★ A **pail** is a bucket. **! pale**.
☆ A **pain** is an unpleasant feeling caused by injury or disease. **! pane**.
✪ A **pair** is a set of two. **! pear**.
✣ **Pale** means 'almost white'. **! pail**.
✹ A **pane** is a piece of glass in a window. **! pain**.

panic
panic *verb*
panics
panicking
panicked
panicky
pannier *noun*
panniers
panorama *noun*
panoramas
panoramic *adjective*
panoramically
pansy *noun*
pansies
pant *verb*
pants
panting
panted
panther *noun*
panthers
panties *plural noun*
pantomime *noun*
pantomimes
pantry *noun*
pantries
pants *plural noun*
paper *noun*
papers
paper *verb*
papers
papering
papered
paperback *noun*
paperbacks
papier mâché
papyrus *noun*
papyri
parable *noun*
parables
parachute *noun*
parachutes
parachutist
parade *noun*
parades
parade *verb*
parades
parading
paraded
paradise
paradox *noun*
paradoxes
paradoxical *adjective*
paradoxically
paraffin
paragraph *noun*
paragraphs
parallel
parallelogram *noun*
parallelograms
paralyse *verb*
paralyses
paralysing
paralysed
paralysis *noun*
paralyses
paralytic *adjective*
paralytically
parapet *noun*
parapets
paraphernalia
paraphrase *verb*
paraphrases
paraphrasing
paraphrased
parasite *noun*
parasites
parasitic *adjective*
parasitically
parasol *noun*
parasols
paratrooper
paratroops *plural noun*
parcel *noun*
parcels
parched
parchment
pardon *verb*
pardons
pardoning
pardoned
pardon *noun*
pardons
pardonable
parent *noun*
parents
parentage
parental
parenthood
parenthesis *noun*
parentheses
parish *noun*
parishes
parishioner *noun*
parishioners
park *noun*
parks
park *verb*
parks
parking
parked
parka *noun*
parkas
parliament *noun*
parliaments
parliamentary
parody *noun*
parodies
parole
parrot *noun*
parrots
parsley
parsnip *noun*
parsnips
parson *noun*
parsons
parsonage *noun*
parsonages
part *noun*
parts

a b c d e f g h i j k l m n o **p** q r s t u v w x y z

part *verb*
parts
parting
parted

partial *adjective*
partially

partiality

participant *noun*
participants

participate *verb*
participates
participating
participated

participation

participle *noun*
participles

particle *noun*
particles

particular *adjective*
particularly

particulars *plural noun*

parting *noun*
partings

partition *noun*
partitions

partly

partner *noun*
partners

partnership

partridge *noun*
partridges

part-time *adjective*

party *noun*
parties

pass *verb*
passes
passing
passed

pass *noun*
passes

passable

passage *noun*
passages

passageway *noun*
passageways

passed★ see **pass**

passenger *noun*
passengers

passer-by *noun*
passers-by

passion *noun*
passions

passionate *adjective*
passionately

passive *adjective*
passively

Passover

passport *noun*
passports

password *noun*
passwords

past☆ *noun, adjective,* and *preposition*

pasta *noun*
pastas

paste *noun*
pastes

paste *verb*
pastes
pasting
pasted

pastel *noun*
pastels

pasteurization

pasteurize *verb*
pasteurizes
pasteurizing
pasteurized

pastille *noun*
pastilles

pastime *noun*
pastimes

pastoral

pastry *noun*
pastries

pasture *noun*
pastures

pasty *noun*
pasties

pasty *adjective*
pastier
pastiest

pat *verb*
pats
patting
patted

pat *noun*
pats

patch *noun*
patches

patch *verb*
patches
patching
patched

patchwork

patchy *adjective*
patchier
patchiest

patent *adjective*
patently

patent *verb*
patents
patenting
patented

patent *noun*
patents

paternal *adjective*
paternally

path *noun*
paths

pathetic *adjective*
pathetically

★ You use **passed** in e.g. *We passed the house.* **! past**.
☆ You use **past** in e.g. *We went past the house.* **! passed**.

patience

patient *adjective*
patiently

patient *noun*
patients

patio *noun*
patios

patriot *noun*
patriots

patriotic *adjective*
patriotically

patriotism

patrol *verb*
patrols
patrolling
patrolled

patrol *noun*
patrols

patron *noun*
patrons

patronage

patronize *verb*
patronizes
patronizing
patronized

patter *verb*
patters
pattering
pattered

patter *noun*
patters

pattern *noun*
patterns

pause *verb*
pauses
pausing
paused

pause *noun*
pauses

pave *verb*
paves
paving
paved

pavement *noun*
pavements

pavilion *noun*
pavilions

paw *noun*
paws

paw *verb*
paws
pawing
pawed

pawn *noun*
pawns

pawn *verb*
pawns
pawning
pawned

pawnbroker *noun*
pawnbrokers

pay *verb*
pays
paying
paid

pay *noun*

payment *noun*
payments

pea *noun*
peas

peace★

peaceful *adjective*
peacefully

peach *noun*
peaches

peacock *noun*
peacocks

peak☆ *noun*
peaks

peak✪ *verb*
peaks
peaking
peaked

peaked

peal✣ *verb*
peals
pealing
pealed

peal✹ *noun*
peals

peanut *noun*
peanuts

pear❉ *noun*
pears

pearl *noun*
pearls

pearly *adjective*
pearlier
pearliest

peasant *noun*
peasants

peasantry

peat

pebble *noun*
pebbles

pebbly *adjective*
pebblier
pebbliest

peck *verb*
pecks
pecking
pecked

★ **Peace** is a time when there is no war. **! piece**.
☆ A **peak** is the top of something. **! peek**.
✪ To **peak** is to reach the highest point. **! peek**.
✣ To **peal** is to make a ringing sound of bells. **! peel**.
✹ A **peal** is a ringing of bells. **! peel**.
❉ A **pear** is a fruit. **! pair**.

a b c d e f g h i j k l m n o p q r s t u v w x y z

peck *noun*
pecks

peckish

peculiar *adjective*
peculiarly

peculiarity *noun*
peculiarities

pedal *noun*
pedals

pedal *verb*
pedals
pedalling
pedalled

peddle★ *verb*
peddles
peddling
peddled

pedestal *noun*
pedestals

pedestrian *noun*
pedestrians

pedestrian *adjective*

pedigree *noun*
pedigrees

pedlar *noun*
pedlars

peek☆ *verb*
peeks
peeking
peeked

peel✪ *noun*
peels

peel✣ *verb*
peels
peeling
peeled

peep *verb*
peeps
peeping
peeped

peep *noun*
peeps

peer✹ *verb*
peers
peering
peered

peer *noun*
peers

peerless

peewit *noun*
peewits

peg *noun*
pegs

peg *verb*
pegs
pegging
pegged

Pekinese *noun*
Pekinese

pelican *noun*
pelicans

pellet *noun*
pellets

pelt *verb*
pelts
pelting
pelted

pelt *noun*
pelts

pen *noun*
pens

penalize *verb*
penalizes
penalizing
penalized

penalty *noun*
penalties

pence see **penny**

pencil *noun*
pencils

pencil *verb*
pencils
pencilling
pencilled

pendant *noun*
pendants

pendulum *noun*
pendulums

penetrate *verb*
penetrates
penetrating
penetrated

penetration

penfriend *noun*
penfriends

penguin *noun*
penguins

penicillin

peninsula *noun*
peninsulas

peninsular

penis *noun*
penises

penitence

penitent

penknife *noun*
penknives

pennant *noun*
pennants

penniless

penny *noun*
pennies *or* pence

★ To **peddle** is to sell things on the street. **! pedal**.
☆ To **peek** is to look secretly at something. **! peak**.
✪ **Peel** is the skin of fruit and vegetables. **! peal**.
✣ To **peel** something is to take the skin off it. **! peal**.
✹ To **peer** is to look closely at something. **! pier**.

pension *noun*
pensions
pensioner *noun*
pensioners
pentagon *noun*
pentagons
pentathlon *noun*
pentathlons
peony *noun*
peonies
people *plural noun*
people *noun*
peoples
pepper *noun*
peppers
peppermint *noun*
peppermints
peppery
perceive *verb*
perceives
perceiving
perceived
per cent
percentage *noun*
percentages
perceptible *adjective*
perceptibly
perception *noun*
perceptions
perceptive *adjective*
perceptively
perch *verb*
perches
perching
perched
perch *noun*
perch
percolator *noun*
percolators
percussion
percussive
perennial *adjective*
perennially
perennial *noun*
perennials
perfect *adjective*
perfectly
perfect *verb*
perfects
perfecting
perfected
perfection
perforate *verb*
perforates
perforating
perforated
perforation *noun*
perforations
perform *verb*
performs
performing
performed
performance *noun*
performances
performer *noun*
performers
perfume *noun*
perfumes
perhaps
peril *noun*
perils
perilous *adjective*
perilously
perimeter *noun*
perimeters
period *noun*
periods
periodic *adjective*
periodically
periodical *noun*
periodicals
periscope *noun*
periscopes
perish *verb*
perishes
perishing
perished
perishable
perm *noun*
perms
perm *verb*
perms
perming
permed
permanence
permanent *adjective*
permanently
permissible
permission
permissive *adjective*
permissively
permissiveness
permit *verb*
permits
permitting
permitted
permit *noun*
permits
perpendicular
perpetual *adjective*
perpetually
perpetuate *verb*
perpetuates
perpetuating
perpetuated
perplex *verb*
perplexes
perplexing
perplexed
perplexity
persecute *verb*
persecutes
persecuting
persecuted
persecution *noun*
persecutions
persecutor *noun*
persecutors
perseverance
persevere *verb*
perseveres
persevering
persevered

persist *verb*
persists
persisting
persisted

persistence

persistent *adjective*
persistently

person★ *noun*
persons *or* people

personal *adjective*
personally

personality *noun*
personalities

personnel *plural noun*

perspective *noun*
perspectives

perspiration

perspire *verb*
perspires
perspiring
perspired

persuade *verb*
persuades
persuading
persuaded

persuasion

persuasive *adjective*
persuasively

perverse *adjective*
perversely

perversion *noun*
perversions

perversity

pervert *verb*
perverts
perverting
perverted

pervert *noun*
perverts

Pesach☆

pessimism

pessimist *noun*
pessimists

pessimistic *adjective*
pessimistically

pest *noun*
pests

pester *verb*
pesters
pestering
pestered

pesticide *noun*
pesticides

pestle *noun*
pestles

pet *noun*
pets

petal *noun*
petals

petition *noun*
petitions

petrify *verb*
petrifies
petrifying
petrified

petrochemical *noun*
petrochemicals

petrol

petroleum

petticoat *noun*
petticoats

pettiness

petty *adjective*
pettier
pettiest
pettily

pew *noun*
pews

pewter

pharmacy *noun*
pharmacies

phase *noun*
phases

phase *verb*
phases
phasing
phased

pheasant *noun*
pheasants

phenomenal *adjective*
phenomenally

phenomenon *noun*
phenomena

philatelist *noun*
philatelists

philately

philosopher *noun*
philosophers

philosophical *adjective*
philosophically

philosophy *noun*
philosophies

phobia *noun*
phobias

> **-phobia**
> *-phobia* makes words meaning 'a strong fear or dislike', e.g. **xenophobia** (a dislike of strangers'). It comes from a Greek word and is only used with other Greek or Latin words.

phoenix *noun*
phoenixes

phone *noun*
phones

★ The normal plural is **people**: *three people came*. **Persons** is formal, e.g. in official reports.

☆ The Hebrew name for Passover. Pronounced *pay-sahk*.

phone *verb*
phones
phoning
phoned

-phone
-phone makes words to do with sound, e.g. **telephone**, **saxophone**. You can sometimes make adjectives by using *-phonic*, e.g. **telephonic**, and nouns by using *-phony*, e.g. **telephony**.

phonecard *noun*
phonecards

phone-in *noun*
phone-ins

phosphorescence

phosphorescent

phosphoric

phosphorus

photo *noun*
photos

photo-
photo- makes words to do with light, e.g. **photograph**, **photocopy**. It is also used in more technical words such as **photochemistry** (the chemistry of light) and as a separate word in **photo** (photograph) and **photo finish** (close finish to a race).

photocopier *noun*
photocopiers

photocopy *noun*
photocopies

photocopy *verb*
photocopies
photocopying
photocopied

photoelectric

photograph *noun*
photographs

photograph *verb*
photographs
photographing
photographed

photographer *noun*
photographers

photographic *adjective*
photographically

photography

phrase *noun*
phrases

phrase *verb*
phrases
phrasing
phrased

physical *adjective*
physically

physician *noun*
physicians

physicist *noun*
physicists

physics

physiological *adjective*
physiologically

physiologist *noun*
physiologists

physiology

pi★

pianist *noun*
pianists

piano *noun*
pianos

piccolo *noun*
piccolos

pick *verb*
picks
picking
picked

pick *noun*
picks

pickaxe *noun*
pickaxes

picket *noun*
pickets

picket *verb*
pickets
picketing
picketed

pickle *noun*
pickles

pickle *verb*
pickles
pickling
pickled

pickpocket *noun*
pickpockets

pick-up *noun*
pick-ups

picnic *noun*
picnics

picnic *verb*
picnics
picnicking
picnicked

picnicker *noun*
picnickers

pictogram *noun*
pictograms

pictorial *adjective*
pictorially

★ **Pi** is a Greek letter, used in mathematics. **! pie**.

a b c d e f g h i j k l m n o **p** q r s t u v w x y z

picture *noun*
pictures

picture *verb*
pictures
picturing
pictured

picturesque

pie★ *noun*
pies

piece☆ *noun*
pieces

piece *verb*
pieces
piecing
pieced

piecemeal

pie chart *noun*
pie charts

pier✪ *noun*
piers

pierce *verb*
pierces
piercing
pierced

pig *noun*
pigs

pigeon *noun*
pigeons

pigeon-hole *noun*
pigeon-holes

piggy *noun*
piggies

piggyback *noun*
piggybacks

piglet *noun*
piglets

pigment *noun*
pigments

pigmy *noun* use **pygmy**

pigsty *noun*
pigsties

pigtail *noun*
pigtails

pike *noun*
pikes

pilchard *noun*
pilchards

pile *noun*
piles

pile *verb*
piles
piling
piled

pilfer *verb*
pilfers
pilfering
pilfered

pilgrim *noun*
pilgrims

pilgrimage *noun*
pilgrimages

pill *noun*
pills

pillage *verb*
pillages
pillaging
pillaged

pillar *noun*
pillars

pillion *noun*
pillions

pillow *noun*
pillows

pillowcase *noun*
pillowcases

pilot *noun*
pilots

pilot *verb*
pilots
piloting
piloted

pimple *noun*
pimples

pimply *adjective*
pimplier
pimpliest

pin *noun*
pins

pin *verb*
pins
pinning
pinned

pinafore *noun*
pinafores

pincer *noun*
pincers

pinch *verb*
pinches
pinching
pinched

pinch *noun*
pinches

pincushion *noun*
pincushions

pine *noun*
pines

pine *verb*
pines
pining
pined

pineapple *noun*
pineapples

ping-pong

★ A **pie** is a food with pastry. **! pi**.
☆ You use **piece** in e.g. *a piece of cake*. **! peace**.
✪ A **pier** is a long building on stilts going into the sea. **! peer**.

pink *adjective*
pinker
pinkest
pink *noun*
pinks
pint *noun*
pints
pioneer *noun*
pioneers
pious *adjective*
piously
pip *noun*
pips
pipe *noun*
pipes
pipe *verb*
pipes
piping
piped
pipeline *noun*
pipelines
piper *noun*
pipers
piracy
pirate *noun*
pirates
pistil★ *noun*
pistils
pistol☆ *noun*
pistols
piston *noun*
pistons
pit *noun*
pits
pit *verb*
pits
pitting
pitted
pitch *noun*
pitches
pitch *verb*
pitches
pitching
pitched
pitch-black
pitcher *noun*
pitchers
pitchfork *noun*
pitchforks
pitfall *noun*
pitfalls
pitiful *adjective*
pitifully
pitiless *adjective*
pitilessly
pity *verb*
pities
pitying
pitied
pity *noun*
pivot *noun*
pivots
pivot *verb*
pivots
pivoting
pivoted
pixie *noun*
pixies
pizza *noun*
pizzas
pizzicato
placard *noun*
placards
place✪ *noun*
places
place *verb*
places
placing
placed
placid *adjective*
placidly
plague *noun*
plagues
plague *verb*
plagues
plaguing
plagued
plaice✣ *noun*
plaice
plaid *noun*
plaids
plain✷ *adjective*
plainer
plainest
plainly
plain *noun*
plains
plain clothes
plainness
plaintiff *noun*
plaintiffs
plaintive
plaintively
plait *noun*
plaits
plait *verb*
plaits
plaiting
plaited
plan *noun*
plans
plan *verb*
plans
planning
planned

★ A **pistil** is a part of a flower. **! pistol**.
☆ A **pistol** is a gun. **! pistil**.
✪ You use **place** in e.g. *a place in the country.* **! plaice**.
✣ A **plaice** is a fish. **! place**.
✷ **Plain** means 'not pretty or decorated'. **! plane**.

plane★ *noun*
planes

plane☆ *verb*
planes
planing
planed

planet *noun*
planets

planetary

plank *noun*
planks

plankton

planner *noun*
planners

plant *noun*
plants

plant *verb*
plants
planting
planted

plantation *noun*
plantations

planter *noun*
planters

plaque *noun*
plaques

plasma

plaster *noun*
plasters

plaster *verb*
plasters
plastering
plastered

plasterer *noun*
plasterers

plaster of Paris

plastic *adjective* and *noun*
plastics

Plasticine

plate *noun*
plates

plate *verb*
plates
plating
plated

plateau *noun*
plateaux

plateful *noun*
platefuls

platform *noun*
platforms

platinum

platoon *noun*
platoons

platypus *noun*
platypuses

play *verb*
plays
playing
played

play *noun*
plays

playback *noun*
playbacks

player *noun*
players

playful *adjective*
playfully

playfulness

playground *noun*
playgrounds

playgroup *noun*
playgroups

playmate *noun*
playmates

play-off *noun*
play-offs

playtime *noun*
playtimes

playwright *noun*
playwrights

plea *noun*
pleas

plead *verb*
pleads
pleading
pleaded

pleasant *adjective*
pleasanter
pleasantest
pleasantly

please *verb*
pleases
pleasing
pleased

pleasurable *adjective*
pleasurably

pleasure *noun*
pleasures

pleat *noun*
pleats

pleated

pledge *verb*
pledges
pledging
pledged

pledge *noun*
pledges

plentiful *adjective*
plentifully

plenty

pliable

pliers *plural noun*

plight *noun*
plights

plod *verb*
plods
plodding
plodded

plodder *noun*
plodders

★ A **plane** is an aeroplane, a level surface, a tool, or a tree. **! plain**.
☆ To **plane** wood is to make it smooth with a tool. **! plain**.

plop *verb*
plops
plopping
plopped

plop *noun*
plops

plot *noun*
plots

plot *verb*
plots
plotting
plotted

plotter *noun*
plotters

plough *noun*
ploughs

plough *verb*
ploughs
ploughing
ploughed

ploughman *noun*
ploughmen

plover *noun*
plovers

pluck *verb*
plucks
plucking
plucked

pluck *noun*

plucky *adjective*
pluckier
pluckiest
pluckily

plug *noun*
plugs

plug *verb*
plugs
plugging
plugged

plum★ *noun*
plums

plumage

plumb☆ *verb*
plumbs
plumbing
plumbed

plumber *noun*
plumbers

plumbing

plume *noun*
plumes

plumed

plump *adjective*
plumper
plumpest

plump *verb*
plumps
plumping
plumped

plunder *verb*
plunders
plundering
plundered

plunder *noun*

plunderer *noun*
plunderers

plunge *verb*
plunges
plunging
plunged

plunge *noun*
plunges

plural *adjective* and *noun*
plurals

plus *preposition*

plus *noun*
pluses

plutonium

plywood

pneumatic

pneumonia

poach *verb*
poaches
poaching
poached

poacher *noun*
poachers

pocket *noun*
pockets

pocket *verb*
pockets
pocketing
pocketed

pocketful *noun*
pocketfuls

pod *noun*
pods

podgy *adjective*
podgier
podgiest

poem *noun*
poems

poet *noun*
poets

poetic *adjective*
poetically

poetry

point *noun*
points

point *verb*
points
pointing
pointed

point-blank *adjective*

pointed *adjective*
pointedly

pointer *noun*
pointers

pointless *adjective*
pointlessly

★ A **plum** is a fruit. **! plumb**.
☆ To **plumb** water is to see how deep it is. **! plum**.

a b c d e f g h i j k l m n o **p** q r s t u v w x y z

poise *noun*

poise *verb*
poises
poising
poised

poison *noun*
poisons

poison *verb*
poisons
poisoning
poisoned

poisoner *noun*
poisoners

poisonous *adjective*
poisonously

poke *verb*
pokes
poking
poked

poke *noun*
pokes

poker *noun*
pokers

polar

Polaroid

pole★ *noun*
poles

police *plural noun*

policeman *noun*
policemen

police officer *noun*
police officers

policewoman *noun*
policewomen

policy *noun*
policies

polio

poliomyelitis

polish *verb*
polishes
polishing
polished

polish *noun*
polishes

polished

polite *adjective*
politer
politest
politely

politeness

political *adjective*
politically

politician *noun*
politicians

politics

polka *noun*
polkas

poll☆ *noun*
polls

pollen

pollute *verb*
pollutes
polluting
polluted

pollution

polo

polo neck *noun*
polo necks

poltergeist *noun*
poltergeists

polygon *noun*
polygons

polystyrene

polythene

pomp

pomposity

pompous *adjective*
pompously

pond *noun*
ponds

ponder *verb*
ponders
pondering
pondered

ponderous *adjective*
ponderously

pony *noun*
ponies

ponytail *noun*
ponytails

pony-trekking

poodle *noun*
poodles

pool *noun*
pools

pool *verb*
pools
pooling
pooled

poor *adjective*
poorer
poorest
poorly

poorly *adjective* and *adverb*

pop *verb*
pops
popping
popped

pop *noun*
pops

popcorn

Pope *noun*
Popes

poplar *noun*
poplars

poppadom *noun*
poppadoms

poppy *noun*
poppies

★ A **pole** is a long thin stick. **! poll**.
☆ A **poll** is a vote in an election. **! pole**.

popular *adjective*
popularly
popularity
popularize *verb*
popularizes
popularizing
popularized
populated
population *noun*
populations
populous
porcelain
porch *noun*
porches
porcupine *noun*
porcupines
pore *noun*
pores
pore★ *verb*
pores
poring
pored
pork
pornographic
pornography
porosity
porous
porpoise *noun*
porpoises
porridge
port *noun*
ports
portable
portcullis *noun*
portcullises
porter *noun*
porters
porthole *noun*
portholes
portion *noun*
portions

portliness
portly *adjective*
portlier
portliest
portrait *noun*
portraits
portray *verb*
portrays
portraying
portrayed
portrayal *noun*
portrayals
pose *verb*
poses
posing
posed
pose *noun*
poses
poser *noun*
posers
posh *adjective*
posher
poshest
position *noun*
positions
positive *adjective*
positively
positive *noun*
positives
posse *noun*
posses
possess *verb*
possesses
possessing
possessed
possession *noun*
possessions
possessive *adjective*
possessively
possessor *noun*
possessors
possibility *noun*
possibilities

possible *adjective*
possibly
post *verb*
posts
posting
posted
post *noun*
posts
postage
postal
postbox *noun*
postboxes
postcard *noun*
postcards
postcode *noun*
postcodes
poster *noun*
posters
postman *noun*
postmen
postmark *noun*
postmarks
post-mortem *noun*
post-mortems
postpone *verb*
postpones
postponing
postponed
postponement *noun*
postponements
postscript *noun*
postscripts
posture *noun*
postures
posy *noun*
posies
pot *noun*
pots
pot *verb*
pots
potting
potted

★ To **pore** over something is to study it closely. **! pour**.

potassium

potato *noun*
potatoes

potency

potent *adjective*
potently

potential *adjective*
potentially

potential *noun*
potentials

pothole *noun*
potholes

potholer *noun*
potholer

potholing

potion *noun*
potions

potter *noun*
potters

potter *verb*
potters
pottering
pottered

pottery *noun*
potteries

potty *adjective*
pottier
pottiest
pottily

potty *noun*
potties

pouch *noun*
pouches

poultry

pounce *verb*
pounces
pouncing
pounced

pound *noun*
pounds

pound *verb*
pounds
pounding
pounded

pour★ *verb*
pours
pouring
poured

pout *verb*
pouts
pouting
pouted

poverty

powder *noun*
powders

powder *verb*
powders
powdering
powdered

powdery

power *noun*
powers

powered

powerful *adjective*
powerfully

powerhouse *noun*
powerhouses

powerless

practicable

practical *adjective*
practically

practice *noun*
practices

practise *verb*
practises
practising
practised

prairie *noun*
prairies

praise *verb*
praises
praising
praised

praise *noun*
praises

pram *noun*
prams

prance *verb*
prances
prancing
pranced

prank *noun*
pranks

prawn *noun*
prawns

pray☆ *verb*
prays
praying
prayed

prayer *noun*
prayers

> **pre-**
> *pre-* makes words meaning 'before', e.g. **pre-date** (to exist before something else), **prefabricated** (made in advance). Many are spelt joined up, but not all.

preach *verb*
preaches
preaching
preached

preacher *noun*
preachers

precarious *adjective*
precariously

precaution *noun*
precautions

★ To **pour** a liquid is to tip it from a jug etc. **! pore**.
☆ To **pray** is to say prayers. **! prey**.

precede *verb*
precedes
preceding
preceded

precedence

precedent *noun*
precedents

precinct *noun*
precincts

precious *adjective*
preciously

precipice *noun*
precipices

précis *noun*
précis

precise *adjective*
precisely

precision

predator *noun*
predators

predatory

predecessor *noun*
predecessors

predict *verb*
predicts
predicting
predicted

predictable *adjective*
predictably

prediction *noun*
predictions

predominance

predominant *adjective*
predominantly

predominate *verb*
predominates
predominating
predominated

preface *noun*
prefaces

prefect *noun*
prefects

prefer *verb*
prefers
preferring
preferred

preferable *adjective*
preferably

preference *noun*
preferences

prefix *noun*
prefixes

pregnancy *noun*
pregnancies

pregnant

prehistoric

prehistory

prejudice *noun*
prejudices

prejudiced

preliminary *adjective* and *noun*
preliminaries

prelude *noun*
preludes

premier *noun*
premiers

première *noun*
premières

premises *plural noun*

premium *noun*
premiums

Premium Bond *noun*
Premium Bonds

preoccupation *noun*
preoccupations

preoccupied

prep

preparation *noun*
preparations

preparatory

prepare *verb*
prepares
preparing
prepared

preposition *noun*
prepositions

prescribe *verb*
prescribes
prescribing
prescribed

prescription *noun*
prescriptions

presence

present *adjective*
presently

present *noun*
presents

present *verb*
presents
presenting
presented

presentation *noun*
presentations

presenter *noun*
presenters

preservation

preservative *noun*
preservatives

preserve *verb*
preserves
preserving
preserved

preside *verb*
presides
presiding
presided

presidency *noun*
presidencies

president *noun*
presidents

presidential *adjective*
presidentially

press *verb*
presses
pressing
pressed

press *noun*
presses

a b c d e f g h i j k l m n o p q r s t u v w x y z

press-up *noun*
press-ups

pressure *noun*
pressures

pressurize *verb*
pressurizes
pressurizing
pressurized

prestige

prestigious *adjective*
prestigiously

presumably

presume *verb*
presumes
presuming
presumed

presumption *noun*
presumptions

presumptuous *adjective*
presumptuously

pretence *noun*
pretences

pretend *verb*
pretends
pretending
pretended

pretender *noun*
pretenders

prettiness

pretty *adjective* and *adverb*
prettier
prettiest
prettily

prevail *verb*
prevails
prevailing
prevailed

prevalent

prevent *verb*
prevents
preventing
prevented

prevention

preventive

preview *noun*
previews

previous *adjective*
previously

prey★ *verb*
preys
preying
preyed

prey *noun*

price *noun*
prices

price *verb*
prices
pricing
priced

priceless

prick *verb*
pricks
pricking
pricked

prick *noun*
pricks

prickle *noun*
prickles

prickly *adjective*
pricklier
prickliest

pride *noun*
prides

priest *noun*
priests

priestess *noun*
priestesses

priesthood

prig *noun*
prigs

priggish *adjective*
priggishly

prim *adjective*
primmer
primmest
primly

primness

primary *adjective*
primarily

primate *noun*
primates

prime *adjective*

prime *verb*
primes
priming
primed

prime *noun*
primes

prime minister *noun*
prime ministers

primer *noun*
primers

primeval

primitive *adjective*
primitively

primrose *noun*
primroses

prince *noun*
princes

princely

princess *noun*
princesses

principal☆ *adjective*
principally

principal✪ *noun*
principals

★ To **prey** on animals is to hunt and kill them. **! pray**.
☆ **Principal** means 'chief' or 'main'. **! principle**.
✪ A **principal** is a head of a college. **! principle**.

principle★ *noun*
principles
print *verb*
prints
printing
printed
print *noun*
prints
printer *noun*
printers
printout *noun*
printouts
priority *noun*
priorities
prise☆ *verb*
prises
prising
prised
prism *noun*
prisms
prison *noun*
prisons
prisoner *noun*
prisoners
privacy
private *adjective*
privately
private *noun*
privates
privatization
privatize *verb*
privatizes
privatizing
privatized
privet
privilege *noun*
privileges
privileged
prize *noun*
prizes

prize✪ *verb*
prizes
prizing
prized
pro *noun*
pros

> **pro-**
> *pro-* makes words meaning 'in favour of', e.g. **pro-choice**. In this type of word you use a hyphen.

probability *noun*
probabilities
probable *adjective*
probably
probation
probationary
probe *verb*
probes
probing
probed
probe *noun*
probes
problem *noun*
problems
procedure *noun*
procedures
proceed *verb*
proceeds
proceeding
proceeded
proceedings *plural noun*
proceeds *plural noun*
process *noun*
processes

process *verb*
processes
processing
processed
procession *noun*
processions
proclaim *verb*
proclaims
proclaiming
proclaimed
proclamation *noun*
proclamations
prod *verb*
prods
prodding
prodded
prodigal *adjective*
prodigally
produce *verb*
produces
producing
produced
produce *noun*
producer *noun*
producers
product *noun*
products
production *noun*
productions
productive *adjective*
productively
productivity
profession *noun*
professions
professional *adjective*
professionally
professional *noun*
professionals
professor *noun*
professors

★ A **principle** is a rule or belief. **! principal**.
☆ To **prise** something is to open it. **! prize**.
✪ To **prize** something is to value it highly. **! prise**.

proficiency

proficient *adjective*
proficiently

profile *noun*
profiles

profit★ *noun*
profits

profit *verb*
profits
profiting
profited

profitable *adjective*
profitably

profound *adjective*
profoundly

profundity

profuse *adjective*
profusely

profusion

program☆ *noun*
programs

program *verb*
programs
programming
programmed

programme☆ *noun*
programmes

progress *noun*

progress *verb*
progresses
progressing
progressed

progression

progressive *adjective*
progressively

prohibit *verb*
prohibits
prohibiting
prohibited

prohibition *noun*
prohibitions

project *noun*
projects

project *verb*
projects
projecting
projected

projection *noun*
projections

projectionist *noun*
projectionists

projector *noun*
projectors

prologue *noun*
prologues

prolong *verb*
prolongs
prolonging
prolonged

promenade *noun*
promenades

prominence

prominent *adjective*
prominently

promise *verb*
promises
promising
promised

promise *noun*
promises

promontory *noun*
promontories

promote *verb*
promotes
promoting
promoted

promoter *noun*
promoter

promotion *noun*
promotions

prompt *adjective*
prompter
promptest
promptly

prompt *verb*
prompts
prompting
prompted

prompter *noun*
prompters

promptness

prone

prong *noun*
prongs

pronoun *noun*
pronouns

pronounce *verb*
pronounces
pronouncing
pronounced

pronouncement *noun*
pronouncements

pronunciation *noun*
pronunciations

proof *adjective* and *noun*
proofs

prop *verb*
props
propping
propped

prop *noun*
props

propaganda

propel *verb*
propels
propelling
propelled

propellant *noun*
propellants

★ A **profit** is extra money made by selling something. **! prophet**.
☆ You use **program** when you are talking about computers. In other meanings you use **programme**.

propeller *noun*
propellers

proper *adjective*
properly

property *noun*
properties

prophecy *noun*
prophecies

prophesy *verb*
prophesies
prophesying
prophesied

prophet★ *noun*
prophets

prophetic *adjective*
prophetically

proportion *noun*
proportions

proportional *adjective*
proportionally

proportionate *adjective*
proportionately

propose *verb*
proposes
proposing
proposed

proposal *noun*
proposals

proprietor *noun*
proprietors

propulsion

prose

prosecute *verb*
prosecutes
prosecuting
prosecuted

prosecution *noun*
prosecutions

prosecutor *noun*
prosecutors

prospect *noun*
prospects

prospect *verb*
prospects
prospecting
prospected

prospector *noun*
prospectors

prosper *verb*
prospers
prospering
prospered

prosperity

prosperous *adjective*
prosperously

prostitute *noun*
prostitutes

protect *verb*
protects
protecting
protected

protection

protective *adjective*
protectively

protector *noun*
protectors

protein *noun*
proteins

protest *verb*
protests
protesting
protested

protest *noun*
protests

protester *noun*
protesters

Protestant *noun*
Protestants

proton *noun*
protons

protoplasm

prototype *noun*
prototypes

protractor *noun*
protractors

protrude *verb*
protrudes
protruding
protruded

protrusion *noun*
protrusions

proud *adjective*
prouder
proudest
proudly

prove *verb*
proves
proving
proved

proverb *noun*
proverbs

proverbial *adjective*
proverbially

provide *verb*
provides
providing
provided

province *noun*
provinces

provincial

provision *noun*
provisions

provisional *adjective*
provisionally

provocative *adjective*
provocatively

provoke *verb*
provokes
provoking
provoked

provocation *noun*
provocations

★ A **prophet** is someone who makes predictions about the future.
! profit.

prow *noun*
prows

prowl *verb*
prowls
prowling
prowled

prowler *noun*
prowlers

prudence

prudent *adjective*
prudently

prune *noun*
prunes

prune *verb*
prunes
pruning
pruned

pry *verb*
pries
prying
pried

psalm *noun*
psalms

pseudonym *noun*
pseudonyms

psychiatric

psychiatrist *noun*
psychiatrists

psychiatry

psychic

psychological *adjective*
psychologically

psychologist *noun*
psychologists

psychology

pub *noun*
pubs

puberty

public *adjective* and *noun*
publicly

publication *noun*
publications

publicity

publicize *verb*
publicizes
publicizing
publicized

publish *verb*
publishes
publishing
published

publisher *noun*
publishers

puck *noun*
pucks

pucker *verb*
puckers
puckering
puckered

pudding *noun*
puddings

puddle *noun*
puddles

puff *verb*
puffs
puffing
puffed

puff *noun*
puffs

puffin *noun*
puffins

pull *verb*
pulls
pulling
pulled

pull *noun*
pulls

pulley *noun*
pulleys

pullover *noun*
pullovers

pulp *noun*
pulps

pulp *verb*
pulps
pulping
pulped

pulpit *noun*
pulpits

pulse *noun*
pulses

pulverize *verb*
pulverizes
pulverizing
pulverized

puma *noun*
pumas

pumice

pump *verb*
pumps
pumping
pumped

pump *noun*
pumps

pumpkin *noun*
pumpkins

pun *noun*
puns

pun *verb*
puns
punning
punned

punch *verb*
punches
punching
punched

punch *noun*
punches

punch *noun*
punches

punchline *noun*
punchlines

punch-up *noun*
punch-ups

punctual *adjective*
punctually

punctuality

punctuate *verb*
punctuates
punctuating
punctuated

punctuation

puncture *noun*
punctures
punish *verb*
punishes
punishing
punished
punishment *noun*
punishments
punk *noun*
punks
punt *noun*
punts
punt *verb*
punts
punting
punted
puny *adjective*
punier
puniest
pup *noun*
pups
pupa *noun*
pupae
pupil *noun*
pupils
puppet *noun*
puppets
puppy *noun*
puppies
purchase *verb*
purchases
purchasing
purchased
purchase *noun*
purchases
purchaser *noun*
purchasers
purdah
pure *adjective*
purer
purest
purely
purge *verb*
purges
purging
purged
purge *noun*
purges
purification
purifier *noun*
purifiers
purify *verb*
purifies
purifying
purified
Puritan★ *noun*
Puritans
puritan *noun*
puritans
puritanical *adjective*
puritanically
purity
purple *noun*
purpose *noun*
purposes
purposely
purr *verb*
purrs
purring
purred
purse *noun*
purses
pursue *verb*
pursues
pursuing
pursued
pursuer *noun*
pursuers
pursuit *noun*
pursuits
pus☆ *noun*
push *verb*
pushes
pushing
pushed
push *noun*
pushes
pushchair *noun*
pushchairs
puss✪ or **pussy** *noun*
pusses *or* pussies
put✣ *verb*
puts
putting
put
putt✹ *verb*
putts
putting
putted
putter *noun*
putters
putty
puzzle *verb*
puzzles
puzzling
puzzled
puzzle *noun*
puzzles
pygmy *noun*
pygmies
pyjamas
pylon *noun*
pylons

★ You use a capital P when you are talking about people in history, and a small p when you mean anyone who is morally strict.
☆ **Pus** is yellow stuff produced in sore places on the body. **! puss**.
✪ **Puss** is a word for a cat. **! pus**.
✣ To **put** something somewhere is to place it there. **! putt**.
✹ To **putt** a ball is to tap it gently. **! put**.

radio *noun*
radios
radioactive
radioactivity
radish *noun*
radishes
radium
radius *noun*
radii
raffle *noun*
raffles
raffle *verb*
raffles
raffling
raffled
raft *noun*
rafts
rafter *noun*
rafters
rag *noun*
rags
rage *noun*
rages
rage *verb*
rages
raging
raged
ragged
ragtime
raid *noun*
raids
raid *verb*
raids
raiding
raided
raider *noun*
raiders
rail *noun*
rails
railings *plural noun*
railway *noun*
railways

rain *verb*
rains
raining
rained
rain *noun*
rains
rainbow *noun*
rainbows
raincoat *noun*
raincoats
raindrop *noun*
raindrops
rainfall
rainforest *noun*
rainforests
raise *verb*
raises
raising
raised
raisin *noun*
raisins
rake *verb*
rakes
raking
raked
rake *noun*
rakes
rally *verb*
rallies
rallying
rallied
rally *noun*
rallies
ram *verb*
rams
ramming
rammed
ram *noun*
rams
Ramadan
ramble *noun*
rambles

ramble *verb*
rambles
rambling
rambled
rambler *noun*
ramblers
ramp *noun*
ramps
rampage *verb*
rampages
rampaging
rampaged
rampage *noun*
ran see **run**
ranch *noun*
ranches
random
rang see **ring**
range *noun*
ranges
range *verb*
ranges
ranging
ranged
ranger★ *noun*
rangers
rank *noun*
ranks
rank *verb*
ranks
ranking
ranked
ransack *verb*
ransacks
ransacking
ransacked
ransom *verb*
ransoms
ransoming
ransomed
ransom *noun*
ransoms

★ You use a capital R when you mean a senior Guide.

rap★ *verb*
raps
rapping
rapped

rap *noun*
raps

rapid *adjective*
rapidly

rapidity

rapids *plural noun*

rare *adjective*
rarer
rarest
rarely

rarity *noun*
rarities

rascal *noun*
rascals

rash *adjective*
rasher
rashest
rashly

rash *noun*
rashes

rasher *noun*
rashers

raspberry *noun*
raspberries

Rastafarian *noun*
Rastafarians

rat *noun*
rats

rate *noun*
rates

rate *verb*
rates
rating
rated

rather

ratio *noun*
ratios

ration *noun*
rations

ration *verb*
rations
rationing
rationed

rational *adjective*
rationally

rationalize *verb*
rationalizes
rationalizing
rationalized

rattle *verb*
rattles
rattling
rattled

rattle *noun*
rattles

rattlesnake *noun*
rattlesnakes

rave *verb*
raves
raving
raved

rave *noun*
raves

raven *noun*
ravens

ravenous *adjective*
ravenously

ravine *noun*
ravines

raw *adjective*
rawer
rawest

ray *noun*
rays

razor *noun*
razors

re-
re- makes words meaning 'again', e.g. **reproduce**. These words are normally spelt joined up, but a few need a hyphen so you don't confuse them with other words, e.g. **re-cover** (to put a new cover on); **recover** has another meaning. You also need a hyphen in words beginning with *e*, e.g. **re-enter**.

reach *verb*
reaches
reaching
reached

reach *noun*
reaches

react *verb*
reacts
reacting
reacted

reaction *noun*
reactions

reactor *noun*
reactors

read☆ *verb*
reads
reading
read

readable

reader *noun*
readers

readily

readiness

reading *noun*
readings

★ To **rap** is to knock loudly. **! wrap**.
☆ To **read** is to look at something written or printed. **! reed**.

a b c d e f g h i j k l m n o p q r s t u v w x y z

ready *adjective*
readier
readiest

real★ *adjective*

realism

realist *noun*
realists

realistic *adjective*
realistically

reality *noun*
realities

realization

realize *verb*
realizes
realizing
realized

really

realm *noun*
realms

reap *verb*
reaps
reaping
reaped

reaper *noun*
reapers

reappear *verb*
reappears
reappearing
reappeared

reappearance *noun*
reappearances

rear *adjective* and *noun*
rears

rear *verb*
rears
rearing
reared

rearrange *verb*
rearranges
rearranging
rearranged

rearrangement *noun*
rearrangements

reason *noun*
reasons

reason *verb*
reasons
reasoning
reasoned

reasonable *adjective*
reasonably

reassurance *noun*
reassurances

reassure *verb*
reassures
reassuring
reassured

rebel *verb*
rebels
rebelling
rebelled

rebel *noun*
rebels

rebellion *noun*
rebellions

rebellious *adjective*
rebelliously

rebound *verb*
rebounds
rebounding
rebounded

rebuild *verb*
rebuilds
rebuilding
rebuilt

recall *verb*
recalls
recalling
recalled

recap *verb*
recaps
recapping
recapped

recapture *verb*
recaptures
recapturing
recaptured

recede *verb*
recedes
receding
receded

receipt *noun*
receipts

receive *verb*
receives
receiving
received

receiver *noun*
receivers

recent *adjective*
recently

receptacle *noun*
receptacles

reception *noun*
receptions

receptionist *noun*
receptionists

recess *noun*
recesses

recession *noun*
recessions

recipe *noun*
recipes

reciprocal *adjective*
reciprocally

reciprocal *noun*
reciprocals

recital *noun*
recitals

recitation *noun*
recitations

recite *verb*
recites
reciting
recited

reckless *adjective*
recklessly

recklessness

★ **Real** means 'true' or 'existing'. **! reel**.

reckon *verb*
reckons
reckoning
reckoned

reclaim *verb*
reclaims
reclaiming
reclaimed

reclamation *noun*
reclamations

recline *verb*
reclines
reclining
reclined

recognition

recognizable *adjective*
recognizably

recognize *verb*
recognizes
recognizing
recognized

recoil *verb*
recoils
recoiling
recoiled

recollect *verb*
recollects
recollecting
recollected

recollection *noun*
recollections

recommend *verb*
recommends
recommending
recommended

recommendation *noun*
recommendations

reconcile *verb*
reconciles
reconciling
reconciled

reconciliation *noun*
reconciliations

reconstruction *noun*
reconstructions

record *noun*
records

record *verb*
records
recording
recorded

recorder *noun*
recorders

recover *verb*
recovers
recovering
recovered

recovery *noun*
recoveries

recreation *noun*
recreations

recreational *adjective*
recreationally

recruit *noun*
recruits

recruit *verb*
recruits
recruiting
recruited

rectangle *noun*
rectangles

rectangular

recur *verb*
recurs
recurring
recurred

recurrence *noun*
recurrences

recycle *verb*
recycles
recycling
recycled

red *adjective*
redder
reddest

red *noun*
reds

redden *verb*
reddens
reddening
reddened

reddish

redeem *verb*
redeems
redeeming
redeemed

redeemer *noun*
redeemers

redemption *noun*
redemptions

redhead *noun*
redheads

reduce *verb*
reduces
reducing
reduced

reduction *noun*
reductions

redundancy *noun*
redundancies

redundant *adjective*
redundantly

reed★ *noun*
reeds

reedy

reef *noun*
reefs

reef knot *noun*
reef knots

reek *verb*
reeks
reeking
reeked

★ A **reed** is a plant or a thin strip. **! read**.

a b c d e f g h i j k l m n o p q r s t u v w x y z

reel★ *noun*
reels
reel *verb*
reels
reeling
reeled
refer *verb*
refers
referring
referred
referee *noun*
referees
referee *verb*
referees
refereeing
refereed
reference *noun*
references
referendum *noun*
referendums
refill *verb*
refills
refilling
refilled
refill *noun*
refills
refine *verb*
refines
refining
refined
refinement *noun*
refinements
refinery *noun*
refineries
reflect *verb*
reflects
reflecting
reflected
reflective *adjective*
reflectively
reflex *noun*
reflexes
reflexive *adjective*
reflexively
reform *verb*
reforms
reforming
reformed
reform *noun*
reforms
reformation *noun*
reformations
Reformation☆
reformer *noun*
reformers
refract *verb*
refracts
refracting
refracted
refraction
refrain *verb*
refrains
refraining
refrained
refrain *noun*
refrains
refresh *verb*
refreshes
refreshing
refreshed
refreshment *noun*
refreshments
refrigerate *verb*
refrigerates
refrigerating
refrigerated
refrigeration
refrigerator *noun*
refrigerators
refuel *verb*
refuels
refuelling
refuelled
refuge *noun*
refuges
refugee *noun*
refugees
refund *verb*
refunds
refunding
refunded
refund *noun*
refunds
refusal
refuse *verb*
refuses
refusing
refused
refuse
regain *verb*
regains
regaining
regained
regard *verb*
regards
regarding
regarded
regard *noun*
regards
regarding *preposition*
regardless
regatta *noun*
regattas
reggae
regiment *noun*
regiments
regimental
region *noun*
regions
regional *adjective*
regionally
register *noun*
registers

★ A **reel** is a cylinder on which something is wound. **! real**.
☆ You use a capital R when you mean the historical religious movement.

register *verb*
registers
registering
registered

registration *noun*
registrations

regret *noun*
regrets

regret *verb*
regrets
regretting
regretted

regretful *adjective*
regretfully

regrettable *adjective*
regrettably

regular *adjective*
regularly

regularity

regulate *verb*
regulates
regulating
regulated

regulation *noun*
regulations

regulator *noun*
regulators

rehearsal *noun*
rehearsals

rehearse *verb*
rehearses
rehearsing
rehearsed

reign★ *verb*
reigns
reigning
reigned

reign *noun*
reigns

rein☆ *noun*
reins

reindeer *noun*
reindeer

reinforce *verb*
reinforces
reinforcing
reinforced

reinforcement *noun*
reinforcements

reject *verb*
rejects
rejecting
rejected

reject *noun*
rejects

rejection *noun*
rejections

rejoice *verb*
rejoices
rejoicing
rejoiced

relate *verb*
relates
relating
related

relation *noun*
relations

relationship *noun*
relationships

relative *adjective*
relatively

relative *noun*
relatives

relax *verb*
relaxes
relaxing
relaxed

relaxation

relay *verb*
relays
relaying
relayed

relay *noun*
relays

release *verb*
releases
releasing
released

release *noun*
releases

relegate *verb*
relegates
relegating
relegated

relegation

relent *verb*
relents
relenting
relented

relentless *adjective*
relentlessly

relevance

relevant *adjective*
relevantly

reliability

reliable *adjective*
reliably

reliance

reliant

relic *noun*
relics

relief *noun*
reliefs

relieve *verb*
relieves
relieving
relieved

religion *noun*
religions

religious *adjective*
religiously

reluctance

★ To **reign** is to rule as a king or queen. **! rein**.
☆ A **rein** is a strap used to guide a horse. **! reign**.

a b c d e f g h i j k l m n o p q r s t u v w x y z

reluctant *adjective*
reluctantly

rely *verb*
relies
relying
relied

remain *verb*
remains
remaining
remained

remainder *noun*
remainders

remains

remark *verb*
remarks
remarking
remarked

remark *noun*
remarks

remarkable *adjective*
remarkably

remedial *adjective*
remedially

remedy *noun*
remedies

remember *verb*
remembers
remembering
remembered

remembrance

remind *verb*
reminds
reminding
reminded

reminder *noun*
reminders

reminisce *verb*
reminisces
reminiscing
reminisced

reminiscence *noun*
reminiscences

reminiscent

remnant *noun*
remnants

remorse

remorseful *adjective*
remorsefully

remorseless *adjective*
remorselessly

remote *adjective*
remoter
remotest
remotely

remoteness

removal *noun*
removals

remove *verb*
removes
removing
removed

Renaissance★

render *verb*
renders
rendering
rendered

rendezvous *noun*
rendezvous

renew *verb*
renews
renewing
renewed

renewable

renewal *noun*
renewals

renown

renowned

rent *noun*
rents

rent *verb*
rents
renting
rented

repair *verb*
repairs
repairing
repaired

repair *noun*
repairs

repay *verb*
repays
repaying
repaid

repayment *noun*
repayments

repeat *verb*
repeats
repeating
repeated

repeat *noun*
repeats

repeatedly

repel *verb*
repels
repelling
repelled

repellent

repent *verb*
repents
repenting
repented

repentance

repentant

repetition *noun*
repetitions

repetitive *adjective*
repetitively

replace *verb*
replaces
replacing
replaced

replacement *noun*
replacements

replay *noun*
replays

★ You use a capital R when you mean the historical period.

replica *noun*
replicas

reply *verb*
replies
replying
replied

reply *noun*
replies

report *verb*
reports
reporting
reported

report *noun*
reports

reporter *noun*
reporters

repossess *verb*
repossesses
repossessing
repossessed

represent *verb*
represents
representing
represented

representation *noun*
representations

representative
adjective and *noun*
representatives

repress *verb*
represses
repressing
repressed

repression *noun*
repressions

repressive *adjective*
repressively

reprieve *verb*
reprieves
reprieving
reprieved

reprieve *noun*
reprieves

reprimand *verb*
reprimands
reprimanding
reprimanded

reprisal *noun*
reprisals

reproach *verb*
reproaches
reproaching
reproached

reproduce *verb*
reproduces
reproducing
reproduced

reproduction *noun*
reproduction

reproductive
adjective
reproductively

reptile *noun*
reptiles

republic *noun*
republics

republican *adjective*
and *noun*
republicans

Republican★
adjective and *noun*
Republicans

repulsion

repulsive *adjective*
repulsively

reputation *noun*
reputations

request *verb*
requests
requesting
requested

request *noun*
requests

require *verb*
requires
requiring
required

requirement *noun*
requirements

reread *verb*
rereads
rereading
reread

rescue *verb*
rescues
rescuing
rescued

rescue *noun*
rescues

rescuer *noun*
rescuers

research *noun*
researches

researcher *noun*
researchers

resemblance *noun*
resemblances

resemble *verb*
resembles
resembling
resembled

resent *verb*
resents
resenting
resented

resentful *adjective*
resentfully

resentment

reservation *noun*
reservations

reserve *verb*
reserves
reserving
reserved

reserve *noun*
reserves

★ You use a capital R when you mean the political party in the USA.

a b c d e f g h i j k l m n o p q **r** s t u v w x y z

reservoir *noun*
reservoirs

reshuffle *noun*
reshuffles

reside *verb*
resides
residing
resided

residence *noun*
residences

resident *noun*
residents

resign *verb*
resigns
resigning
resigned

resignation *noun*
resignations

resin *noun*
resins

resinous

resist *verb*
resists
resisting
resisted

resistance *noun*
resistances

resistant

resolute *adjective*
resolutely

resolution *noun*
resolutions

resolve *verb*
resolves
resolving
resolved

resort *noun*
resorts

resort *verb*
resorts
resorting
resorted

resound *verb*
resounds
resounding
resounded

resource *noun*
resources

respect *verb*
respects
respecting
respected

respect *noun*
respects

respectability

respectable *adjective*
respectably

respectful *adjective*
respectfully

respective *adjective*
respectively

respiration

respirator *noun*
respirators

respiratory

respond *verb*
responds
responding
responded

response *noun*
responses

responsibility *noun*
responsibilities

responsible *adjective*
responsibly

rest *verb*
rests
resting
rested

rest *noun*
rests

restaurant *noun*
restaurants

restful *adjective*
restfully

restless *adjective*
restlessly

restlessness

restoration *noun*
restorations

restore *verb*
restores
restoring
restored

restrain *verb*
restrains
restraining
restrained

restraint *noun*
restraints

restrict *verb*
restricts
restricting
restricted

restriction *noun*
restrictions

restrictive *adjective*
restrictively

result *verb*
results
resulting
resulted

result *noun*
results

resume *verb*
resumes
resuming
resumed

resumption *noun*
resumptions

resuscitate *verb*
resuscitates
resuscitating
resuscitated

retail *verb*
retails
retailing
retailed

retail *noun*

retain *verb*
retains
retaining
retained

retina *noun*
retinas

retire *verb*
retires
retiring
retired

retirement

retort *verb*
retorts
retorting
retorted

retort *noun*
retorts

retrace *verb*
retraces
retracing
retraced

retreat *verb*
retreats
retreating
retreated

retrievable *adjective*
retrievably

retrieval *noun*
retrievals

retrieve *verb*
retrieves
retrieving
retrieved

retriever *noun*
retrievers

return *verb*
returns
returning
returned

return *noun*
returns

reunion *noun*
reunions

rev *verb*
revs
revving
revved

rev *noun*
revs

reveal *verb*
reveals
revealing
revealed

revelation *noun*
revelations

revenge

revenue *noun*
revenues

revere *verb*
reveres
revering
revered

reverence

Reverend★

reverent★ *adjective*
reverently

reversal *noun*
reversals

reverse *verb*
reverses
reversing
reversed

reverse *noun*
reverses

reversible *adjective*
reversibly

review *verb*
reviews
reviewing
reviewed

review☆ *noun*
reviews

reviewer *noun*
reviewers

revise *verb*
revises
revising
revised

revision *noun*
revisions

revival *noun*
revivals

revive *verb*
revives
reviving
revived

revolt *verb*
revolts
revolting
revolted

revolt *noun*
revolts

revolution *noun*
revolutions

revolutionary
adjective and *noun*
revolutionaries

revolutionize *verb*
revolutionizes
revolutionizing
revolutionized

revolve *verb*
revolves
revolving
revolved

revolver *noun*
revolvers

revue✪ *noun*
revues

★ You use **Reverend** as a title of a member of the clergy, and **reverent** as an ordinary word meaning 'showing respect'.
☆ A **review** is a piece of writing about a film, play, etc. **! revue**.
✪ A **revue** is an entertainment of short sketches. **! review**.

reward *verb*
rewards
rewarding
rewarded

reward *noun*
rewards

rewind *verb*
rewinds
rewinding
rewound

rewrite *verb*
rewrites
rewriting
rewrote
rewritten

rheumatic

rheumatism

rhinoceros *noun*
rhinoceroses
rhinoceros

rhododendron *noun*
rhododendrons

rhombus *noun*
rhombuses

rhubarb

rhyme *verb*
rhymes
rhyming
rhymed

rhyme *noun*
rhymes

rhythm *noun*
rhythms

rhythmic or **rhythmical** *adjective*
rhythmically

rib *noun*
ribs

ribbon *noun*
ribbons

rice

rich *adjective*
richer
richest
richly

riches *plural noun*

richness

rick *noun*
ricks

rickety

rickshaw *noun*
rickshaws

ricochet *verb*
ricochets
ricocheting
ricocheted

rid *verb*
rids
ridding
rid

riddance

riddle *noun*
riddles

ride *verb*
rides
riding
rode
ridden

ride *noun*
rides

rider *noun*
riders

ridge *noun*
ridges

ridicule *verb*
ridicules
ridiculing
ridiculed

ridiculous *adjective*
ridiculously

rifle *noun*
rifles

rift *noun*
rifts

rig *verb*
rigs
rigging
rigged

rigging

right *adjective*
rightly

right★ *noun*
rights

right☆ *verb*
rights
righting
righted

righteous *adjective*
righteously

righteousness

rightful *adjective*
rightfully

right-handed

rightness

rigid *adjective*
rigidly

rigidity

rim *noun*
rims

rind *noun*
rinds

ring *noun*
rings

ring✪ *verb*
rings
ringing
rang
rung

★ A **right** is something you are entitled to. **! rite**, **write**.

☆ To **right** something is to make it right. **! rite**, **write**.

✪ The past tense is **rang** and the past participle is **rung** when you mean 'to make a sound like a bell'. **! wring**.

a b c d e f g h i j k l m n o p q **r** s t u v w x y z

ring★ *verb*
rings
ringing
ringed

ring *noun*
rings

ringleader *noun*
ringleaders

ringlet *noun*
ringlets

ringmaster *noun*
ringmasters

rink *noun*
rinks

rinse *verb*
rinses
rinsing
rinsed

rinse *noun*
rinses

riot *verb*
riots
rioting
rioted

riot *noun*
riots

riotous *adjective*
riotously

rip *verb*
rips
ripping
ripped

rip *noun*
rips

ripe *adjective*
riper
ripest

ripen *verb*
ripens
ripening
ripened

ripeness

rip-off *noun*
rip-offs

ripple *noun*
ripples

ripple *verb*
ripples
rippling
rippled

rise *verb*
rises
rising
rose
risen

rise *noun*
rises

risk *verb*
risks
risking
risked

risk *noun*
risks

risky *adjective*
riskier
riskiest
riskily

risotto *noun*
risottos

rissole *noun*
rissoles

rite☆ *noun*
rites

ritual *noun*
rituals

rival *noun*
rivals

rival *verb*
rivals
rivalling
rivalled

rivalry *noun*
rivalries

river *noun*
rivers

rivet *noun*
rivets

rivet *verb*
rivets
riveting
riveted

road✪ *noun*
roads

roadroller *noun*
roadrollers

roadside *noun*
roadsides

roadway *noun*
roadways

roam *verb*
roams
roaming
roamed

roar *verb*
roars
roaring
roared

roar *noun*
roars

roast *verb*
roasts
roasting
roasted

rob *verb*
robs
robbing
robbed

★ The past tense and past participle is **ringed** when you mean 'to put a ring round something'. **! wring**.

☆ A **rite** is a ceremony or ritual. **! right**, **write**.

✪ A **road** is a hard surface for traffic to use. **! rode**.

robber *noun*
robbers

robbery *noun*
robberies

robe *noun*
robes

robin *noun*
robins

robot *noun*
robots

robust *adjective*
robustly

rock *verb*
rocks
rocking
rocked

rock *noun*
rocks

rocker *noun*
rockers

rockery *noun*
rockeries

rocket *noun*
rockets

rocky *adjective*
rockier
rockiest
rockily

rod *noun*
rods

rode★ see **ride**

rodent *noun*
rodents

rodeo *noun*
rodeos

rogue *noun*
rogues

roguish *adjective*
roguishly

role☆ *noun*
roles

roll *verb*
rolls
rolling
rolled

roll✪ *noun*
rolls

roller *noun*
rollers

Roman *adjective* and *noun*
Romans

Roman Catholic *noun*
Roman Catholics

romance *noun*
romances

Roman numeral

romantic *adjective*
romantically

Romany

romp *verb*
romps
romping
romped

romp *noun*
romps

rompers *plural noun*

roof *noun*
roofs

rook *noun*
rooks

room *noun*
rooms

roomful *adjective*
roomfuls

roomy *adjective*
roomier
roomiest
roomily

roost *noun*
roosts

root✣ *noun*
roots

root *verb*
roots
rooting
rooted

rope *noun*
ropes

rose *noun*
roses

rose see **rise**

rosette *noun*
rosettes

rosy *adjective*
rosier
rosiest
rosily

rot *verb*
rots
rotting
rotted

rot *noun*

rota *noun*
rotas

rotary

rotate *verb*
rotates
rotating
rotated

rotation *noun*
rotations

rotor *noun*
rotors

rotten

★ **Rode** is the past tense of **ride**. **! road**.
☆ A **role** is a part in a play or film. **! roll**.
✪ A **roll** is a small loaf of bread or an act of rolling. **! role**.
✣ A **root** is the part of a plant that grows underground. **! route**.

rottenness

rottweiler *noun*
rottweilers

rough *adjective*
rougher
roughest
roughly

roughness

roughage

roughen *verb*
roughens
roughening
roughened

round *adjective, adverb,* and *preposition*
rounder
roundest
roundly

round *noun*
rounds

round *verb*
rounds
rounding
rounded

roundabout *adjective* and *noun*
roundabouts

rounders *noun*

Roundhead *noun*
Roundheads

rouse *verb*
rouses
rousing
roused

rout *verb*
routs
routing
routed

rout *noun*
routs

route★ *noun*
routes

routine *noun*
routines

routine *adjective*
routinely

rove *verb*
roves
roving
roved

rover *noun*
rovers

row☆ *noun*
rows

row✪ *verb*
rows
rowing
rowed

rowdiness

rowdy *adjective*
rowdier
rowdiest
rowdily

rower *noun*
rowers

rowlock *noun*
rowlocks

royal *adjective*
royally

royalty

rub *verb*
rubs
rubbing
rubbed

rub *noun*
rubs

rubber *noun*
rubbers

rubbery

rubbish

rubble

ruby *noun*
rubies

rucksack *noun*
rucksacks

rudder *noun*
rudders

ruddy *adjective*
ruddier
ruddiest

rude *adjective*
ruder
rudest
rudely

rudeness

ruffian *noun*
ruffians

ruffle *verb*
ruffles
ruffling
ruffled

rug *noun*
rugs

rugby✣

rugged *adjective*
ruggedly

rugger

★ A **route** is the way you go to get to a place. **! root**.
☆ A **row** is a line of people or things and rhymes with ‘go’. A **row** is also a noise or argument and rhymes with ‘cow’.
✪ To **row** means to use oars to make a boat move and rhymes with ‘go’.
✣ You can use a small r when you mean the game.

a b c d e f g h i j k l m n o p q r s t u v w x y z

ruin *verb*
ruins
ruining
ruined

ruin *noun*
ruins

ruinous *adjective*
ruinously

rule *noun*
rules

rule *verb*
rules
ruling
ruled

ruler *noun*
rulers

ruling *noun*
rulings

rum *noun*
rums

rumble *verb*
rumbles
rumbling
rumbled

rumble *noun*
rumbles

rummage *verb*
rummages
rummaging
rummaged

rummy

rumour *noun*
rumours

rump *noun*
rumps

run *verb*
runs
running
ran
run

run *noun*
runs

runaway *noun*
runaways

rung *noun*
rungs

rung see **ring**

runner *noun*
runners

runner-up *noun*
runners-up

runny *adjective*
runnier
runniest
runnily

runway *noun*
runways

rural

rush *verb*
rushes
rushing
rushed

rush *noun*
rushes

rusk *noun*
rusks

rust *noun*

rust *verb*
rusts
rusting
rusted

rustic

rustle *verb*
rustles
rustling
rustled

rustler *noun*
rustlers

rusty *adjective*
rustier
rustiest
rustily

rut *noun*
ruts

ruthless *adjective*
ruthlessly

ruthlessness

rutted

rye★ *noun*

Ss

sabbath *noun*
sabbaths

sabotage *noun*

sabotage *verb*
sabotages
sabotaging
sabotaged

saboteur *noun*
saboteurs

sac☆ *noun*
sacs

saccharin

sachet *noun*
sachets

sack✪ *noun*
sacks

sack *verb*
sacks
sacking
sacked

sacred

sacrifice *noun*
sacrifices

sacrificial *adjective*
sacrificially

★ **Rye** is a type of cereal or bread. **! wry**.
☆ A **sac** is a bag-like part of an animal or plant. **! sack**.
✪ A **sack** is a large bag. **! sac**.

sacrifice *verb*
sacrifices
sacrificing
sacrificed

sad *adjective*
sadder
saddest
sadly

sadness

sadden *verb*
saddens
saddening
saddened

saddle *noun*
saddles

saddle *verb*
saddles
saddling
saddled

sadist *noun*
sadists

sadism

sadistic *adjective*
sadistically

safari *noun*
safaris

safe *adjective*
safer
safest
safely

safe *noun*
safes

safeguard *noun*
safeguards

safety

sag *verb*
sags
sagging
sagged

saga *noun*
sagas

sago

said see **say**

sail *verb*
sails
sailing
sailed

sail★ *noun*
sails

sailboard *noun*
sailboards

sailor *noun*
sailors

saint *noun*
saints

saintly *adjective*
saintlier
saintliest

sake

salaam *interjection*

salad *noun*
salads

salami *noun*
salamis

salary *noun*
salaries

sale☆ *noun*
sales

salesman *noun*
salesmen

salesperson *noun*
salespersons

saleswoman *noun*
saleswomen

saline

saliva

sally *verb*
sallies
sallying
sallied

salmon *noun*
salmon

salon *noun*
salons

saloon *noun*
saloons

salt *noun*

salt *verb*
salts
salting
salted

salty *adjective*
saltier
saltiest

salute *verb*
salutes
saluting
saluted

salute *noun*
salutes

salvage *verb*
salvages
salvaging
salvaged

salvation

same

samosa *noun*
samosas

sample *noun*
samples

sample *verb*
samples
sampling
sampled

sanctuary *noun*
sanctuaries

sand *noun*
sands

sand *verb*
sands
sanding
sanded

sander *noun*
sanders

★ A **sail** is a sheet that catches the wind to make a boat go. **! sale**.
☆ You use **sale** in e.g. *The house is for sale.* **! sail**.

a b c d e f g h i j k l m n o p q r **s** t u v w x y z

sandal *noun*
sandals
sandbag *noun*
sandbags
sandpaper
sands *plural noun*
sandstone
sandwich *noun*
sandwiches
sandy *adjective*
sandier
sandiest
sane *adjective*
saner
sanest
sanely
sang see **sing**
sanitary
sanitation
sanity
sank see **sink**
Sanskrit
sap *noun*
sap *verb*
saps
sapping
sapped
sapling *noun*
saplings
sapphire *noun*
sapphires
sarcasm
sarcastic *adjective*
sarcastically
sardine *noun*
sardines
sari *noun*
saris
sash *noun*
sashes
sat see **sit**

satchel *noun*
satchels
satellite *noun*
satellites
satin
satire *noun*
satires
satirical *adjective*
satirically
satirist *noun*
satirists
satisfaction
satisfactory *adjective*
satisfactorily
satisfy *verb*
satisfies
satisfying
satisfied
saturate *verb*
saturates
saturating
saturated
saturation
Saturday *noun*
Saturdays
sauce★ *noun*
sauces
saucepan *noun*
saucepans
saucer *noun*
saucers
saucy *adjective*
saucier
sauciest
saucily
sauna *noun*
saunas
saunter *verb*
saunters
sauntering
sauntered
sausage *noun*
sausages

savage *adjective*
savagely
savage *noun*
savages
savage *verb*
savages
savaging
savaged
savagery
savannah *noun*
savannahs
save *verb*
saves
saving
saved
saver *noun*
savers
savings *plural noun*
saviour *noun*
saviours
savoury
saw *noun*
saws
saw *verb*
saws
sawing
sawed
sawn
saw see **see**
sawdust
saxophone *noun*
saxophones
say *verb*
says
saying
said
say *noun*
saying *noun*
sayings
scab *noun*
scabs

★ A **sauce** is a liquid you put on food. **! source**.

scabbard *noun*
scabbards
scaffold *noun*
scaffolds
scaffolding
scald *verb*
scalds
scalding
scalded
scale *noun*
scales
scale *verb*
scales
scaling
scaled
scales *plural noun*
scaly *adjective*
scalier
scaliest
scalp *noun*
scalps
scalp *verb*
scalps
scalping
scalped
scamper *verb*
scampers
scampering
scampered
scampi *plural noun*
scan *verb*
scans
scanning
scanned
scan *noun*
scans
scandal *noun*
scandals
scandalous *adjective*
scandalous
scanner *noun*
scanners

scanty *adjective*
scantier
scantiest
scantily
scapegoat *noun*
scapegoats
scar *noun*
scars
scar *verb*
scars
scarring
scarred
scarce *adjective*
scarcer
scarcest
scarcely
scarcity *noun*
scarcities
scare *verb*
scares
scaring
scared
scare *noun*
scares
scarecrow *noun*
scarecrows
scarf *noun*
scarves
scarlet
scary *adjective*
scarier
scariest
scarily
scatter *verb*
scatters
scattering
scattered
scene★ *noun*
scenes
scenery
scent☆ *noun*
scents

scent *verb*
scents
scenting
scented
sceptic *noun*
sceptics
sceptical *adjective*
sceptically
scepticism
schedule *noun*
schedules
scheme *noun*
schemes
scheme *verb*
schemes
scheming
schemed
schemer *noun*
schemers
scholar *noun*
scholars
scholarly
scholarship *noun*
scholarships
school *noun*
schools
schoolboy *noun*
schoolboys
schoolchild *noun*
schoolchildren
schoolgirl *noun*
schoolgirls
schoolteacher *noun*
schoolteachers
schooner *noun*
schooners
science
scientific *adjective*
scientifically
scientist *noun*
scientists

★ A **scene** is a place or part of a play. **! seen**.
☆ A **scent** is a smell or perfume. **! cent**, **sent**.

scissors *plural noun*

scoff *verb*
scoffs
scoffing
scoffed

scold *verb*
scolds
scolding
scolded

scone *noun*
scones

scoop *noun*
scoops

scoop *verb*
scoops
scooping
scooped

scooter *noun*
scooters

scope

scorch *verb*
scorches
scorching
scorched

score *noun*
scores

score *verb*
scores
scoring
scored

scorer *noun*
scorers

scorn *noun*

scorn *verb*
scorns
scorning
scorned

scorpion *noun*
scorpions

Scot *noun*
Scots

scoundrel *noun*
scoundrels

scour *verb*
scours
scouring
scoured

Scout★ *noun*
Scouts

scout *noun*
scouts

scowl *verb*
scowls
scowling
scowled

scramble *verb*
scrambles
scrambling
scrambled

scramble *noun*
scrambles

scrap *verb*
scraps
scrapping
scrapped

scrap *noun*
scraps

scrape *verb*
scrapes
scraping
scraped

scrape *noun*
scrapes

scraper *noun*
scrapers

scrappy *adjective*
scrappier
scrappiest
scrappily

scratch *verb*
scratches
scratching
scratched

scratch *noun*
scratches

scrawl *verb*
scrawls
scrawling
scrawled

scrawl *noun*
scrawls

scream *verb*
screams
screaming
screamed

scream *noun*
screams

screech *verb*
screeches
screeching
screeched

screech *noun*
screeches

screen *noun*
screens

screen *verb*
screens
screening
screened

screw *noun*
screws

screw *verb*
screws
screwing
screwed

screwdriver *noun*
screwdrivers

scribble *verb*
scribbles
scribbling
scribbled

scribble *noun*
scribbles

scribbler *noun*
scribblers

★ You use a capital S when you mean a member of the Scout Association.

script *noun*
scripts
scripture *noun*
scriptures
scroll *noun*
scrolls
scrotum *noun*
scrotums *or* scrota
scrounge *verb*
scrounges
scrounging
scrounged
scrounger *noun*
scroungers
scrub *verb*
scrubs
scrubbing
scrubbed
scrub *noun*
scruffy *adjective*
scruffier
scruffiest
scruffily
scrum *noun*
scrums
scrummage *noun*
scrummages
scrutinize *verb*
scrutinizes
scrutinizing
scrutinized
scrutiny *noun*
scrutinies
scuba diving
scuffle *noun*
scuffles
scuffle *verb*
scuffles
scuffling
scuffled
scullery *noun*
sculleries
sculptor *noun*
sculptors
sculpture *noun*
sculptures
scum
scurry *verb*
scurries
scurrying
scurried
scurvy
scuttle *verb*
scuttles
scuttling
scuttled
scuttle *noun*
scuttles
scythe *noun*
scythes
sea★ *noun*
seas
seabed
seafarer *noun*
seafarers
seafaring
seafood
seagull *noun*
seagulls
sea horse *noun*
sea horses
seal *verb*
seals
sealing
sealed
seal *noun*
seals
sea lion *noun*
sea lions
seam☆ *noun*
seams
seaman *noun*
seamen
seamanship
seaplane *noun*
seaplanes
seaport *noun*
seaports
search *verb*
searches
searching
searched
search *noun*
searches
searcher *noun*
searchers
searchlight *noun*
searchlights
seashore *noun*
seashores
seasick
seasickness
seaside
season *noun*
seasons
season *verb*
seasons
seasoning
seasoned
seasonal *adjective*
seasonally
seasoning *noun*
seasonings
seat *noun*
seats
seat *verb*
seats
seating
seated
seat belt *noun*
seat belts
seaward *adjective* and *adverb*
seawards *adverb*

★ A **sea** is an area of salt water. **! see**.
☆ A **seam** is a line of stitching in cloth. **! seem**.

a b c d e f g h i j k l m n o p q r **s** t u v w x y z

seaweed *noun*
seaweeds

secateurs *plural noun*

secluded

seclusion

second *adjective*
secondly

second *noun*
seconds

second *verb*
seconds
seconding
seconded

secondary

second-hand *adjective*

secrecy

secret *adjective*
secretly

secret *noun*
secrets

secretary *noun*
secretaries

secrete *verb*
secretes
secreting
secreted

secretion *noun*
secretions

secretive *adjective*
secretively

secretiveness

sect *noun*
sects

section *noun*
sections

sectional

sector *noun*
sectors

secure *adjective*
securer
securest
securely

secure *verb*
secures
securing
secured

security

sedate *adjective*
sedately

sedation

sedative *noun*
sedatives

sediment

sedimentary

see★ *verb*
sees
seeing
saw
seen

seed *noun*
seeds

seedling *noun*
seedlings

seek *verb*
seeks
seeking
sought

seem☆ *verb*
seems
seeming
seemed

seemingly

seen✪ see **see**

seep *verb*
seeps
seeping
seeped

seepage

see-saw *noun*
see-saws

seethe *verb*
seethes
seething
seethed

segment *noun*
segments

segmented

segregate *verb*
segregates
segregating
segregated

segregation

seismograph *noun*
seismographs

seize *verb*
seizes
seizing
seized

seizure *noun*
seizures

seldom

select *verb*
selects
selecting
selected

select *adjective*

self *noun*
selves

self-confidence

self-confident *adjective*
self-confidently

self-conscious *adjective*
self-consciously

self-contained

selfish *adjective*
selfishly

★ You use **see** in e.g. *I can't see anything.* **! sea**.
☆ You use **seem** in e.g. *they seem tired.* **! seam**.
✪ **Seen** is the past participle of **see**. **! scene**.

selfishness
selfless *adjective*
selflessly
self-service
sell★ *verb*
sells
selling
sold
semaphore
semen

semi-
semi- makes words meaning 'half', e.g. **semi-automatic**, **semi-skimmed**. A few words are spelt joined up, e.g. **semicircle**, **semicolon**, but most of them have hyphens.

semibreve *noun*
semibreves
semicircle *noun*
semicircles
semicircular
semicolon *noun*
semicolons
semi-detached
semi-final *noun*
semi-finals
semi-finalist *noun*
semi-finalists
semitone *noun*
semitones
semolina
senate
senator *noun*
senators
send *verb*
sends
sending
sent
senior *adjective* and *noun*
seniors
seniority
sensation *noun*
sensations
sensational *adjective*
sensationally
sense *noun*
senses
sense *verb*
senses
sensing
sensed
senseless *adjective*
senselessly
sensible *adjective*
sensibly
sensitive *adjective*
sensitively
sensitivity *noun*
sensitivities
sensitize *verb*
sensitizes
sensitizing
sensitized
sensor *noun*
sensors
sent☆ see **send**
sentence *noun*
sentences
sentence *verb*
sentences
sentencing
sentenced
sentiment *noun*
sentiments
sentimental *adjective*
sentimentally
sentimentality
sentinel *noun*
sentinels
sentry *noun*
sentries
separable
separate *adjective*
separately
separate *verb*
separates
separating
separated
separation *noun*
separations
September *noun*
Septembers
septic
sequel *noun*
sequels
sequence *noun*
sequences
sequin *noun*
sequins
serene *adjective*
serenely
serenity
sergeant *noun*
sergeants
sergeant major *noun*
sergeant majors
serial✪ *noun*
serials
series *noun*
series
serious *adjective*
seriously
seriousness

★ To **sell** something means 'to exchange it for money'. **! cell**.
☆ You use **sent** in e.g. *he was sent home*. **! cent**, **scent**.
✪ A **serial** is a story or programme in separate parts. **! cereal**.

a b c d e f g h i j k l m n o p q r **s** t u v w x y z

sermon *noun*
sermons

serpent *noun*
serpents

servant *noun*
servants

serve *verb*
serves
serving
served

server *noun*
servers

serve *noun*
serves

service *noun*
services

service *verb*
services
servicing
serviced

serviette *noun*
serviettes

session *noun*
sessions

set *verb*
sets
setting
set

set *noun*
sets

set square *noun*
set squares

sett★ *noun*
setts

settee *noun*
settees

setting *noun*
settings

settle *verb*
settles
settling
settled

settlement *noun*
settlements

settler *noun*
settlers

set-up *noun*
set-ups

seven

seventeen

seventeenth

seventh *adjective* and *noun*
seventhly

seventieth

seventy *adjective* and *noun*
seventies

sever *verb*
severs
severing
severed

several *adjective*
severally

severe *adjective*
severer
severest
severely

severity

sew☆ *verb*
sews
sewing
sewed
sewn

sewage

sewer *noun*
sewers

sex *noun*
sexes

sexism

sexist *adjective* and *noun*
sexists

sextet *noun*
sextets

sexual *adjective*
sexually

sexuality

sexy *adjective*
sexier
sexiest
sexily

shabbiness

shabby *adjective*
shabbier
shabbiest
shabbily

shack *noun*
shacks

shade *noun*
shades

shade *verb*
shades
shading
shaded

shadow *noun*
shadows

shadow *verb*
shadows
shadowing
shadowed

shadowy

shady *adjective*
shadier
shadiest

shaft *noun*
shafts

shaggy *adjective*
shaggier
shaggiest
shaggily

★ A **sett** is a badger's burrow.
☆ To **sew** is to work with a needle and thread. **! sow**.

shake *verb*
shakes
shaking
shook
shaken

shake★ *noun*
shakes

shaky *adjective*
shakier
shakiest
shakily

shall *verb*
should

shallow *adjective*
shallower
shallowest
shallowly

sham *noun*
shams

shamble *verb*
shambles
shambling
shambled

shambles *noun*

shame *verb*
shames
shaming
shamed

shame *noun*

shameful *adjective*
shamefully

shameless *adjective*
shamelessly

shampoo *noun*
shampoos

shampoo *verb*
shampoos
shampooing
shampooed

shamrock

shandy *noun*
shandies

shan't *verb*

shanty *noun*
shanties

shape *noun*
shapes

shape *verb*
shapes
shaping
shaped

shapeless *adjective*
shapelessly

shapely *adjective*
shapelier
shapeliest

share *noun*
shares

share *verb*
shares
sharing
shared

shark *noun*
sharks

sharp *adjective*
sharper
sharpest
sharply

sharp *noun*
sharps

sharpen *verb*
sharpens
sharpening
sharpened

sharpener *noun*
sharpeners

sharpness

shatter *verb*
shatters
shattering
shattered

shave *verb*
shaves
shaving
shaved

shave *noun*
shaves

shaver *noun*
shavers

shavings *plural noun*

shawl *noun*
shawls

she

sheaf *noun*
sheaves

shear☆ *verb*
shears
shearing
sheared
shorn

shearer *noun*
shearers

shears *plural noun*

sheath *noun*
sheaths

sheathe *verb*
sheathes
sheathing
sheathed

shed *noun*
sheds

shed *verb*
sheds
shedding
shed

she'd *verb*

sheen

sheep *noun*
sheep

sheepdog *noun*
sheepdogs

sheepish *adjective*
sheepishly

★ To **shake** is to tremble or quiver. **! sheikh**.
☆ To **shear** is to cut wool from a sheep. **! sheer**.

sheer★ *adjective*
sheerer
sheerest

sheet *noun*
sheets

sheikh *noun*
sheikhs

shelf *noun*
shelves

shell *noun*
shells

shell *verb*
shells
shelling
shelled

she'll *verb*

shellfish *noun*
shellfish

shelter *noun*
shelters

shelter *verb*
shelters
sheltering
sheltered

shelve *verb*
shelves
shelving
shelved

shepherd *noun*
shepherds

sherbet *noun*
sherbets

sheriff *noun*
sheriffs

sherry *noun*
sherries

she's *verb*

shield *noun*
shields

shield *verb*
shields
shielding
shielded

shift *noun*
shifts

shift *verb*
shifts
shifting
shifted

shilling *noun*
shillings

shimmer *verb*
shimmers
shimmering
shimmered

shin *noun*
shins

shine *verb*
shines
shining
shone
shined

shine *noun*

shingle

shiny *adjective*
shinier
shiniest

> **-ship**
> *-ship* makes nouns, e.g. **friendship**. Other noun suffixes are **-dom**, **-hood**, **-ment**, and **-ness**.

ship *noun*
ships

ship *verb*
ships
shipping
shipped

shipping

shipwreck *noun*
shipwrecks

shipwrecked

shipyard *noun*
shipyards

shire *noun*
shires

shirk *verb*
shirks
shirking
shirked

shirt *noun*
shirts

shiver *verb*
shivers
shivering
shivered

shiver *noun*
shivers

shivery

shoal *noun*
shoals

shock *verb*
shocks
shocking
shocked

shock *noun*
shocks

shoddy *adjective*
shoddier
shoddiest
shoddily

shoe *noun*
shoes

shoelace *noun*
shoelaces

shoestring *noun*
shoestrings

shone see **shine**

shook see **shake**

shoot *verb*
shoots
shooting
shot

★ You use **sheer** in e.g. *sheer joy*. **! shear**.

shoot★ *noun*
shoots
shop *noun*
shops
shop *verb*
shops
shopping
shopped
shopkeeper *noun*
shopkeepers
shoplifter *noun*
shoplifters
shopper *noun*
shoppers
shopping
shore *noun*
shores
shorn see **shear**
short *adjective*
shorter
shortest
shortly
shortness
shortage *noun*
shortages
shortbread
shortcake *noun*
shortcakes
shortcoming *noun*
shortcomings
shorten *verb*
shortens
shortening
shortened
shorthand
short-handed
shortly
shorts *plural noun*
short-sighted
shot *noun*
shots
shot see **shoot**

shotgun *noun*
shotguns
should
shoulder *noun*
shoulders
shoulder *verb*
shoulders
shouldering
shouldered
shout *verb*
shouts
shouting
shouted
shout *noun*
shouts
shove *verb*
shoves
shoving
shoved
shovel *noun*
shovels
shovel *verb*
shovels
shovelling
shovelled
show *verb*
shows
showing
showed
shown
show *noun*
shows
shower *noun*
showers
shower *verb*
showers
showering
showered
showery
showjumper *noun*
showjumpers
showjumping
showman *noun*
showmen

showmanship
showroom *noun*
showrooms
showiness
showy *adjective*
showier
showiest
showily
shrank see **shrink**
shrapnel
shred *noun*
shreds
shred *verb*
shreds
shredding
shredded
shrew *noun*
shrews
shrewd *adjective*
shrewder
shrewdest
shrewdly
shrewdness
shriek *verb*
shrieks
shrieking
shrieked
shriek *noun*
shrieks
shrill *adjective*
shriller
shrillest
shrilly
shrillness
shrimp *noun*
shrimps
shrine *noun*
shrines
shrink *verb*
shrinks
shrinking
shrank
shrunk

★ To **shoot** is to fire at someone with a gun. **! chute**.

a b c d e f g h i j k l m n o p q r s t u v w x y z

shrinkage

shrivel *verb*
shrivels
shrivelling
shrivelled

shroud *noun*
shrouds

shroud *verb*
shrouds
shrouding
shrouded

Shrove Tuesday

shrub *noun*
shrubs

shrubbery *noun*
shrubberies

shrug *verb*
shrugs
shrugging
shrugged

shrug *noun*
shrugs

shrunk see **shrink**

shrunken *adjective*

shudder *verb*
shudders
shuddering
shuddered

shudder *noun*
shudders

shuffle *verb*
shuffles
shuffling
shuffled

shuffle *noun*
shuffles

shunt *verb*
shunts
shunting
shunted

shunter *noun*
shunters

shut *verb*
shuts
shutting
shut

shutter *noun*
shutters

shuttle *noun*
shuttles

shuttlecock *noun*
shuttlecocks

shy *adjective*
shyer
shyest
shyly

Siamese

sick *adjective*
sicker
sickest

sicken *verb*
sickens
sickening
sickened

sickly *adjective*
sicklier
sickliest

sickness *noun*
sicknesses

side *noun*
sides

side *verb*
sides
siding
sided

sideboard *noun*
sideboards

sidecar *noun*
sidecars

sideline *noun*
sidelines

sideshow *noun*
sideshows

sideways

siding *noun*
sidings

siege *noun*
sieges

sieve *noun*
sieves

sift *verb*
sifts
sifting
sifted

sigh *verb*
sighs
sighing
sighed

sigh *noun*
sighs

sight★ *noun*
sights

sight *verb*
sights
sighting
sighted

sightseer *noun*
sightseers

sightseeing

sign *verb*
signs
signing
signed

sign *noun*
signs

signal *noun*
signals

signal *verb*
signals
signalling
signalled

signaller *noun*
signallers

signalman *noun*
signalmen

signature *noun*
signatures

★ A **sight** is something you see. **! site**.

signet★ *noun*
signets
significance
significant *adjective*
significantly
signify *verb*
signifies
signifying
signified
signing
signpost *noun*
signposts
Sikh *noun*
Sikhs
silence *noun*
silences
silence *verb*
silences
silencing
silenced
silencer *noun*
silencers
silent *adjective*
silently
silhouette *noun*
silhouettes
silicon
silk
silken
silkworm *noun*
silkworms
silky *adjective*
silkier
silkiest
silkily
sill *noun*
sills
silliness
silly *adjective*
sillier
silliest
sillily

silver
silvery
similar *adjective*
similarly
similarity
simile *noun*
similes
simmer *verb*
simmers
simmering
simmered
simple *adjective*
simpler
simplest
simplicity
simplification
simplify *verb*
simplifies
simplifying
simplified
simply
simulate *verb*
simulates
simulating
simulated
simulation *noun*
simulations
simulator *noun*
simulators
simultaneous *adjective*
simultaneously
sin *noun*
sins
sin *verb*
sins
sinning
sinned
since *preposition, adverb,* and *conjunction*

sincere *adjective*
sincerer
sincerest
sincerely
sincerity
sinew *noun*
sinews
sinful *adjective*
sinfully
sinfulness
sing *verb*
sings
singing
sang
sung
singer *noun*
singers
singe *verb*
singes
singeing
singed
single *adjective*
singly
single *noun*
singles
single *verb*
singles
singling
singled
single-handed
singular *adjective*
singularly
singular *noun*
singulars
sinister *adjective*
sinisterly
sink *verb*
sinks
sinking
sank *or* sunk
sunk
sink *noun*
sinks

★ A **signet** is a seal worn in a ring. **! cygnet**.

a b c d e f g h i j k l m n o p q r **s** t u v w x y z

sinner *noun*
sinners

sinus *noun*
sinuses

sip *verb*
sips
sipping
sipped

siphon *noun*
siphons

siphon *verb*
siphons
siphoning
siphoned

sir

siren *noun*
sirens

sister *noun*
sisters

sisterly

sister-in-law *noun*
sisters-in-law

sit *verb*
sits
sitting
sat

sitter *noun*
sitters

site★ *noun*
sites

site *verb*
sites
siting
sited

sit-in *noun*
sit-ins

situated

situation *noun*
situations

six *noun*
sixes

sixpence *noun*
sixpences

sixteen *noun*
sixteens

sixteenth

sixth

sixthly

sixtieth

sixty *noun*
sixties

size *noun*
sizes

size *verb*
sizes
sizing
sized

sizeable

sizzle *verb*
sizzles
sizzling
sizzled

skate *verb*
skates
skating
skated

skate☆ *noun*
skates *or* skate

skateboard *noun*
skateboards

skater *noun*
skaters

skeletal *adjective*
skeletally

skeleton *noun*
skeletons

sketch *noun*
sketches

sketch *verb*
sketches
sketching
sketched

sketchy *adjective*
sketchier
sketchiest
sketchily

skewer *noun*
skewers

ski *verb*
skis
skiing
skied
ski´d

ski *noun*
skis

skid *verb*
skids
skidding
skidded

skid *noun*
skids

skier *noun*
skiers

skilful *adjective*
skilfully

skill *noun*
skills

skilled

skim *verb*
skims
skimming
skimmed

skimp *verb*
skimps
skimping
skimped

skimpy *adjective*
skimpier
skimpiest
skimpily

skin *noun*
skins

★ A **site** is a place where something will be built. **! sight**.
☆ The plural is **skate** when you mean the fish.

skin *verb*
skins
skinning
skinned

skinny *adjective*
skinnier
skinniest

skint

skip *verb*
skips
skipping
skipped

skip *noun*
skips

skipper *noun*
skippers

skirt *noun*
skirts

skirt *verb*
skirts
skirting
skirted

skirting *noun*
skirtings

skit *noun*
skits

skittish *adjective*
skittishly

skittle *noun*
skittles

skull *noun*
skulls

skunk *noun*
skunks

sky *noun*
skies

skylark *noun*
skylarks

skylight *noun*
skylights

skyscraper *noun*
skyscrapers

slab *noun*
slabs

slack *adjective*
slacker
slackest
slackly

slacken *verb*
slackens
slackening
slackened

slackness

slacks *plural noun*

slag heap *noun*
slag heaps

slain see **slay**

slam *verb*
slams
slamming
slammed

slang

slant *verb*
slants
slanting
slanted

slant *noun*
slants

slap *verb*
slaps
slapping
slapped

slap *noun*
slaps

slapstick

slash *verb*
slashes
slashing
slashed

slash *noun*
slashes

slat *noun*
slats

slate *noun*
slates

slaty *adjective*
slatier
slatiest

slaughter *verb*
slaughters
slaughtering
slaughtered

slaughter *noun*

slaughterhouse *noun*
slaughterhouses

slave *noun*
slaves

slave *verb*
slaves
slaving
slaved

slavery

slay★ *verb*
slays
slaying
slew
slain

sled *noun*
sleds

sledge *noun*
sledges

sledgehammer *noun*
sledgehammers

sleek *adjective*
sleeker
sleekest
sleekly

sleep *verb*
sleeps
sleeping
slept

sleep *noun*

sleeper *noun*
sleepers

sleepiness

sleepless

★ To **slay** people is to kill them. **! sleigh**.

a b c d e f g h i j k l m n o p q r s t u v w x y z

sleepwalker *noun*
sleepwalkers

sleepwalking

sleepy *adjective*
sleepier
sleepiest
sleepily

sleet

sleeve *noun*
sleeves

sleeveless

sleigh★ *noun*
sleighs

slender *adjective*
slenderer
slenderest

slept see **sleep**

slew see **slay**

slice *noun*
slices

slice *verb*
slices
slicing
sliced

slick *adjective*
slicker
slickest
slickly

slick *noun*
slicks

slide *verb*
slides
sliding
slid

slide *noun*
slides

slight *adjective*
slighter
slightest
slightly

slim *adjective*
slimmer
slimmest
slimly

slim *verb*
slims
slimming
slimmed

slime

slimmer *noun*
slimmers

slimy *adjective*
slimier
slimiest

sling *verb*
slings
slinging
slung

sling *noun*
slings

slink *verb*
slinks
slinking
slunk

slip *verb*
slips
slipping
slipped

slip *noun*
slips

slipper *noun*
slippers

slippery

slipshod

slit *noun*
slits

slit *verb*
slits
slitting
slit

slither *verb*
slithers
slithering
slithered

sliver *noun*
slivers

slog *verb*
slogs
slogging
slogged

slog *noun*
slogs

slogan *noun*
slogans

slop *verb*
slops
slopping
slopped

slope *verb*
slopes
sloping
sloped

slope *noun*
slopes

sloppiness

sloppy *adjective*
sloppier
sloppiest
sloppily

slops *plural noun*

slosh *verb*
sloshes
sloshing
sloshed

slot *noun*
slots

sloth *noun*
sloths

slouch *verb*
slouches
slouching
slouched

slovenly

★ A **sleigh** is a vehicle for sliding on snow. **! slay**.

slow *adjective*
slower
slowest
slowly
slow *verb*
slows
slowing
slowed
slowcoach *noun*
slowcoaches
slowness
sludge
slug *noun*
slugs
slum *noun*
slums
slumber
slumber *verb*
slumbers
slumbering
slumbered
slump *verb*
slumps
slumping
slumped
slump *noun*
slumps
slung see **sling**
slunk see **slink**
slur *noun*
slurs
slush
slushy *adjective*
slushier
slushiest
slushily
sly *adjective*
slyer
slyest
slyly
slyness
smack *verb*
smacks
smacking
smacked
smack *noun*
smacks
small *adjective*
smaller
smallest
smallpox
smart *adjective*
smarter
smartest
smartly
smart *verb*
smarts
smarting
smarted
smarten *verb*
smartens
smartening
smartened
smartness
smash *verb*
smashes
smashing
smashed
smash *noun*
smashes
smashing
smear *verb*
smears
smearing
smeared
smear *noun*
smears
smell *verb*
smells
smelling
smelt *or* smelled
smell *noun*
smells
smelly *adjective*
smellier
smelliest
smelt *verb*
smelts
smelting
smelted
smile *noun*
smiles
smile *verb*
smiles
smiling
smiled
smith *noun*
smiths
smithereens *plural noun*
smock *noun*
smocks
smog
smoke *noun*
smoke *verb*
smokes
smoking
smoked
smokeless
smoker *noun*
smokers
smoky *adjective*
smokier
smokiest
smooth *adjective*
smoother
smoothest
smoothly
smooth *verb*
smooths
smoothing
smoothed
smoothness
smother *verb*
smothers
smothering
smothered
smoulder *verb*
smoulders
smouldering
smouldered
smudge *verb*
smudges
smudging
smudged

a b c d e f g h i j k l m n o p q r **s** t u v w x y z

a b c d e f g h i j k l m n o p q r s t u v w x y z

smudge *noun*
smudges

smuggle *verb*
smuggles
smuggling
smuggled

smuggler *noun*
smugglers

smut *noun*
smuts

smutty *adjective*
smuttier
smuttiest
smuttily

snack *noun*
snacks

snag *noun*
snags

snail *noun*
snails

snake *noun*
snakes

snaky *adjective*
snakier
snakiest

snap *verb*
snaps
snapping
snapped

snap *noun*
snaps

snappy *adjective*
snappier
snappiest
snappily

snapshot *noun*
snapshots

snare *noun*
snares

snare *verb*
snares
snaring
snared

snarl *verb*
snarls
snarling
snarled

snarl *noun*
snarls

snatch *verb*
snatches
snatching
snatched

snatch *noun*
snatches

sneak *verb*
sneaks
sneaking
sneaked

sneak *noun*
sneaks

sneaky *adjective*
sneakier
sneakiest
sneakily

sneer *verb*
sneers
sneering
sneered

sneeze *verb*
sneezes
sneezing
sneezed

sneeze *noun*
sneezes

sniff *verb*
sniffs
sniffing
sniffed

sniff *noun*
sniffs

snigger *verb*
sniggers
sniggering
sniggered

snigger *noun*
sniggers

snip *verb*
snips
snipping
snipped

snip *noun*
snips

snipe *verb*
snipes
sniping
sniped

sniper *noun*
snipers

snippet *noun*
snippets

snivel *verb*
snivels
snivelling
snivelled

snob *noun*
snobs

snobbery

snobbish *adjective*
snobbishly

snooker

snoop *verb*
snoops
snooping
snooped

snooper *noun*
snoopers

snore *verb*
snores
snoring
snored

snorkel *noun*
snorkels

snort *verb*
snorts
snorting
snorted

snort *noun*
snorts

snout *noun*
snouts

snow *noun*

snow *verb*
snows
snowing
snowed

snowball *noun*
snowballs

snowdrop *noun*
snowdrops

snowflake *noun*
snowflakes

snowman *noun*
snowmen

snowplough *noun*
snowploughs

snowshoe *noun*
snowshoes

snowstorm *noun*
snowstorms

snowy *adjective*
snowier
snowiest

snub *verb*
snubs
snubbing
snubbed

snuff

snug *adjective*
snugger
snuggest
snugly

snuggle *verb*
snuggles
snuggling
snuggled

soak *verb*
soaks
soaking
soaked

so-and-so *noun*
so-and-so´s

soap *noun*
soaps

soapiness *noun*

soapy *adjective*
soapier
soapiest
soapily

soar★ *verb*
soars
soaring
soared

sob *verb*
sobs
sobbing
sobbed

sob *noun*
sobs

sober *adjective*
soberly

sobriety

so-called

soccer

sociability

sociable *adjective*
sociably

social *adjective*
socially

socialism

socialist *noun*
socialists

society *noun*
societies

sociological *adjective*
sociologically

sociologist *noun*
sociologists

sociology

sock *noun*
socks

sock *verb*
socks
socking
socked

socket *noun*
sockets

soda

sodium

sofa *noun*
sofas

soft *adjective*
softer
softest
softly

soften *verb*
softens
softening
softened

softness

software

soggy *adjective*
soggier
soggiest
soggily

soil *noun*

soil *verb*
soils
soiling
soiled

solar

sold see **sell**

solder *noun*

solder *verb*
solders
soldering
soldered

soldier *noun*
soldiers

sole☆ *noun*
soles

sole *adjective*
solely

solemn *adjective*
solemnly

solemnity

★ To **soar** is to rise or fly high. **! sore**.
☆ A **sole** is a sh or a part of a shoe. **! soul**.

solicitor *noun*
solicitors
solid *adjective*
solidly
solid *noun*
solids
solidify *verb*
solidifies
solidifying
solidified
solidity
soliloquy *noun*
soliloquies
solitary
solitude
solo *noun*
solos
soloist *noun*
soloists
solstice *noun*
solstices
solubility
soluble *adjective*
solubly
solution *noun*
solutions
solve *verb*
solves
solving
solved
solvent *adjective* and *noun*
solvents
sombre *adjective*
sombrely
some★ *adjective* and *pronoun*
somebody
somehow
someone
somersault *noun*
somersaults
something
sometime
sometimes
somewhat
somewhere
son☆ *noun*
sons
sonar *noun*
sonars
song *noun*
songs
songbird *noun*
songbirds
sonic *adjective*
sonically
sonnet *noun*
sonnets
soon *adverb*
sooner
soonest
soot
soothe *verb*
soothes
soothing
soothed
sooty *adjective*
sootier
sootiest
sophisticated
sophistication
sopping
soppy *adjective*
soppier
soppiest
soppily
soprano *noun*
sopranos
sorcerer *noun*
sorcerers
sorceress *noun*
sorceresses
sorcery
sore✪ *adjective*
sorer
sorest
sorely
sore *noun*
sores
soreness
sorrow *noun*
sorrows
sorrowful *adjective*
sorrowfully
sorry *adjective*
sorrier
sorriest
sort *noun*
sorts
sort *verb*
sorts
sorting
sorted
sought see **seek**
soul✣ *noun*
souls
sound *noun*
sounds
sound *verb*
sounds
sounding
sounded
sound *adjective*
sounder
soundest
soundly

★ You use **some** in e.g. *Have some cake.* **! sum**.
☆ A **son** is a male child. **! sun**.
✪ You use **sore** in e.g. *I've got a sore tooth.* **! soar**.
✣ A **soul** is a person's spirit. **! sole**.

soundness
soundtrack *noun*
soundtracks
soup *noun*
soups
sour *adjective*
sourer
sourest
sourly
source★ *noun*
sources
sourness
south *adjective* and *adverb*
south☆ *noun*
south-east *noun and adjective*
southerly *adjective* and *noun*
southerlies
southern *adjective*
southerner *noun*
southerners
southward *adjective* and *adverb*
southwards *adverb*
south-west *noun* and *adjective*
souvenir *noun*
souvenirs
sovereign *noun*
sovereigns
sow✪ *verb*
sows
sowing
sowed
sown
sow *noun*
sows

sower *noun*
sowers
soya bean *noun*
soya beans
space *noun*
spaces
space *verb*
spaces
spacing
spaced
spacecraft *noun*
spacecraft
spaceman *noun*
spacemen
spaceship *noun*
spaceships
spacewoman *noun*
spacewomen
spacious *adjective*
spaciously
spaciousness
spade *noun*
spades
spaghetti
span *verb*
spans
spanning
spanned
span *noun*
spans
spaniel *noun*
spaniels
spank *verb*
spanks
spanking
spanked
spanner *noun*
spanners
spar *noun*
spars

spar *verb*
spars
sparring
sparred
spare *verb*
spares
sparing
spared
spare *adjective* and *noun*
spares
sparing *adjective*
sparingly
spark *noun*
sparks
spark *verb*
sparks
sparking
sparked
sparkle *verb*
sparkles
sparkling
sparkled
sparkler *noun*
sparklers
sparrow *noun*
sparrows
sparse *adjective*
sparser
sparsest
sparsely
sparseness
spastic *noun*
spastics
spat see **spit**
spatter *verb*
spatters
spattering
spattered
spawn *noun*

★ The **source** is where something comes from. **! sauce**.
☆ You use a capital S in **the South**, when you mean a particular region.
✪ To **sow** is to put seed in the ground. **! sew**.

a b c d e f g h i j k l m n o p q r s t u v w x y z

spawn *verb*
spawns
spawning
spawned

speak *verb*
speaks
speaking
spoke
spoken

speaker *noun*
speakers

spear *noun*
spears

spear *verb*
spears
spearing
speared

special *adjective*
specially

specialist *noun*
specialists

speciality *noun*
specialities

specialization

specialize *verb*
specializes
specializing
specialized

species *noun*
species

specific *adjective*
specifically

specification *noun*
specifications

specify *verb*
specifies
specifying
specified

specimen *noun*
specimens

speck *noun*
specks

speckled

spectacle *noun*
spectacles

spectacular *adjective*
spectacularly

spectator *noun*
spectators

spectre *noun*
spectres

spectrum *noun*
spectra

speech *noun*
speeches

speechless

speed *noun*
speeds

speed★ *verb*
speeds
speeding
sped *or* speeded

speedboat *noun*
speedboats

speedometer *noun*
speedometers

speedway *noun*
speedways

speedy *adjective*
speedier
speediest
speedily

spell *verb*
spells
spelling
spelt
spelled

spell *noun*
spells

spelling *noun*
spellings

spend *verb*
spends
spending
spent

sperm *noun*
sperms *or* sperm

sphere *noun*
spheres

spherical *adjective*
spherically

spice *noun*
spices

spicy *adjective*
spicier
spiciest

spider *noun*
spiders

spied see **spy**

spike *noun*
spikes

spiky *adjective*
spikier
spikiest

spill☆ *verb*
spills
spilling
spilt *or* spilled

spill *noun*
spills

spin *verb*
spins
spinning
spun

★ You use **sped** in e.g. *Cars sped past* and **speeded** in e.g. *They speeded up the process.*

☆ You use **spilled** in e.g. *I spilled the milk*. You use **spilt** in e.g. *I can see spilt milk*. You use **spilled** or **spilt** in e.g. *I have spilled/spilt the milk.*

spin *noun*
spins
spinach
spindle *noun*
spindles
spin-drier *noun*
spin-driers
spine *noun*
spines
spinal
spin-off *noun*
spin-offs
spinster *noun*
spinsters
spiny *adjective*
spiniest
spiniest
spiral *adjective*
spirally
spire *noun*
spires
spirit *noun*
spirits
spiritual *adjective*
spiritually
spiritual *noun*
spirituals
spiritualism
spiritualist *noun*
spiritualists
spit *verb*
spits
spitting
spat
spit *noun*
spits
spite
spiteful *adjective*
spitefully
spittle

splash *verb*
splashes
splashing
splashed
splash *noun*
splashes
splashdown *noun*
splashdowns
splendid *adjective*
splendidly
splendour
splint *noun*
splints
splinter *noun*
splinters
splinter *verb*
splinters
splintering
splintered
split *verb*
splits
splitting
split
split *noun*
splits
splutter *verb*
splutters
spluttering
spluttered
spoil★ *verb*
spoils
spoiling
spoilt *or* spoiled
spoils *plural noun*
spoilsport *noun*
spoilsports
spoke *noun*
spokes
spoke see **speak**
spoken see **speak**

spokesperson *noun*
spokespersons
sponge *noun*
sponges
sponge *verb*
sponges
sponging
sponged
sponger *noun*
spongers
sponginess *noun*
spongy *adjective*
spongier
spongiest
spongily
sponsor *noun*
sponsors
sponsorship *noun*
sponsorships
spontaneity
spontaneous *adjective*
spontaneously
spooky *adjective*
spookier
spookiest
spookily
spool *noun*
spools
spoon *noun*
spoons
spoon *verb*
spoons
spooning
spooned
spoonful *noun*
spoonfuls
sport *noun*
sports
sporting

★ You use **spoiled** in e.g. *They spoiled the party*. You use **spoilt** in e.g. *a spoilt child*. You use **spoiled** or **spoilt** in e.g. *They have spoiled/spoilt the party*.

a b c d e f g h i j k l m n o p q r s t u v w x y z

sportsman *noun*
sportsmen

sportsmanship

sportswoman *noun*
sportswomen

spot *noun*
spots

spot *verb*
spots
spotting
spotted

spotless *adjective*
spotlessly

spotlight *noun*
spotlights

spotter *noun*
spotters

spotty *adjective*
spottier
spottiest
spottily

spout *noun*
spouts

spout *verb*
spouts
spouting
spouted

sprain *verb*
sprains
spraining
sprained

sprain *noun*
sprains

sprang see **spring**

sprawl *verb*
sprawls
sprawling
sprawled

spray *verb*
sprays
spraying
sprayed

spray *noun*
sprays

spread *verb*
spreads
spreading
spread

spread *noun*
spreads

spreadsheet *noun*
spreadsheets

sprightliness

sprightly *adjective*
sprightlier
sprightliest

spring *verb*
springs
springing
sprang
sprung

spring *noun*
springs

springboard *noun*
springboards

spring-clean *verb*
spring-cleans
spring-cleaning
spring-cleaned

springtime

springy *adjective*
springier
springiest

sprinkle *verb*
sprinkles
sprinkling
sprinkled

sprinkler *noun*
sprinklers

sprint *verb*
sprints
sprinting
sprinted

sprinter *noun*
sprinters

sprout *verb*
sprouts
sprouting
sprouted

sprout *noun*
sprouts

spruce *noun*
spruces

spruce *adjective*
sprucer
sprucest

sprung see **spring**

spud *noun*
spuds

spun see **spin**

spur *noun*
spurs

spur *verb*
spurs
spurring
spurred

spurt *verb*
spurts
spurting
spurted

spurt *noun*
spurts

spy *noun*
spies

spy *verb*
spies
spying
spied

squabble *verb*
squabbles
squabbling
squabbled

squabble *noun*
squabbles

squad *noun*
squads

squadron *noun*
squadrons

squalid *adjective*
squalidly

squall *noun*
squalls

squally *adjective*
squallier
squalliest

squalor

squander *verb*
squanders
squandering
squandered

square *adjective*
squarely

square *noun*
squares

square *verb*
squares
squaring
squared

squareness

squash *verb*
squashes
squashing
squashed

squash *noun*
squashes

squat *verb*
squats
squatting
squatted

squat *adjective*
squatter
squattest
squatly

squatter *noun*
squatters

squaw *noun*
squaws

squawk *verb*
squawks
squawking
squawked

squawk *noun*
squawks

squeak *verb*
squeaks
squeaking
squeaked

squeak *noun*
squeaks

squeaky *adjective*
squeakier
squeakiest
squeakily

squeal *verb*
squeals
squealing
squealed

squeal *noun*
squeals

squeeze *verb*
squeezes
squeezing
squeezed

squeeze *noun*
squeezes

squeezer *noun*
squeezers

squelch *verb*
squelches
squelching
squelched

squelch *noun*
squelches

squid *noun*
squid
squids

squint *verb*
squints
squinting
squinted

squint *noun*
squints

squire *noun*
squires

squirm *verb*
squirms
squirming
squirmed

squirrel *noun*
squirrels

squirt *verb*
squirts
squirting
squirted

stab *verb*
stabs
stabbing
stabbed

stab *noun*
stabs

stability

stabilize *verb*
stabilizes
stabilizing
stabilized

stabilizer *noun*
stabilizers

stable *adjective*
stabler
stablest
stably

stable *noun*
stables

stack *verb*
stacks
stacking
stacked

stack *noun*
stacks

stadium *noun*
stadiums *or* stadia

staff *noun*
staffs

stag *noun*
stags

stage *noun*
stages

stage *verb*
stages
staging
staged

stagecoach *noun*
stagecoaches

a b c d e f g h i j k l m n o p q r s t u v w x y z

stagger *verb*
staggers
staggering
staggered

stagnant *adjective*
stagnantly

stain *noun*
stains

stain *verb*
stains
staining
stained

stainless

stair★ *noun*
stairs

staircase *noun*
staircases

stake☆ *noun*
stakes

stake *verb*
stakes
staking
staked

stalactite *noun*
stalactites

stalagmite *noun*
stalagmites

stale *adjective*
staler
stalest

stalk *noun*
stalks

stalk *verb*
stalks
stalking
stalked

stall *noun*
stalls

stall *verb*
stalls
stalling
stalled

stallion *noun*
stallions

stalls *plural noun*

stamen *noun*
stamens

stamina

stammer *verb*
stammers
stammering
stammered

stammer *noun*
stammers

stamp *noun*
stamps

stamp *verb*
stamps
stamping
stamped

stampede *noun*
stampedes

stand *verb*
stands
standing
stood

stand *noun*
stands

standard *adjective*
and *noun*
standards

standardize *verb*
standardizes
standardizing
standardized

standby *noun*
standbys

standstill *noun*
standstills

stank see **stink**

stanza *noun*
stanzas

staple *noun*
staples

staple *adjective*

stapler *noun*
staplers

star *noun*
stars

starry *adjective*
starrier
starriest
starrily

star *verb*
stars
starring
starred

starboard

starch *noun*
starches

starchy *adjective*
starchier
starchiest

stare✪ *verb*
stares
staring
stared

starfish *noun*
starfish *or* starfishes

starling *noun*
starlings

start *verb*
starts
starting
started

start *noun*
starts

starter *noun*
starters

★ A **stair** is one of a set of steps. **! stare**.
☆ A **stake** is a pointed stick or post. **! steak**.
✪ To **stare** is to look at something without moving your eyes. **! stair**.

startle *verb*
startles
startling
startled

starvation

starve *verb*
starves
starving
starved

state *noun*
states

state *verb*
states
stating
stated

stateliness

stately *adjective*
statelier
stateliest

statement *noun*
statements

statesman *noun*
statesmen

statesmanship

stateswoman *noun*
stateswomen

static *adjective*
statically

station *noun*
stations

station *verb*
stations
stationing
stationed

stationary★ *adjective*

stationery☆ *noun*

stationmaster *noun*
stationmasters

statistic *noun*
statistics

statistical *adjective*
statistically

statistician *noun*
statisticians

statistics

statue *noun*
statues

status *noun*
statuses

staunch *adjective*
stauncher
staunchest
staunchly

stave *noun*
staves

stave *verb*
staves
staving
staved
stove

stay *verb*
stays
staying
stayed

stay *noun*
stays

steadiness

steady *adjective*
steadier
steadiest
steadily

steady *verb*
steadies
steadying
steadied

steak✪ *noun*
steaks

steal✣ *verb*
steals
stealing
stole
stolen

stealth

stealthy *adjective*
stealthier
stealthiest
stealthily

steam *noun*

steam *verb*
steams
steaming
steamed

steamy *adjective*
steamier
steamiest
steamily

steamer *noun*
steamers

steamroller *noun*
steamrollers

steamship *noun*
steamships

steed *noun*
steeds

steel *noun*

steel✹ *verb*
steels
steeling
steeled

steely *adjective*
steelier
steeliest

steep *adjective*
steeper
steepest
steeply

★ **Stationary** means 'not moving'. **! stationery**.
☆ **Stationery** means 'paper and envelopes'. **! stationary**.
✪ A **steak** is a thick slice of meat. **! stake**.
✣ To **steal** is to take something that is not yours. **! steel**.
✹ To **steel** yourself is to find courage to do something hard. **! steal**.

a b c d e f g h i j k l m n o p q r s t u v w x y z

steepness

steeple *noun*
steeples

steeplechase *noun*
steeplechases

steeplejack *noun*
steeplejacks

steer *verb*
steers
steering
steered

steer *noun*
steers

stem *noun*
stems

stem *verb*
stems
stemming
stemmed

stench *noun*
stenches

stencil *noun*
stencils

step★ *noun*
steps

step *verb*
steps
stepping
stepped

stepchild *noun*
stepchildren

stepfather *noun*
stepfathers

stepladder *noun*
stepladders

stepmother *noun*
stepmothers

steppe☆ *noun*
steppes

stereo *adjective* and *noun*
stereos

stereophonic *adjective*
stereophonically

sterile

sterility

sterilization

sterilize *verb*
sterilizes
sterilizing
sterilized

sterling

stern *noun*
sterns

stern *adjective*
sterner
sternest
sternly

sternness

stethoscope *noun*
stethoscopes

stew *verb*
stews
stewing
stewed

stew *noun*
stews

steward *noun*
stewards

stewardess *noun*
stewardesses

stick *verb*
sticks
sticking
stuck

stick *noun*
sticks

sticker *noun*
stickers

stickiness

stickleback *noun*
sticklebacks

sticky *adjective*
stickier
stickiest
stickily

stiff *adjective*
stiffer
stiffest
stiffly

stiffen *verb*
stiffens
stiffening
stiffened

stiffness

stifle *verb*
stifles
stifling
stifled

stile *noun*
stiles

still *adjective*
stiller
stillest

still *adverb*

still *verb*
stills
stilling
stilled

stillness

stilts

stimulant *noun*
stimulants

stimulate *verb*
stimulates
stimulating
stimulated

stimulation

stimulus *noun*
stimuli

sting *noun*
stings

★ A **step** is a movement of the feet or part of a stair. **! steppe**.
☆ A **steppe** is a grassy plain. **! step**.

sting *verb*
stings
stinging
stung

stingy *adjective*
stingier
stingiest
stingily

stink *noun*
stinks

stink *verb*
stinks
stinking
stank
stunk

stir *verb*
stirs
stirring
stirred

stir *noun*
stirs

stirrup *noun*
stirrups

stitch *noun*
stitches

stoat *noun*
stoats

stock *noun*
stocks

stock *verb*
stocks
stocking
stocked

stockade *noun*
stockades

stockbroker *noun*
stockbrokers

stocking *noun*
stockings

stockpile *noun*
stockpiles

stocks *plural noun*

stocky *adjective*
stockier
stockiest
stockily

stodgy *adjective*
stodgier
stodgiest
stodgily

stoke *verb*
stokes
stoking
stoked

stole *noun*
stoles

stole see **steal**

stolen see **steal**

stomach *noun*
stomachs

stomach *verb*
stomachs
stomaching
stomached

stone *noun*
stones *or* stone

stone *verb*
stones
stoning
stoned

stony *adjective*
stonier
stoniest

stood see **stand**

stool *noun*
stools

stoop *verb*
stoops
stooping
stooped

stop *verb*
stops
stopping
stopped

stop *noun*
stops

stoppage *noun*
stoppages

stopper *noun*
stoppers

stopwatch *noun*
stopwatches

storage

store *verb*
stores
storing
stored

store *noun*
stores

storey★ *noun*
storeys

stork *noun*
storks

storm *noun*
storms

storm *verb*
storms
storming
stormed

stormy *adjective*
stormier
stormiest
stormily

story☆ *noun*
stories

stout *adjective*
stouter
stoutest
stoutly

stoutness

stove *noun*
stoves

★ A **storey** is a floor of a building. **! story**.
☆ You use **story** in e.g. *read me a story.* **! storey**.

a b c d e f g h i j k l m n o p q r s t u v w x y z

stove see **stave**

stow *verb*
stows
stowing
stowed

stowaway *noun*
stowaways

straddle *verb*
straddles
straddling
straddled

straggle *verb*
straggles
straggling
straggled

straggler *noun*
stragglers

straggly *adjective*
stragglier
straggliest

straight★ *adjective*
straighter
straightest

straighten *verb*
straightens
straightening
straightened

straightforward *adjective*
straightforwardly

strain *verb*
strains
straining
strained

strain *noun*
strains

strainer *noun*
strainers

strait☆ *noun*
straits

straits✪ *plural noun*

strand *noun*
strands

stranded

strange *adjective*
stranger
strangest
strangely

strangeness

stranger *noun*
strangers

strangle *verb*
strangles
strangling
strangled

strangler *noun*
stranglers

strangulation

strap *noun*
straps

strap *verb*
straps
strapping
strapped

strategic *adjective*
strategically

strategist *noun*
strategists

strategy *noun*
strategies

stratum *noun*
strata

straw *noun*
straws

strawberry *noun*
strawberries

stray *verb*
strays
straying
strayed

stray *adjective*

streak *noun*
streaks

streak *verb*
streaks
streaking
streaked

streaky *adjective*
streakier
streakiest
streakily

stream *noun*
streams

stream *verb*
streams
streaming
streamed

streamer *noun*
streamers

streamline *verb*
streamlines
streamlining
streamlined

street *noun*
streets

strength *noun*
strengths

strengthen *verb*
strengthens
strengthening
strengthened

strenuous *adjective*
strenuously

stress *noun*
stresses

stress *verb*
stresses
stressing
stressed

stretch *verb*
stretches
stretching
stretched

★ **Straight** means 'not curving or bending'. **! strait**.
☆ A **strait** is a narrow stretch of water. **! straight**.
✪ You use **straits** in the phrase *in dire straits*.

stretch *noun*
stretches

stretcher *noun*
stretchers

strew *verb*
strews
strewing
strewed
strewn

stricken

strict *adjective*
stricter
strictest
strictly

strictness

stride *verb*
strides
striding
strode
stridden

stride *noun*
strides

strife

strike *verb*
strikes
striking
struck

strike *noun*
strikes

striker *noun*
strikers

striking *adjective*
strikingly

string *noun*
strings

string *verb*
strings
stringing
strung

stringiness

stringy *adjective*
stringier
stringiest
stringily

strip *verb*
strips
stripping
stripped

strip *noun*
strips

stripe *noun*
stripes

striped

stripy *adjective*
stripier
stripiest

strive *verb*
strives
striving
strove
striven

strobe *noun*
strobes

strode see **stride**

stroke *noun*
strokes

stroke *verb*
strokes
stroking
stroked

stroll *verb*
strolls
strolling
strolled

stroll *noun*
strolls

strong *adjective*
stronger
strongest
strongly

stronghold *noun*
strongholds

strove see **strive**

struck see **strike**

structural *adjective*
structurally

structure *noun*
structures

struggle *verb*
struggles
struggling
struggled

struggle *noun*
struggles

strum *verb*
strums
strumming
strummed

strung see **string**

strut *verb*
struts
strutting
strutted

strut *noun*
struts

stub *verb*
stubs
stubbing
stubbed

stub *noun*
stubs

stubble

stubborn *adjective*
stubbornly

stubbornness

stuck see **stick**

stuck-up

stud *noun*
studs

student *noun*
students

studio *noun*
studios

studious *adjective*
studiously

study *verb*
studies
studying
studied

study *noun*
studies

stuff *noun*

stuff *verb*
stuffs
stuffing
stuffed

stuffiness

stuffing *noun*
stuffings

stuffy *adjective*
stuffier
stuffiest
stuffily

stumble *verb*
stumbles
stumbling
stumbled

stump *noun*
stumps

stump *verb*
stumps
stumping
stumped

stun *verb*
stuns
stunning
stunned

stung see **sting**

stunk see **stink**

stunt *noun*
stunts

stupendous *adjective*
stupendously

stupid *adjective*
stupider
stupidest
stupidly

stupidity

sturdiness

sturdy *adjective*
sturdier
sturdiest
sturdily

stutter *verb*
stutters
stuttering
stuttered

stutter *noun*
stutters

sty★ *noun*
sties

style *noun*
styles

style *verb*
styles
styling
styled

stylish *adjective*
stylishly

stylus *noun*
styluses

subcontinent *noun*
subcontinents

subdivide *verb*
subdivides
subdividing
subdivided

subdivision *noun*
subdivisions

subdue *verb*
subdues
subduing
subdued

subject *adjective* and *noun*
subjects

subject *verb*
subjects
subjecting
subjected

subjective *adjective*
subjectively

submarine *noun*
submarines

submerge *verb*
submerges
submerging
submerged

submersion

submission *noun*
submissions

submissive *adjective*
submissively

submit *verb*
submits
submitting
submitted

subordinate *adjective* and *noun*
subordinates

subordinate *verb*
subordinates
subordinating
subordinated

subordination

subscribe *verb*
subscribes
subscribing
subscribed

subscriber *noun*
subscribers

subscription *noun*
subscriptions

subsequent *adjective*
subsequently

subside *verb*
subsides
subsiding
subsided

subsidence

subsidize *verb*
subsidizes
subsidizing
subsidized

subsidy *noun*
subsidies

★ A **sty** is a place for pigs or a swelling on the eye. In the second meaning you can also use *stye*, plural *styes*.

substance *noun*
substances

substantial *adjective*
substantially

substitute *verb*
substitutes
substituting
substituted

substitute *noun*
substitutes

substitution *noun*
substitutions

subtle *adjective*
subtler
subtlest
subtly

subtlety *noun*
subtleties

subtract *verb*
subtracts
subtracting
subtracted

subtraction *noun*
subtractions

suburb *noun*
suburbs

suburban

suburbia

subway *noun*
subways

succeed *verb*
succeeds
succeeding
succeeded

success *noun*
successes

successful *adjective*
successfully

succession *noun*
successions

successive *adjective*
successively

successor *noun*
successors

such

suck *verb*
sucks
sucking
sucked

suck *noun*
sucks

suction

sudden *adjective*
suddenly

suddenness

suds *plural noun*

sue *verb*
sues
suing
sued

suede

suet

suffer *verb*
suffers
suffering
suffered

sufficiency

sufficient *adjective*
sufficiently

suffix *noun*
suffixes

suffocate *verb*
suffocates
suffocating
suffocated

suffocation

sugar

sugary

suggest *verb*
suggests
suggesting
suggested

suggestion *noun*
suggestions

suicidal *adjective*
suicidally

suicide *noun*
suicides

suit★ *noun*
suits

suit *verb*
suits
suiting
suited

suitability

suitable *adjective*
suitably

suitcase *noun*
suitcases

suite☆ *noun*
suites

suitor *noun*
suitors

sulk *verb*
sulks
sulking
sulked

sulkiness

sulky *adjective*
sulkier
sulkiest
sulkily

sullen *adjective*
sullenly

sullenness

sulphur

sulphuric acid

sultan *noun*
sultans

sultana *noun*
sultanas

★ A **suit** is a set of matching clothes. **! suite**.
☆ A **suite** is a set of furniture or a group of rooms. **! suit**.

a b c d e f g h i j k l m n o p q r s t u v w x y z

sum★ *noun*
sums

sum *verb*
sums
summing
summed

summarize *verb*
summarizes
summarizing
summarized

summary *noun*
summaries

summer *noun*
summers

summertime

summit *noun*
summits

summon *verb*
summons
summoning
summoned

summons *noun*
summonses

sun☆ *noun*
suns

sun *verb*
suns
sunning
sunned

sunbathe *verb*
sunbathes
sunbathing
sunbathed

sunburn

sunburned or **sunburnt**

sundae✪ *noun*
sundaes

Sunday✣ *noun*
Sundays

sundial *noun*
sundials

sunflower *noun*
sunflowers

sung see **sing**

sunglasses

sunk see **sink**

sunlight

sunlit

sunny *adjective*
sunnier
sunniest
sunnily

sunrise *noun*
sunrises

sunset *noun*
sunsets

sunshade *noun*
sunshades

sunshine

sunspot *noun*
sunspots

sunstroke

suntan *noun*
suntans

suntanned

super

> **super-**
> *super-* makes words meaning 'very good' or 'extra', e.g. **supermarket**, **supermodel**. They are normally spelt joined up.

superb *adjective*
superbly

superficial *adjective*
superficially

superfluous *adjective*
superfluously

superintend *verb*
superintends
superintending
superintended

superintendent *noun*
superintendents

superior *adjective* and *noun*
superiors

superiority

superlative *adjective*
superlatively

superlative *noun*
superlatives

supermarket *noun*
supermarkets

supernatural *adjective*
supernaturally

supersonic *adjective*
supersonically

superstition *noun*
superstitions

superstitious *adjective*
superstitiously

supervise *verb*
supervises
supervising
supervised

supervision

supervisor

supper *noun*
suppers

★ A **sum** is an amount or total. **! some**.
☆ A **sun** is a large star. **! son**.
✪ A **sundae** is a cocktail of fruit and ice cream. **! Sunday**.
✣ **Sunday** is a day of the week. **! sundae**.

supple *adjective*
supplier
supplest
supplely

supplement *noun*
supplements

supplementary

suppleness

supply *verb*
supplies
supplying
supplied

supplier *noun*
suppliers

supply *noun*
supplies

support *verb*
supports
supporting
supported

support *noun*
supports

supporter *noun*
supporters

suppose *verb*
supposes
supposing
supposed

supposedly

supposition *noun*
suppositions

suppress *verb*
suppresses
suppressing
suppressed

suppression

supremacy

supreme *adjective*
supremely

sure *adjective*
surer
surest
surely

surf *noun*

surf *verb*
surfs
surfing
surfed

surface *noun*
surfaces

surface *verb*
surfaces
surfacing
surfaced

surfboard *noun*
surfboards

surfer *noun*
surfers

surge *verb*
surges
surging
surged

surge *noun*
surges

surgeon *noun*
surgeons

surgery *noun*
surgeries

surgical *adjective*
surgically

surname *noun*
surnames

surpass *verb*
surpasses
surpassing
surpassed

surplus *noun*
surpluses

surprise *verb*
surprises
surprising
surprised

surprise *noun*
surprises

surrender *verb*
surrenders
surrendering
surrendered

surrender *noun*
surrenders

surround *verb*
surrounds
surrounding
surrounded

surroundings *plural noun*

survey *noun*
surveys

survey *verb*
surveys
surveying
surveyed

surveyor *noun*
surveyors

survival

survive *verb*
survives
surviving
survived

survivor *noun*
survivors

suspect *verb*
suspects
suspecting
suspected

suspect *noun*
suspects

suspend *verb*
suspends
suspending
suspended

suspense

suspension *noun*
suspensions

suspicion *noun*
suspicions

suspicious *adjective*
suspiciously

sustain *verb*
sustains
sustaining
sustained

swagger *verb*
swaggers
swaggering
swaggered

swallow *verb*
swallows
swallowing
swallowed

swallow *noun*
swallows

swam see **swim**

swamp *verb*
swamps
swamping
swamped

swamp *noun*
swamps

swampy *adjective*
swampier
swampiest

swan *noun*
swans

swank *verb*
swanks
swanking
swanked

swap *verb*
swaps
swapping
swapped

swap *noun*
swaps

swarm *noun*
swarms

swarm *verb*
swarms
swarming
swarmed

swastika *noun*
swastikas

swat★ *verb*
swats
swatting
swatted

swatter *noun*
swatters

sway *verb*
sways
swaying
swayed

swear *verb*
swears
swearing
swore
sworn

sweat *verb*
sweats
sweating
sweated

sweat *noun*

sweater *noun*
sweaters

sweatshirt *noun*
sweatshirts

sweaty *adjective*
sweatier
sweatiest
sweatily

swede *noun*
swedes

sweep *verb*
sweeps
sweeping
swept

sweep *noun*
sweeps

sweeper *noun*
sweepers

sweet *adjective*
sweeter
sweetest
sweetly

sweet *noun*
sweets

sweetcorn

sweeten *verb*
sweetens
sweetening
sweetened

sweetener *noun*
sweeteners

sweetheart *noun*
sweethearts

sweetness

swell *verb*
swells
swelling
swelled
swollen

swell *noun*
swells

swelling *noun*
swellings

swelter *verb*
swelters
sweltering
sweltered

swept see **sweep**

swerve *verb*
swerves
swerving
swerved

swerve *noun*
swerves

swift *adjective*
swifter
swiftest
swiftly

swift *noun*
swifts

swiftness

swill *verb*
swills
swilling
swilled

swill *noun*

★ To **swat** an insect is to hit it. **! swot**.

swim *verb*
swims
swimming
swam
swum

swim *noun*
swims

swimmer *noun*
swimmers

swimsuit *noun*
swimsuits

swindle *verb*
swindles
swindling
swindled

swindler *noun*
swindlers

swindle *noun*
swindles

swine *noun*
swine *or* swines

swing *verb*
swings
swinging
swung

swing *noun*
swings

swipe *verb*
swipes
swiping
swiped

swipe *noun*
swipes

swirl *verb*
swirls
swirling
swirled

swirl *noun*
swirls

swish *verb*
swishes
swishing
swished

swish *noun*
swishes

Swiss roll *noun*
Swiss rolls

switch *verb*
switches
switching
switched

switch *noun*
switches

switchboard *noun*
switchboards

swivel *verb*
swivels
swivelling
swivelled

swollen see **swell**

swoon *verb*
swoons
swooning
swooned

swoop *verb*
swoops
swooping
swooped

swoop *noun*
swoops

swop *verb*
swops
swopping
swopped

sword *noun*
swords

swore see **swear**

sworn see **swear**

swot★ *verb*
swots
swotting
swotted

swot *noun*
swots

swum see **swim**

swung see **swing**

sycamore *noun*
sycamores

syllabic *adjective*
syllabically

syllable *noun*
syllables

syllabus *noun*
syllabuses

symbol *noun*
symbols

symbolic *adjective*
symbolically

symbolism

symbolize *verb*
symbolizes
symbolizing
symbolized

symmetrical *adjective*
symmetrically

symmetry

sympathetic *adjective*
sympathetically

sympathize *verb*
sympathizes
sympathizing
sympathized

sympathy *noun*
sympathies

symphonic *adjective*
symphonically

symphony *noun*
symphonies

symptom *noun*
symptoms

symptomatic *adjective*
symptomatically

synagogue *noun*
synagogues

synchronization

★ To **swot** is to study hard. **! swat**.

a b c d e f g h i j k l m n o p q r **s** t u v w x y z

a b c d e f g h i j k l m n o p q r s t u v w x y z

tentacle *noun*
tentacles

tenth

tenthly

tepid

term *noun*
terms

term *verb*
terms
terming
termed

terminal *noun*
terminals

terminate *verb*
terminates
terminating
terminated

termination *noun*
terminations

terminus *noun*
termini

terrace *noun*
terraces

terrapin *noun*
terrapins

terrible *adjective*
terribly

terrier *noun*
terriers

terrific *adjective*
terrifically

terrify *verb*
terrifies
terrifying
terrified

territorial *adjective*
territorially

territory *noun*
territories

terror *noun*
terrors

terrorism

terrorist *adjective* and *noun*
terrorists

terrorize *verb*
terrorizes
terrorizing
terrorized

tessellation *noun*
tessellations

test *noun*
tests

test *verb*
tests
testing
tested

testament *noun*
testaments

testicle *noun*
testicles

testify *verb*
testifies
testifying
testified

testimonial *noun*
testimonials

testimony *noun*
testimonies

testy *adjective*
testier
testiest

tether *verb*
tethers
tethering
tethered

tether *noun*
tethers

text *noun*
texts

textbook *noun*
textbooks

textile *noun*
textiles

texture *noun*
textures

than

thank *verb*
thanks
thanking
thanked

thankful *adjective*
thankfully

thankless *adjective*
thanklessly

thanks *plural noun*

that *adjective, pronoun,* and *conjunction*

thatch *noun*

thatch *verb*
thatches
thatching
thatched

thatcher *noun*
thatchers

thaw *verb*
thaws
thawing
thawed

theatre *noun*
theatres

theatrical *adjective*
theatrically

thee

theft *noun*
thefts

their★

theirs☆

them

★ You use **their** in e.g. *this is their house.* **! there**, **they´re**.
☆ You use **theirs** in e.g. *the house is theirs.* Note that there is no apostrophe in this word.

theme *noun*
themes
theme park *noun*
theme parks
themselves
then
theologian *noun*
theologians
theological *adjective*
theologically
theology
theorem *noun*
theorems
theoretical *adjective*
theoretically
theory *noun*
theories
therapist *noun*
therapists
therapy *noun*
therapies
there★ *adverb*
thereabouts
therefore
thermal *adjective*
thermally
thermometer *noun*
thermometers
Thermos *noun*
Thermoses
thermostat *noun*
thermostats
thermostatic *adjective*
thermostatically
thesaurus *noun*
thesauri *or* thesauruses
these
they
they'd *verb*
they'll *verb*
they're☆ *verb*
they've *verb*
thick *adjective*
thicker
thickest
thickly
thicken *verb*
thickens
thickening
thickened
thicket *noun*
thickets
thickness *noun*
thicknesses
thief *noun*
thieves
thigh *noun*
thighs
thimble *noun*
thimbles
thin *adjective*
thinner
thinnest
thinly
thin *verb*
thins
thinning
thinned
thine
thing *noun*
things
think *verb*
thinks
thinking
thought
thinker *noun*
thinkers
thinness
third
thirdly
Third World
thirst
thirsty *adjective*
thirstier
thirstiest
thirstily
thirteen
thirteenth
thirtieth
thirty *noun*
thirties
this
thistle *noun*
thistles
thorn *noun*
thorns
thorny *adjective*
thornier
thorniest
thorough *adjective*
thoroughly
thoroughness
those
thou
though
thought *noun*
thoughts
thought see **think**
thoughtful *adjective*
thoughtfully
thoughtfulness
thoughtless *adjective*
thoughtlessly
thoughtlessness
thousand *noun*
thousands
thousandth

★ You use **there** in e.g. *Look over there.* **! their**, **they´re**.
☆ **They´re** is short for *they are.* **! their**, **there**.

a b c d e f g h i j k l m n o p q r s t u v w x y z

thrash★ *verb*
thrashes
thrashing
thrashed

thread *noun*
threads

thread *verb*
threads
threading
threaded

threadbare

threat *noun*
threats

threaten *verb*
threatens
threatening
threatened

three *noun*
threes

three-dimensional *adjective*
three-dimensionally

thresh☆ *verb*
threshes
threshing
threshed

threshold *noun*
thresholds

threw see **throw**

thrift

thrifty *adjective*
thriftier
thriftiest
thriftily

thrill *noun*
thrills

thrill *verb*
thrills
thrilling
thrilled

thriller *noun*
thrillers

thrive *verb*
thrives
thriving
thrived *or* throve *or* thriven

throat *noun*
throats

throb *verb*
throbs
throbbing
throbbed

throb *noun*
throbs

throne *noun*
thrones

throng *noun*
throngs

throttle *verb*
throttles
throttling
throttled

throttle *noun*
throttles

through

throughout

throve see **thrive**

throw *verb*
throws
throwing
threw
thrown

throw *noun*
throws

thrush *noun*
thrushes

thrust *verb*
thrusts
thrusting
thrust

thud *noun*
thuds

thud *verb*
thuds
thudding
thudded

thumb *noun*
thumbs

thump *verb*
thumps
thumping
thumped

thump *noun*
thumps

thunder *noun*

thunder *verb*
thunders
thundering
thundered

thunderous *adjective*
thunderously

thunderstorm *noun*
thunderstorms

Thursday *noun*
Thursdays

thus

thy

tick *verb*
ticks
ticking
ticked

tick *noun*
ticks

ticket *noun*
tickets

tickle *verb*
tickles
tickling
tickled

ticklish *adjective*
ticklishly

tidal

tiddler *noun*
tiddlers

★ To **thrash** someone is to beat them. **! thresh**.
☆ To **thresh** corn is to beat it to separate the grain. **! thrash**.

tiddlywink *noun*
tiddlywinks

tide *noun*
tides

tide *verb*
tides
tiding
tided

tidiness

tidy *adjective*
tidier
tidiest
tidily

tie *verb*
ties
tying
tied

tie *noun*
ties

tie-break *noun*
tie-breaks

tiger *noun*
tigers

tight *adjective*
tighter
tightest
tightly

tighten *verb*
tightens
tightening
tightened

tightness

tightrope *noun*
tightropes

tights *plural noun*

tigress *noun*
tigresses

tile *noun*
tiles

tiled

till *preposition* and *conjunction*

till *noun*
tills

till *verb*
tills
tilling
tilled

tiller *noun*
tillers

tilt *verb*
tilts
tilting
tilted

tilt *noun*
tilts

timber *noun*
timbers

time *noun*
times

time *verb*
times
timing
timed

timer *noun*
timers

times

timetable *noun*
timetables

timid *adjective*
timidly

timidity

timing

timpani *plural noun*

tin *noun*
tins

tin *verb*
tins
tinning
tinned

tingle *verb*
tingles
tingling
tingled

tingle *noun*
tingles

tinker *verb*
tinkers
tinkering
tinkered

tinker *noun*
tinkers

tinkle *verb*
tinkles
tinkling
tinkled

tinkle *noun*
tinkles

tinny *adjective*
tinnier
tinniest
tinnily

tinsel

tint *noun*
tints

tint *verb*
tints
tinting
tinted

tiny *adjective*
tinier
tiniest

tip *verb*
tips
tipping
tipped

tip *noun*
tips

tiptoe *verb*
tiptoes
tiptoeing
tiptoed

tiptoe *noun*

tire★ *verb*
tires
tiring
tired

★ To **tire** is to become tired. **! tyre**.

a b c d e f g h i j k l m n o p q r s **t** u v w x y z

a b c d e f g h i j k l m n o p q r s t u v w x y z

tired
tireless *adjective*
tirelessly
tiresome *adjective*
tiresomely
tissue *noun*
tissues
tit *noun*
tits
titbit *noun*
titbits
title *noun*
titles
titter *verb*
titters
tittering
tittered
to★ *preposition*
toad *noun*
toads
toadstool *noun*
toadstools
toast *verb*
toasts
toasting
toasted
toast *noun*
toasts
toaster *noun*
toasters
tobacco *noun*
tobaccos
tobacconist *noun*
tobacconists
toboggan *noun*
toboggans
tobogganing
today
toddler *noun*
toddlers
toe☆ *noun*
toes
toffee *noun*
toffees
toga *noun*
togas
together
toil *verb*
toils
toiling
toiled
toilet *noun*
toilets
token *noun*
tokens
told see **tell**
tolerable *adjective*
tolerably
tolerance
tolerant *adjective*
tolerantly
tolerate *verb*
tolerates
tolerating
tolerated
toll *noun*
tolls
toll *verb*
tolls
tolling
tolled
tomahawk *noun*
tomahawks
tomato *noun*
tomatoes
tomb *noun*
tombs
tomboy *noun*
tomboys
tombstone *noun*
tombstones
tomcat *noun*
tomcats
tommy-gun *noun*
tommy-guns
tomorrow
tom-tom *noun*
tom-toms
ton✪ *noun*
tons
tonal *adjective*
tonally
tone *noun*
tones
tone *verb*
tones
toning
toned
tone-deaf
tongs *plural noun*
tongue *noun*
tongues
tonic *noun*
tonics
tonight
tonne✣ *noun*
tonnes
tonsillitis
tonsils *plural noun*
too✸ *adverb*
took see **take**
tool *noun*
tools
tooth *noun*
teeth

★ You use **to** in e.g. *go to bed* or *I want to stay.* **! too**, **two**.
☆ A **toe** is a part of a foot. **! tow**.
✪ A **ton** is a non-metric unit of weight. **! tonne**.
✣ A **tonne** is a metric unit of weight. **! ton**.
✸ You use **too** in e.g. *it´s too late* or *I want to come too.* **! to**, **two**.

toothache
toothbrush *noun*
toothbrushes
toothed
toothpaste *noun*
toothpastes
top *noun*
tops
top *verb*
tops
topping
topped
topic *noun*
topics
topical *adjective*
topically
topicality
topless
topmost
topping *noun*
toppings
topple *verb*
topples
toppling
toppled
topsy-turvy
torch *noun*
torches
tore see **tear**
toreador *noun*
toreadors
torment *verb*
torments
tormenting
tormented
torment *noun*
torments
tormentor *noun*
tormentors
torn see **tear**
tornado *noun*
tornadoes

torpedo *noun*
torpedoes
torpedo *verb*
torpedoes
torpedoing
torpedoed
torrent *noun*
torrents
torrential *adjective*
torrentially
torso *noun*
torsos
tortoise *noun*
tortoises
torture *verb*
tortures
torturing
tortured
torture *noun*
tortures
torturer *noun*
torturers
Tory *noun*
Tories
toss *verb*
tosses
tossing
tossed
toss *noun*
tosses
total *noun*
totals
total *adjective*
totally
total *verb*
totals
totalling
totalled
totalitarian
totem pole *noun*
totem poles

totter *verb*
totters
tottering
tottered
touch *verb*
touches
touching
touched
touch *noun*
touches
touchy *adjective*
touchier
touchiest
touchily
tough *adjective*
tougher
toughest
toughly
toughen *verb*
toughens
toughening
toughened
toughness
tour *noun*
tours
tourism
tourist *noun*
tourists
tournament *noun*
tournaments
tow★ *verb*
tows
towing
towed
tow *noun*
toward or **towards**
towel *noun*
towels
towelling
tower *noun*
towers

★ To **tow** something is to pull it along. **! toe**.

a b c d e f g h i j k l m n o p q r s **t** u v w x y z

tower *verb*
towers
towering
towered

town *noun*
towns

towpath *noun*
towpaths

toxic *adjective*
toxically

toy *noun*
toys

toy *verb*
toys
toying
toyed

toyshop *noun*
toyshops

trace *noun*
traces

trace *verb*
traces
tracing
traced

traceable

track *noun*
tracks

track *verb*
tracks
tracking
tracked

tracker *noun*
trackers

tracksuit *noun*
tracksuits

tract *noun*
tracts

traction

tractor *noun*
tractors

trade *noun*
trades

trade *verb*
trades
trading
traded

trademark *noun*
trademarks

trader *noun*
traders

tradesman *noun*
tradesmen

trade union *noun*
trade unions

tradition *noun*
traditions

traditional *adjective*
traditionally

traffic *noun*

traffic *verb*
traffics
trafficking
trafficked

tragedy *noun*
tragedies

tragic *adjective*
tragically

trail *noun*
trails

trail *verb*
trails
trailing
trailed

trailer *noun*
trailers

train *noun*
trains

train *verb*
trains
training
trained

trainer *noun*
trainers

traitor *noun*
traitors

tram *noun*
trams

tramp *noun*
tramps

tramp *verb*
tramps
tramping
tramped

trample *verb*
tramples
trampling
trampled

trampoline *noun*
trampolines

trance *noun*
trances

tranquil *adjective*
tranquilly

tranquillity★

tranquillizer *noun*
tranquillizers

transact *verb*
transacts
transacting
transacted

transaction *noun*
transactions

transatlantic

transfer *verb*
transfers
transferring
transferred

transfer *noun*
transfers

transferable

transference

transform *verb*
transforms
transforming
transformed

transformation *noun*
transformations

★ Note that there are two ls in this word.

transformer *noun*
transformers
transfusion *noun*
transfusions
transistor *noun*
transistors
transition *noun*
transitions
transitional *adjective*
transitionally
transitive *adjective*
transitively
translate *verb*
translates
translating
translated
translation *noun*
translations
translator *noun*
translators
translucent
transmission *noun*
transmissions
transmit *verb*
transmits
transmitting
transmitted
transmitter *noun*
transmitters
transparency *noun*
transparencies
transparent *adjective*
transparently
transpire *verb*
transpires
transpiring
transpired
transplant *verb*
transplants
transplanting
transplanted
transplant *noun*
transplants
transplantation *noun*
transplantations

transport *verb*
transports
transporting
transported
transportation
transport
transporter *noun*
transporters
trap *verb*
traps
trapping
trapped
trap *noun*
traps
trapdoor *noun*
trapdoors
trapeze *noun*
trapezes
trapezium *noun*
trapeziums
trapezoid *noun*
trapezoids
trapper *noun*
trappers
trash
trashy *adjective*
trashier
trashiest
trashily
travel *verb*
travels
travelling
travelled
travel *noun*
traveller *noun*
travellers
traveller's cheque *noun*
traveller´s cheques
trawler *noun*
trawlers
tray *noun*
trays
treacherous *adjective*
treacherously

treachery
treacle
tread *verb*
treads
treading
trod
trodden
tread *noun*
treads
treason
treasure *noun*
treasures
treasure *verb*
treasures
treasuring
treasured
treasurer *noun*
treasurers
treasury *noun*
treasuries
treat *verb*
treats
treating
treated
treat *noun*
treats
treatment *noun*
treatments
treaty *noun*
treaties
treble *adjective* and *noun*
trebles
treble *verb*
trebles
trebling
trebled
tree *noun*
trees
trek *verb*
treks
trekking
trekked
trek *noun*
treks

a b c d e f g h i j k l m n o p q r s t u v w x y z

trellis *noun*
trellises

tremble *verb*
trembles
trembling
trembled

tremble *noun*
trembles

tremendous *adjective*
tremendously

tremor *noun*
tremors

trench *noun*
trenches

trend *noun*
trends

trendiness

trendy *adjective*
trendier
trendiest
trendily

trespass *verb*
trespasses
trespassing
trespassed

trespasser *noun*
trespassers

trestle *noun*
trestles

trial *noun*
trials

triangle *noun*
triangles

triangular

tribal *adjective*
tribally

tribe *noun*
tribes

tribesman *noun*
tribesmen

tributary *noun*
tributaries

tribute *noun*
tributes

trick *noun*
tricks

trick *verb*
tricks
tricking
tricked

trickery

trickster *noun*
tricksters

trickle *verb*
trickles
trickling
trickled

trickle *noun*
trickles

tricky *adjective*
trickier
trickiest
trickily

tricycle *noun*
tricycles

tried see **try**

trifle *noun*
trifles

trifle *verb*
trifles
trifling
trifled

trifling

trigger *noun*
triggers

trigger *verb*
triggers
triggering
triggered

trillion *noun*
trillions

trim *adjective*
trimmer
trimmest
trimly

trim *verb*
trims
trimming
trimmed

trim *noun*
trims

Trinity★

trio *noun*
trios

trip *verb*
trips
tripping
tripped

trip *noun*
trips

tripe

triple *adjective*
triply

triple *noun*
triples

triple *verb*
triples
tripling
tripled

triplet *noun*
triplets

tripod *noun*
tripods

triumph *noun*
triumphs

triumphant *adjective*
triumphantly

trivial *adjective*
trivially

triviality *noun*
trivialities

trod see **tread**

trodden see **tread**

★ You use a capital T when you mean the three persons of God in Christianity.

troll *noun*
trolls

trolley *noun*
trolleys

trombone *noun*
trombones

troop *noun*
troops

troop *verb*
troops
trooping
trooped

troops *plural noun*

trophy *noun*
trophies

tropic *noun*
tropics

tropical *adjective*

trot *verb*
trots
trotting
trotted

trot *noun*
trots

trouble *noun*
troubles

trouble *verb*
troubles
troubling
troubled

troublesome

trough *noun*
troughs

trousers *plural noun*

trout *noun*
trout

trowel *noun*
trowels

truancy *noun*
truancies

truant *noun*
truants

truce *noun*
truces

truck *noun*
trucks

trudge *verb*
trudges
trudging
trudged

true *adjective*
truer
truest
truly

trump *noun*
trumps

trump *verb*
trumps
trumping
trumped

trumpet *noun*
trumpets

trumpet *verb*
trumpets
trumpeting
trumpeted

trumpeter *noun*
trumpeters

truncheon *noun*
truncheons

trundle *verb*
trundles
trundling
trundled

trunk *noun*
trunks

trunks *plural noun*

trust *verb*
trusts
trusting
trusted

trust

trustful *adjective*
trustfully

trustworthy *adjective*
trustworthily

trusty *adjective*
trustier
trustiest
trustily

truth *noun*
truths

truthful *adjective*
truthfully

truthfulness

try *verb*
tries
trying
tried

try *noun*
tries

T-shirt *noun*
T-shirts

tub *noun*
tubs

tuba *noun*
tubas

tube *noun*
tubes

tuber *noun*
tubers

tubing

tubular

tuck *verb*
tucks
tucking
tucked

tuck *noun*
tucks

Tuesday *noun*
Tuesdays

tuft *noun*
tufts

tug *noun*
tugs

tug *verb*
tugs
tugging
tugged

tulip *noun*
tulips

a b c d e f g h i j k l m n o p q r s t u v w x y z

tumble *verb*
tumbles
tumbling
tumbled

tumble *noun*
tumbles

tumble-drier *noun*
tumble-driers

tumbler *noun*
tumblers

tummy *noun*
tummies

tumour *noun*
tumours

tumult

tumultuous *adjective*
tumultuously

tuna *noun*
tuna *or* tunas

tundra

tune *noun*
tunes

tune *verb*
tunes
tuning
tuned

tuneful *adjective*
tunefully

tunic *noun*
tunics

tunnel *noun*
tunnels

tunnel *verb*
tunnels
tunnelling
tunnelled

turban *noun*
turbans

turbine *noun*
turbines

turbulence

turbulent *adjective*
turbulently

turf *noun*
turfs *or* turves

turkey *noun*
turkeys

Turkish bath *noun*
Turkish baths

Turkish delight

turmoil

turn *verb*
turns
turning
turned

turn *noun*
turns

turncoat *noun*
turncoats

turnip *noun*
turnips

turnover *noun*
turnovers

turnstile *noun*
turnstiles

turntable *noun*
turntables

turpentine

turquoise

turret *noun*
turrets

turtle *noun*
turtles

tusk *noun*
tusks

tussle *verb*
tussles
tussling
tussled

tussle *noun*
tussles

tutor *noun*
tutors

tweak *verb*
tweaks
tweaking
tweaked

tweak *noun*
tweaks

tweed

tweezers *plural noun*

twelve *noun*
twelves

twelfth

twentieth

twenty *noun*
twenties

twice

twiddle *verb*
twiddles
twiddling
twiddled

twiddle *noun*
twiddles

twig *noun*
twigs

twig *verb*
twigs
twigging
twigged

twilight

twin *noun*
twins

twin *verb*
twins
twinning
twinned

twine

twinkle *verb*
twinkles
twinkling
twinkled

twinkle *noun*
twinkles

twirl *verb*
twirls
twirling
twirled

twirl *noun*
twirls

twist *verb*
twists
twisting
twisted

twist *noun*
twists

twister *noun*
twisters

twitch *verb*
twitches
twitching
twitched

twitch *noun*
twitches

twitter *verb*
twitters
twittering
twittered

two★ *adjective* and *noun*
twos

tying see **tie**

type *noun*
types

type *verb*
types
typing
typed

typewriter *noun*
typewriters

typewritten

typhoon *noun*
typhoons

typical *adjective*
typically

typist *noun*
typists

tyranny *noun*
tyrannies

tyrannical *adjective*
tyrannically

tyrant *noun*
tyrants

tyre☆ *noun*
tyres

Uu

udder *noun*
udders

ugliness

ugly *adjective*
uglier
ugliest

ulcer *noun*
ulcers

ultimate *adjective*
ultimately

ultraviolet

umbilical cord *noun*
umbilical cords

umbrella *noun*
umbrellas

umpire *noun*
umpires

un-
un- makes words meaning 'not', e.g. **unable**, **unhappiness**. Some of these words have special meanings, e.g. **unprofessional**. See the note at **non-**.

unable

unaided

unanimity

unanimous *adjective*
unanimously

unavoidable *adjective*
unavoidably

unaware

unawares

unbearable *adjective*
unbearably

unbelievable *adjective*
unbelievably

unblock *verb*
unblocks
unblocking
unblocked

unborn

uncalled for

uncanny *adjective*
uncannier
uncanniest

uncertain *adjective*
uncertainly

uncertainty

uncle *noun*
uncles

uncomfortable *adjective*
uncomfortably

uncommon *adjective*
uncommonly

unconscious *adjective*
unconsciously

unconsciousness

uncontrollable *adjective*
uncontrollably

uncountable

uncouth

★ You use **two** in e.g. *two people* or *there are two of them.* **! to**, **too**.
☆ A **tyre** is a rubber cover for a wheel. **! tire**.

a b c d e f g h i j k l m n o p q r s t u v w x y z

uncover *verb*
uncovers
uncovering
uncovered

undecided

undeniable *adjective*
undeniably

under

underarm *adjective*

underclothes *plural noun*

underdeveloped

underdone

underfoot

undergo *verb*
undergoes
undergoing
underwent
undergone

undergraduate *noun*
undergraduates

underground *adjective* and *noun*
undergrounds

undergrowth

underhand

underlie *verb*
underlies
underlying
underlay
underlain

underline *verb*
underlines
underlining
underlined

undermine *verb*
undermines
undermining
undermined

underneath *preposition*

underpants *plural noun*

underpass *noun*
underpasses

underprivileged

understand *verb*
understands
understanding
understood

understandable *adjective*
understandably

understanding

undertake *verb*
undertakes
undertaking
undertook
undertaken

undertaker *noun*
undertakers

undertaking *noun*
undertakings

underwater

underwear

underworld

undesirable *adjective*
undesirably

undeveloped

undo *verb*
undoes
undoing
undid
undone

undoubted *adjective*
undoubtedly

undress *verb*
undresses
undressing
undressed

unearth *verb*
unearths
unearthing
unearthed

unearthly

unease

uneasiness

uneasy *adjective*
uneasier
uneasiest
uneasily

uneatable

unemployed

unemployment

uneven *adjective*
unevenly

unevenness

unexpected *adjective*
unexpectedly

unfair *adjective*
unfairly

unfairness

unfaithful *adjective*
unfaithfully

unfamiliar

unfamiliarity

unfasten *verb*
unfastens
unfastening
unfastened

unfavourable *adjective*
unfavourably

unfinished

unfit

unfold *verb*
unfolds
unfolding
unfolded

unforgettable *adjective*
unforgettably

unforgivable *adjective*
unforgivably

unfortunate *adjective*
unfortunately

unfreeze *verb*
unfreezes
unfreezing
unfroze
unfrozen

unfriendliness
unfriendly
ungrateful *adjective*
ungratefully
unhappiness
unhappy *adjective*
unhappier
unhappiest
unhappily
unhealthy *adjective*
unhealthier
unhealthiest
unhealthily
unheard-of
unicorn *noun*
unicorns
unification
uniform *noun*
uniforms
uniform *adjective*
uniformly
uniformed
uniformity
unify *verb*
unifies
unifying
unified
unimportance
unimportant
uninhabited
unintentional *adjective*
unintentionally
uninterested
uninteresting
union *noun*
unions
unique *adjective*
uniquely
uniqueness
unisex
unison
unit *noun*
units
unite *verb*
unites
uniting
united
unity *noun*
unities
universal *adjective*
universally
universe
university *noun*
universities
unjust *adjective*
unjustly
unkind *adjective*
unkinder
unkindest
unkindly
unkindness
unknown
unleaded
unless
unlike
unlikely *adjective*
unlikelier
unlikeliest
unload *verb*
unloads
unloading
unloaded
unlock *verb*
unlocks
unlocking
unlocked
unlucky *adjective*
unluckier
unluckiest
unluckily
unmistakable *adjective*
unmistakably
unnatural *adjective*
unnaturally
unnecessary *adjective*
unnecessarily
unoccupied
unpack *verb*
unpacks
unpacking
unpacked
unpleasant *adjective*
unpleasantly
unpleasantness
unplug *verb*
unplugs
unplugging
unplugged
unpopular *adjective*
unpopularly
unpopularity
unravel *verb*
unravels
unravelling
unravelled
unreal
unreasonable *adjective*
unreasonably
unrest
unroll *verb*
unrolls
unrolling
unrolled
unruliness
unruly *adjective*
unrulier
unruliest
unscrew *verb*
unscrews
unscrewing
unscrewed
unseemly
unseen
unselfish *adjective*
unselfishly
unselfishness
unsightly
unskilled

a b c d e f g h i j k l m n o p q r s t u v w x y z

unsound *adjective*
unsoundly

unsteadiness

unsteady *adjective*
unsteadier
unsteadiest
unsteadily

unsuccessful *adjective*
unsuccessfully

unsuitable *adjective*
unsuitably

unthinkable *adjective*
unthinkably

untidiness

untidy *adjective*
untidier
untidiest
untidily

untie *verb*
unties
untying
untied

until

untimely

unto

untold

untoward

untrue *adjective*
untruly

untruthful *adjective*
untruthfully

unused

unusual *adjective*
unusually

unwanted

unwell

unwilling *adjective*
unwillingly

unwillingness

unwind *verb*
unwinds
unwinding
unwound

unwrap *verb*
unwraps
unwrapping
unwrapped

unzip *verb*
unzips
unzipping
unzipped

update *verb*
updates
updating
updated

upgrade *verb*
upgrades
upgrading
upgraded

upheaval *noun*
upheavals

uphill

uphold *verb*
upholds
upholding
upheld

upholstery

upkeep

uplands *plural noun*

upon

upper

upright *adjective*
uprightly

upright *noun*
uprights

uprising *noun*
uprisings

uproar *noun*
uproars

upset *verb*
upsets
upsetting
upset

upset *noun*
upsets

upshot

upside down

upstairs

upstart *noun*
upstarts

upstream *adjective*

uptake

uptight

upward *adjective* and *adverb*

upwards *adverb*

uranium

urban

urbanization

urbanize *verb*
urbanizes
urbanizing
urbanized

urchin *noun*
urchins

Urdu

urge *verb*
urges
urging
urged

urge *noun*
urges

urgency

urgent *adjective*
urgently

urinary

urinate *verb*
urinates
urinating
urinated

urination

urine

urn *noun*
urns

> **-us**
> Most nouns ending in *-us* come from Latin words, e.g. **bonus** and **terminus**. They normally have plurals ending in *-uses*, e.g. **bonuses** and **terminuses**. Some more technical words have plurals ending in *-i*, e.g. **nucleus** - **nuclei**.

usable

usage *noun*
usages

use *verb*
uses
using
used

use *noun*
uses

useful *adjective*
usefully

usefulness

useless *adjective*
uselessly

uselessness

user *noun*
users

user-friendly *adjective*
user-friendlier
user-friendliest

usher *noun*
ushers

usher *verb*
ushers
ushering
ushered

usherette *noun*
usherettes

usual *adjective*
usually

usurp *verb*
usurps
usurping
usurped

usurper *noun*
usurpers

utensil *noun*
utensils

uterus *noun*
uteri

utilization

utilize *verb*
utilizes
utilizing
utilized

utmost

utter *adjective*

utter *verb*
utters
uttering
uttered

utterance *noun*
utterances

utterly *adverb*

U-turn *noun*
U-turns

Vv

vacancy *noun*
vacancies

vacant *adjective*
vacantly

vacate *verb*
vacates
vacating
vacated

vacation *noun*
vacations

vaccinate *verb*
vaccinates
vaccinating
vaccinated

vaccination *noun*
vaccinations

vaccine *noun*
vaccines

vacuum *noun*
vacuums

vagina *noun*
vaginas

vague *adjective*
vaguer
vaguest
vaguely

vagueness

vain★ *adjective*
vainer
vainest
vainly

vale☆ *noun*
vales

valentine *noun*
valentines

valiant *adjective*
valiantly

valid *adjective*
validly

validity

valley *noun*
valleys

valour

valuable *adjective*
valuably

valuables *plural noun*

★ **Vain** means 'conceited' or 'proud'. **! vane**, **vein**.
☆ A **vale** is a valley. **! veil**.

a b c d e f g h i j k l m n o p q r s t u v w x y z

valuation *noun*
valuations
value *noun*
values
value *verb*
values
valuing
valued
valueless
valuer *noun*
valuers
valve *noun*
valves
vampire *noun*
vampires
van *noun*
vans
vandal *noun*
vandals
vandalism
vane★ *noun*
vanes
vanilla
vanish *verb*
vanishes
vanishing
vanished
vanity
vanquish *verb*
vanquishes
vanquishing
vanquished
vaporize *verb*
vaporizes
vaporizing
vaporized
vapour *noun*
vapours
variable *adjective*
variably
variable *noun*
variables
variation *noun*
variations
varied
variety *noun*
varieties
various *adjective*
variously
varnish *noun*
varnishes
varnish *verb*
varnishes
varnishing
varnished
vary *verb*
varies
varying
varied
vase *noun*
vases
vast *adjective*
vastly
vastness
vat *noun*
vats
vault *verb*
vaults
vaulting
vaulted
vault *noun*
vaults
veal
vector *noun*
vectors
Veda
veer *verb*
veers
veering
veered
vegan *noun*
vegans
vegetable *noun*
vegetables
vegetarian *noun*
vegetarians
vegetate *verb*
vegetates
vegetating
vegetated
vegetation
vehicle *noun*
vehicles
veil☆ *noun*
veils
veil *verb*
veils
veiling
veiled
vein✪ *noun*
veins
velocity *noun*
velocities
velvet
velvety
vendetta *noun*
vendettas
vendor *noun*
vendors
venerable *adjective*
venerably
venereal disease *noun*
venereal diseases
venetian blind *noun*
venetian blinds
vengeance
venison

★ A **vane** is a pointer that shows which way the wind is blowing. **! vain**, **vein**.
☆ A **veil** is a covering for the face. **! vale**.
✪ A **vein** carries blood to the heart. **! vain**, **vane**.

Venn diagram *noun*
Venn diagrams
venom
venomous *adjective*
venomously
vent *noun*
vents
ventilate *verb*
ventilates
ventilating
ventilated
ventilation
ventilator *noun*
ventilators
ventriloquism
ventriloquist *noun*
ventriloquists
venture *verb*
ventures
venturing
ventured
venture *noun*
ventures
veranda *noun*
verandas
verb *noun*
verbs
verdict *noun*
verdicts
verge *verb*
verges
verging
verged
verge *noun*
verges
verification
verify *verb*
verifies
verifying
verified
vermin
verruca *noun*
verrucas
versatile
versatility
verse *noun*
verses
version *noun*
versions
versus
vertebra *noun*
vertebrae
vertebrate *noun*
vertebrates
vertex *noun*
vertices
vertical *adjective*
vertically
very
Vesak
vessel *noun*
vessels
vest *noun*
vests
vested *adjective*
vested
vestment *noun*
vestments
vestry *noun*
vestries
vet *noun*
vets
veteran *noun*
veterans
veterinary
veto *verb*
vetoes
vetoing
vetoed
veto *noun*
vetoes
vex *verb*
vexes
vexing
vexed
vexation
via
viaduct *noun*
viaducts
vibrate *verb*
vibrates
vibrating
vibrated
vibration *noun*
vibrations
vicar *noun*
vicars
vicarage *noun*
vicarages
vice *noun*
vices
vice-president *noun*
vice-presidents
vice versa
vicinity *noun*
vicinities
vicious *adjective*
viciously
viciousness
victim *noun*
victims
victimize *verb*
victimizes
victimizing
victimized
victor *noun*
victors
Victorian *adjective*
and *noun*
Victorians
victorious *adjective*
victoriously
victory *noun*
victories
video *noun*
videos
video *verb*
videoes
videoing
videoed
videotape *noun*
videotapes

view *noun*
views

view *verb*
views
viewing
viewed

viewer *noun*
viewers

vigilance

vigilant *adjective*
vigilantly

vigorous *adjective*
vigorously

vigour

Viking *noun*
Vikings

vile *adjective*
viler
vilest
vilely

villa *noun*
villas

village *noun*
villages

villager *noun*
villagers

villain *noun*
villains

villainous *adjective*
villainously

villainy

vine *noun*
vines

vinegar

vineyard *noun*
vineyards

vintage *noun*
vintages

vinyl

viola *noun*
violas

violate *verb*
violates
violating
violated

violation *noun*
violations

violator *noun*
violators

violence

violent *adjective*
violently

violet *noun*
violets

violin *noun*
violins

violinist *noun*
violinists

viper *noun*
vipers

virgin *noun*
virgins

virginity

virtual *adjective*
virtually

virtue *noun*
virtues

virtuous *adjective*
virtuously

virus *noun*
viruses

visa *noun*
visas

visibility

visible *adjective*
visibly

vision *noun*
visions

visit *verb*
visits
visiting
visited

visit *noun*
visits

visitor *noun*
visitors

visor *noun*
visors

visual *adjective*
visually

visualize *verb*
visualizes
visualizing
visualized

vital *adjective*
vitally

vitality

vitamin *noun*
vitamins

vivid *adjective*
vividly

vividness

vivisection *noun*
vivisections

vixen *noun*
vixens

vocabulary *noun*
vocabularies

vocal *adjective*
vocally

vocalist *noun*
vocalists

vocation *noun*
vocations

vocational *adjective*
vocationally

vodka *noun*
vodkas

voice *noun*
voices

voice *verb*
voices
voicing
voiced

volcanic

volcano *noun*
volcanoes

vole *noun*
voles

volley *noun*
volleys

volleyball

volt *noun*
volts

voltage *noun*
voltages

volume *noun*
volumes

voluntary *adjective*
voluntarily

volunteer *verb*
volunteers
volunteering
volunteered

volunteer *noun*
volunteers

vomit *verb*
vomits
vomiting
vomited

vote *verb*
votes
voting
voted

vote *noun*
votes

voter *noun*
voters

vouch *verb*
vouches
vouching
vouched

voucher *noun*
vouchers

vow *noun*
vows

vow *verb*
vows
vowing
vowed

vowel *noun*
vowels

voyage *noun*
voyages

voyager *noun*
voyagers

vulgar *adjective*
vulgarly

vulnerable *adjective*
vulnerably

vulture *noun*
vultures

vulva *noun*
vulvas

Ww

wad *noun*
wads

waddle *verb*
waddles
waddling
waddled

waddle *noun*
waddles

wade *verb*
wades
wading
waded

wafer *noun*
wafers

wag *verb*
wags
wagging
wagged

wag *noun*
wags

wage *noun*
wages

wage *verb*
wages
waging
waged

wager *noun*
wagers

wager *verb*
wagers
wagering
wagered

waggle *verb*
waggles
waggling
waggled

wagon *noun*
wagons

wagtail *noun*
wagtails

wail *verb*
wails
wailing
wailed

wail★ *noun*
wails

waist☆ *noun*
waists

waistcoat *noun*
waistcoats

wait✪ *verb*
waits
waiting
waited

wait *noun*
waits

waiter *noun*
waiters

★ A **wail** is a loud sad cry. **! whale**.
☆ A person's **waist** is the narrow part around their middle. **! waste**.
✪ To **wait** is to delay, pause, or rest. **! weight**.

a b c d e f g h i j k l m n o p q r s t u **v** **w** x y z

a b c d e f g h i j k l m n o p q r s t u v **w** x y z

waitress *noun*
waitresses

waive★ *verb*
waives
waiving
waived

wake *verb*
wakes
waking
woke
woken

wake *noun*
wakes

waken *verb*
wakens
wakening
wakened

walk *verb*
walks
walking
walked

walk *noun*
walks

walkabout *noun*
walkabouts

walker *noun*
walkers

walkie-talkie *noun*
walkie-talkies

Walkman *noun*
Walkmans

wall *noun*
walls

wall *verb*
walls
walling
walled

wallaby *noun*
wallabies

wallet *noun*
wallets

wallflower *noun*
wallflowers

wallop *verb*
wallops
walloping
walloped

wallow *verb*
wallows
wallowing
wallowed

wallpaper *noun*
wallpapers

walnut *noun*
walnuts

walrus *noun*
walruses

waltz *noun*
waltzes

waltz *verb*
waltzes
waltzing
waltzed

wand *noun*
wands

wander *verb*
wanders
wandering
wandered

wanderer *noun*
wanderers

wane *verb*
wanes
waning
waned

wangle *verb*
wangles
wangling
wangled

want *verb*
wants
wanting
wanted

want *noun*
wants

war *noun*
wars

warble *verb*
warbles
warbling
warbled

warble *noun*
warbles

warbler *noun*
warblers

ward *noun*
wards

ward *verb*
wards
warding
warded

warden *noun*
wardens

warder *noun*
warders

wardrobe *noun*
wardrobes

ware☆ *noun*
wares

warehouse *noun*
warehouses

warfare

warhead *noun*
warheads

wariness

warlike

warm *adjective*
warmer
warmest
warmly

★ To **waive** a right is to say you do not need it. **! wave**.
☆ **Wares** are manufactured goods. **! wear**, **where**.

warm *verb*
warms
warming
warmed

warmth

warn *verb*
warns
warning
warned

warning *noun*
warnings

warp *verb*
warps
warping
warped

warp *noun*
warps

warrant *noun*
warrants

warrant *verb*
warrants
warranting
warranted

warren *noun*
warrens

warrior *noun*
warriors

warship *noun*
warships

wart *noun*
warts

wary *adjective*
warier
wariest
warily

was

wash *verb*
washes
washing
washed

wash *noun*
washes

washable

washbasin *noun*
washbasins

washer *noun*
washers

washing

washing-up

wash-out *noun*
wash-outs

wasn't *verb*

wasp *noun*
wasps

wastage

waste★ *verb*
wastes
wasting
wasted

waste *adjective* and *noun*
wastes

wasteful *adjective*
wastefully

watch *verb*
watches
watching
watched

watch *noun*
watches

watchdog *noun*
watchdogs

watcher *noun*
watchers

watchful *adjective*
watchfully

watchfulness

watchman *noun*
watchmen

water *noun*
waters

water *verb*
waters
watering
watered

watercolour *noun*
watercolours

watercress

waterfall *noun*
waterfalls

waterlogged

watermark *noun*
watermarks

waterproof

water-skiing

watertight

waterway *noun*
waterways

waterworks *noun*
waterworks

watery

watt☆ *noun*
watts

wave✪ *verb*
waves
waving
waved

wave *noun*
waves

waveband *noun*
wavebands

wavelength *noun*
wavelengths

waver *verb*
wavers
wavering
wavered

★ To **waste** something is to use more of it than is needed. **! waist**.
☆ A **watt** is a unit of electricity. **! what**.
✪ To **wave** is to move your arm in greeting. **! waive**.

a b c d e f g h i j k l m n o p q r s t u v w x y z

wavy *adjective*
wavier
waviest
wavily

wax *noun*
waxes

wax *verb*
waxes
waxing
waxed

waxwork *noun*
waxworks

waxy *adjective*
waxier
waxiest

way★ *noun*
ways

weak☆ *adjective*
weaker
weakest
weakly

weakness

weaken *verb*
weakens
weakening
weakened

weakling *noun*
weaklings

wealth

wealthy *adjective*
wealthier
wealthiest
wealthily

weapon *noun*
weapons

wear✪ *verb*
wears
wearing
wore
worn

wear *noun*

wearer *noun*
wearers

weariness

weary *adjective*
wearier
weariest
wearily

weasel *noun*
weasels

weather *noun*

weather *verb*
weathers
weathering
weathered

weathercock *noun*
weathercocks

weave✣ *verb*
weaves
weaving
weaved *or* wove
woven

weaver *noun*
weavers

web *noun*
webs

webbed

website *noun*
websites

wed *verb*
weds
wedding
wedded
wed

we'd *verb*

wedding *noun*
weddings

wedge *noun*
wedges

wedge *verb*
wedges
wedging
wedged

Wednesday *noun*
Wednesdays

weed *noun*
weeds

weed *verb*
weeds
weeding
weeded

weedy *adjective*
weedier
weediest
weedily

week✸ *noun*
weeks

weekday *noun*
weekdays

weekend *noun*
weekends

weekly *adjective* and *adverb*

weep *verb*
weeps
weeping
wept

★ You use **way** in e.g. *can you tell me the way?* **! weigh**, **whey**.
☆ **Weak** means 'not strong'. **! week**.
✪ To **wear** clothes is to be dressed in them. **! ware**, **where**.
✣ The past tense is **weaved** in e.g. *she weaved her way through the crowd* and **wove** in e.g. *she wove a shawl*.
✸ A **week** is a period of seven days. **! weak**.

weft

weigh★ *verb*
weighs
weighing
weighed

weight☆ *noun*
weights

weightless

weightlifting

weighty *adjective*
weightier
weightiest
weightily

weir *noun*
weirs

weird *adjective*
weirder
weirdest
weirdly

weirdness

welcome *noun*
welcomes

welcome *verb*
welcomes
welcoming
welcomed

weld *verb*
welds
welding
welded

welder *noun*
welders

welfare

well *noun*
wells

well *adjective* and *adverb*
better
best

we'll *verb*

well-being

wellington boots *plural noun*

well-known

went see **go**

wept see **weep**

were see **are**

we're *verb*

werewolf *noun*
werewolves

west *adjective* and *adverb*

west✪ *noun*

westerly *adjective* and *noun*
westerlies

western *adjective*

western *noun*
westerns

westward *adjective* and *adverb*

westwards *adverb*

wet *adjective*
wetter
wettest

wet *verb*
wets
wetting
wetted

wetness

we've *abbreviation*

whack *verb*
whacks
whacking
whacked

whack *noun*
whacks

whale✣ *noun*
whales

whaler *noun*
whalers

whaling

wharf *noun*
wharves *or* wharfs

what✹

whatever

wheat

wheel *noun*
wheels

wheel *verb*
wheels
wheeling
wheeled

wheelbarrow *noun*
wheelbarrows

wheelchair *noun*
wheelchairs

wheeze *verb*
wheezes
wheezing
wheezed

whelk *noun*
whelks

when

whenever *conjunction*

★ You use **weigh** in e.g. *how much do you weigh?* **! way**, **whey**.
☆ **Weight** is how heavy something is. **! wait**.
✪ You use a capital W in **the West**, when you mean a particular region.
✣ A **whale** is a large sea mammal. **! wail**.
✹ You use **what** in e.g. *what are they doing?* or *I don´t know what you mean.* **! watt**.

where★
whereabouts
whereas
whereupon
wherever
whether *conjunction*
whey☆
which✪
whichever
whiff *noun*
whiffs
while *adjective* and *noun*
while *verb*
whiles
whiling
whiled
whilst *conjunction*
whimper *verb*
whimpers
whimpering
whimpered
whimper *noun*
whimpers
whine *verb*
whines
whining
whined
whine✣ *noun*
whines
whinny *verb*
whinnies
whinnying
whinnied
whip *noun*
whips

whip *verb*
whips
whipping
whipped
whirl *verb*
whirls
whirling
whirled
whirl *noun*
whirls
whirlpool *noun*
whirlpools
whirlwind *noun*
whirlwinds
whirr *verb*
whirrs
whirring
whirred
whirr *noun*
whirrs
whisk *verb*
whisks
whisking
whisked
whisk *noun*
whisks
whisker *noun*
whiskers
whisky *noun*
whiskies
whisper *verb*
whispers
whispering
whispered
whisper *noun*
whispers
whist

whistle *verb*
whistles
whistling
whistled
whistle *noun*
whistles
whistler *noun*
whistlers
white *adjective*
whiter
whitest
whiteness
whitish
white *noun*
whites
whiten *verb*
whitens
whitening
whitened
whitewash *noun*
whitewash *verb*
whitewashes
whitewashing
whitewashed
Whitsun
Whit Sunday
whiz *verb*
whizzes
whizzing
whizzed
who
whoever
whole✸ *adjective*
wholly
whole *noun*
wholes
wholefood *noun*
wholefoods

★ You use **where** in e.g. *where are you?* **! ware**, **wear**.
☆ **Whey** is a watery liquid from milk. **! way**, **weigh**.
✪ You use **which** in e.g. *which one is that?* **! witch**.
✣ A **whine** is a high piercing sound. **! wine**.
✸ You use **whole** in e.g. *I saw the whole lm.* **! hole**.

wholemeal
wholesale *adjective*
wholesome
wholly
whom
whoop *noun*
whoops
whoopee *interjection*
whooping cough
who's★ *verb*
whose☆ *adjective*
why
wick *noun*
wicks
wicked *adjective*
wickeder
wickedest
wickedly
wickedness
wicker
wickerwork
wicket *noun*
wickets
wicketkeeper *noun*
wicketkeepers
wide *adjective* and *adverb*
wider
widest
widely
widen *verb*
widens
widening
widened
widespread
widow *noun*
widows
widower *noun*
widowers

width *noun*
widths
wield *verb*
wields
wielding
wielded
wife *noun*
wives
wig *noun*
wigs
wiggle *verb*
wiggles
wiggling
wiggled
wiggle *noun*
wiggles
wigwam *noun*
wigwams
wild *adjective*
wilder
wildest
wildly
wilderness *noun*
wildernesses
wildness
wildlife
wilful *adjective*
wilfully
wilfulness
wiliness
will *verb*
would
will *noun*
wills
willing *adjective*
willingly
willingness
willow *noun*
willows

wilt *verb*
wilts
wilting
wilted
wily *adjective*
wilier
wiliest
wimp *noun*
wimps
win *verb*
wins
winning
won
win *noun*
wins
wince *verb*
winces
wincing
winced
winch *noun*
winches
winch *verb*
winches
winching
winched
wind *noun*
winds
wind *verb*
winds
winding
wound
windfall *noun*
windfalls
windmill *noun*
windmills
window *noun*
windows
windpipe *noun*
windpipes

★ You use **who's** in *who's* (who is) *that?* and *I don't know who's* (who has) *done it.* **! whose**.
☆ You use **whose** in *whose is this?* and *I don't know whose it is.* **! who's**.

a b c d e f g h i j k l m n o p q r s t u v **w** x y z

worry *noun*
worries

worse *adjective* and *adverb*

worsen *verb*
worsens
worsening
worsened

worship *verb*
worships
worshipping
worshipped

worship *noun*

worshipper *noun*
worshippers

worst *adjective* and *adverb*

worth

worthiness

worthless *adjective*
worthlessly

worthwhile

worthy *adjective*
worthier
worthiest
worthily

would★ see **will**

wouldn't *verb*

wound *noun*
wounds

wound *verb*
wounds
wounding
wounded

wound see **wind**

wove see **weave**

woven see **weave**

wrap☆ *verb*
wraps
wrapping
wrapped

wrap *noun*
wraps

wrapper *noun*
wrappers

wrapping *noun*
wrappings

wrath

wrathful *adjective*
wrathfully

wreath *noun*
wreaths

wreathe *verb*
wreathes
wreathing
wreathed

wreck *verb*
wrecks
wrecking
wrecked

wreck *noun*
wrecks

wreckage *noun*
wreckages

wrecker *noun*
wreckers

wren *noun*
wrens

wrench *verb*
wrenches
wrenching
wrenched

wrench *noun*
wrenches

wrestle *verb*
wrestles
wrestling
wrestled

wrestler *noun*
wrestlers

wretch *noun*
wretches

wretched *adjective*
wretchedly

wriggle *verb*
wriggles
wriggling
wriggled

wriggle *noun*
wriggles

wriggly *adjective*
wrigglier
wriggliest

wring✪ *verb*
wrings
wringing
wrung

wrinkle *noun*
wrinkles

wrinkle *verb*
wrinkles
wrinkling
wrinkled

wrist *noun*
wrists

wristwatch *noun*
wristwatches

write✣ *verb*
writes
writing
wrote
written

writer *noun*
writers

★ You use **would** in e.g. *would you like to come to tea?* **! wood**.
☆ To **wrap** something is to cover it in paper etc. **! rap**.
✪ To **wring** something is to squeeze it hard. **! ring**.
✣ You use **write** in e.g. *to write a letter*. **! right**, **rite**.

writhe *verb*
writhes
writhing
writhed

writing *noun*
writings

written see **write**

wrong *adjective* and *adverb*
wrongly

wrong *noun*
wrongs

wrong *verb*
wrongs
wronging
wronged

wrote see **write**

wrung see **wring**

wry★ *adjective*
wryer
wryest

Xx

xenophobia

Xmas *noun*
Xmases

X-ray *noun*
X-rays

X-ray *verb*
X-rays
X-raying
X-rayed

xylophone *noun*
xylophones

Yy

-y and **-ey**
Nouns ending in *-y* following a consonant, e.g. **story**, make plurals ending in *-ies*, e.g. **stories**, and verbs, e.g. **try**, make forms in *-ies* and *-ied*, e.g. **tries**, **tried**. Nouns ending in *-ey*, e.g. **journey**, make plurals ending in *-eys*, e.g. **journeys**.

yacht *noun*
yachts

yachtsman *noun*
yachtsmen

yachtswoman *noun*
yachtswomen

yam *noun*
yams

yank *verb*
yanks
yanking
yanked

yap *verb*
yaps
yapping
yapped

yap *noun*
yaps

yard *noun*
yards

yard *noun*
yards

yarn *noun*
yarns

yawn *verb*
yawns
yawning
yawned

yawn *noun*
yawns

year *noun*
years

yearly *adjective* and *adverb*

yearn *verb*
yearns
yearning
yearned

yeast

yell *noun*
yells

yell *verb*
yells
yelling
yelled

yellow *adjective* and *noun*
yellower
yellowest

yelp *verb*
yelps
yelping
yelped

yelp *noun*
yelps

yen☆ *noun*
yens *or* yen

yeoman *noun*
yeomen

★ You use **wry** in e.g. *a wry smile.* **! rye**.
☆ The plural is **yens** when you mean 'a longing' and **yen** for Japanese money.

a b c d e f g h i j k l m n o p q r s t u v w x y z

yesterday *adjective* and *noun*
yesterdays
yet
yeti *noun*
yetis
yew★ *noun*
yews
yield *verb*
yields
yielding
yielded
yield *noun*
yields
yippee
yodel *verb*
yodels
yodelling
yodelled
yodeller *noun*
yodellers
yoga
yoghurt *noun*
yoghurts
yoke☆ *noun*
yokes
yoke *verb*
yokes
yoking
yoked
yolk✪ *noun*
yolks
Yom Kippur
yonder
you✣
you'd *verb*
you'll *verb*
young *adjective*
younger
youngest
young *plural noun*
youngster *noun*
youngsters
your
you're *abbreviation*
yours
yourself *pronoun*
yourselves
youth *noun*
youths
youthful *adjective*
youthfully
you've *abbreviation*
yo-yo *noun*
yo-yos
yuppie *noun*
yuppies

Zz

zany *adjective*
zanier
zaniest
zanily
zap *verb*
zaps
zapping
zapped
zeal
zealous *adjective*
zealously
zebra *noun*
zebras
zenith *noun*
zeniths
zero *noun*
zeros
zest
zigzag *noun*
zigzags
zigzag *verb*
zigzags
zigzagging
zigzagged
zinc
zip *noun*
zips
zip *verb*
zips
zipping
zipped
zodiac
zombie *noun*
zombies
zone *noun*
zones
zoo *noun*
zoos
zoological *adjective*
zoologically
zoologist *noun*
zoologists
zoology
zoom *verb*
zooms
zooming
zoomed

★ A **yew** is a tree. **! ewe**, **you**.
☆ A **yoke** is a piece of wood put across animals pulling a cart. **! yolk**.
✪ A **yolk** is the yellow part of an egg. **! yoke**.
✣ You use **you** in e.g. *I love you.* **! ewe**, **yew**.

OXFORD
Dictionaries and Thesauruses for home and school

Oxford Very First Dictionary

Oxford First Dictionary
Oxford First Thesaurus

Oxford Junior Illustrated Dictionary
Oxford Junior Illustrated Thesaurus

Oxford Junior Dictionary
Oxford Junior Thesaurus

Oxford Primary Dictionary
Oxford Primary Thesaurus

Oxford Children's Dictionary
Oxford Children's Thesaurus

Oxford Concise School Dictionary
Oxford Concise School Thesaurus

Oxford School Dictionary
Oxford School Thesaurus

Oxford Pocket School Dictionary
Oxford Pocket School Thesaurus

Oxford Mini School Dictionary
Oxford Mini School Thesaurus

Oxford Student's Dictionary

Large print

Oxford Young Reader's Dictionary
Oxford Young Reader's Spelling Dictionary